CONTENTS

SIT
DOWN
AND
CHEER

SIT DOWN AND CHEER

MARTIN KELNER

BLOOMSBURY
LONDON • NEW DELHI • NEW YORK • SYDNEY

Bloomsbury Publishing Plc
50 Bedford Square
London WC1B 3DP

www.bloomsbury.com

Bloomsbury Publishing, London, New Delhi, New York and Sydney

A CIP catalogue record for this book is available from the British Library

ISBN 9781408129234

10 9 8 7 6 5 4 3 2 1

Typeset by seagulls.net
Printed in Great Britain by Clays Ltd, St Ives plc

ONE

NOT BEING THERE

The trouble with most histories of sport is that they are written by people who were there. Any idiot with a press card – don't get me wrong, many of these idiots I count as personal friends – can tell you what the atmosphere is like on a big night of European Cup football in the San Siro, or capture the sights and sounds of thoroughbred racehorses charging over the fences at Aintree, or report the collected speeches of gold medal winners at the Olympic games. And any athlete with a decent ghost writer can describe the goals, the runs, the knockouts, the booze, the sex, the drugs, and (for a disturbing number of former tennis professionals these days) the rock 'n' roll.

But to chronicle the last sixty colourful, tempestuous years of sport through the eyes of those who were present at its epoch-making events is to ignore a multi-channel elephant in the corner of the room. Because without the unholy union between sport and television, the sporting landscape we look out on today would be unrecognisable. The story of sport needs to be written by someone who stayed at home and watched, and my credentials to be its author are impeccable.

I have made a kind of career out of watching sport on TV. Apologies if that does a disservice to those of you in real careers like medicine, the law, or online pornography, but for the past fourteen years, the *Guardian* newspaper has paid me to produce a column based, sometimes rather loosely, on televised sport. Before that, I watched a good deal on an amateur basis, going back to the mid-1950s when the whole business started in earnest.

I only realised what an immense social history I was sitting on when I appeared on a sporting discussion programme on BBC Radio Five Live with some much younger contributors and was asked about the build-up to the 1966 World Cup final. 'What build-up?' I was forced to reply. We were excited, of course, largely because there was to be live football on TV, a rarity in those days, but there were no special supplements in the papers, no dedicated sports sections, it did not occupy our every waking moment.

Looking at the TV schedules for Friday 29 July 1966, the eve of the great match, I note the BBC manages a half-hour show, *World Cup Report*, at 7pm ('Meet the teams and the personalities who play tomorrow'), allocating precisely twenty minutes less screen time to the Match of the Century than to *The Hippodrome Circus, Great Yarmouth*, which occupies the peak-time slot at 8pm.

ITV has no World Cup preview at all, scheduling *Ready Steady Go* against the BBC's meet-the-teams programme. I can't say for certain, but I suspect I may have been watching ITV. As a teenager in 1966, pop music took precedence over almost everything.

Nor was there any great hoop-la on TV after the triumph. The BBC granted *Grandstand* a whole twenty minutes extra, to round up the momentous events of the day. Had West Germany not equalised in the final minute, we should all have been enjoying the Laurel and Hardy short *County Hospital* on the BBC by 5.20 (one of the best, as it happens, where Stan brings hard-boiled eggs and nuts to Ollie's bedside), followed by Susan Hampshire and others discussing the latest releases on *Juke Box Jury*. Even less time for post-match hosannas was allowed by ITV, who scheduled *Robin Hood* at 5.15pm – in other words, allocating the World Cup final slightly less time than Sky in 2012 would grant a mid-table Premier League match.

But, of course, we were all busy buzzing round the streets of London in E-Type Jags after the match with Rita Tushingham and Simon Dee, drinking whisky and Coke with Paul McCartney and Jane Asher in Le Kilt Club, or at the very least having a knees-up at one of the many street parties, our Union Jack-bedecked trestle tables groaning under the weight of light ale, pop for the kiddies, and commemorative cakes and pies.

Well, not in suburban Manchester we weren't. The Swinging Sixties did not arrive in Manchester until around 1974. Frankly, where we lived it may as well have still been wartime. The air-raid shelters down the bottom of our road had still not been demolished – possibly in case of Luftwaffe reprisals for Geoff Hurst's dubious second goal – and the country, particularly the North, as is customary, was going through the worst economic crisis since the last worst economic crisis.

In the *Daily Express* on World Cup final morning, the only indication there was a big match on – apart from the team news on the back page – was a story about the government barring players' wives from the post-match banquet and cocktail party (bunch of Normas and Susans coming down from the North with their beehive hair-dos, who did they think they were? FIFA officials' wives were fine, by the way), and a display ad for a hair oil called Vitalis picturing Bobby Moore, and bearing the slogan, 'The very best of luck England and Bobby Moore. We'll be behind you'. The lead story was about prime minister Harold Wilson's bibulous economics minister George Brown turning up two hours late for a scheduled TV appearance to explain the government's wage freeze, because he 'forgot'. The *Express* speculated this might signal the end of his career.

It did not stop the minister getting a seat for the match, though. The documentary feature *Goal! World Cup 1966* has a lovely sequence, which cuts from the throng on Wembley Way to the seats – armchairs, really – being prepared for the VIPs. A tartan rug is spread over the back of each seat, and the name of the dignitary is placed on it: Harold Wilson, George Brown, Sir Stanley Rous, President of the FA, and Her Majesty The Queen of course.* Whatever *Time* magazine said in its famous

---

* To the chagrin of BBC director Alec Weeks, *Goal!* is the only colour record of the final, although the technology was available to the BBC at the time. The film boasts a fine, wry script by the journalist Brian Glanville and quirky narration by Nigel Patrick.

Swinging London issue three months earlier, and whatever iconoclasm was implied in British films of the period, deference was still alive and well in 1966 England.

In case you were in any doubt what different times those were, the throng all appear to be wearing demob suits (cheap suits given to military people in advance of their re-entry into civilian life), and sensible shoes buffed up with a decent helping of Cherry Blossom, a million miles away from the baseball-booted, replica-shirted, be-jeaned crowd you might see these days. They did not seem dressed for a party.

As far as the TV coverage went, the 1966 World Cup remains Britain's most watched broadcast, with an audience of 32.3 million, just pipping Princess Diana's funeral in 1997, but nowhere was it discussed at the time as a television event. There were TV writers around then – notably Philip Purser at the *Sunday Telegraph* and Nancy Banks Smith, later a much-loved fixture at the *Guardian* but then at the original, pre-Murdoch *Sun*. But they tended to focus on programmes made specifically for television: drama and comedy mostly. No one in 1966 had yet grasped the way reality, in the shape of sport, and television could interact.

Nor had anyone caught on to the comic potential of sports broadcasters. There was nobody doing what I try to do in the *Guardian*, and Giles Smith does in *The Times*, and Clive James was doing before either of us in the *Observer*. Even Wolstenholme's famously felicitous valediction, 'They think it's all over. It is now', failed to make any impact on the press or public. It was only when highlights of the match were replayed some months later on the *BBC Sports Personality of the Year* programme and on various year-end round-ups that Wolstenholme's words began to register a little, but I wager it was the 1980s before anybody looked at a dessert trolley and said, 'They think it's pavlova. It is now.'

At the start of the television age in Britain, the 1950s and 1960s, the effects of the twentieth century's two world wars were still being keenly felt. It was some years before Britain was ready to abandon the stiff upper lip that had seen us through two epic international contests. It was not about to be jettisoned in the cause of football. For an article in *Intel-*

ligent Life magazine in 2010, the journalist Tim de Lisle unearthed the fact that on the Monday after England's triumph, the front-page splash in Britain's biggest-selling newspaper, the *Daily Mirror*, announced, 'A BOUNCING BABY GIRL FOR PRINCESS ALEX'. 'Winning the World Cup,' wrote de Lisle, 'was not as big as the birth of Marina Ogilvy, the Queen's first cousin once removed.'

By 1990, a ticker-tape parade and Beatles-style airport welcome were being bestowed on England's semi-final *losers*, not because of their stumbling, rather fortunate, progress to fourth place *(fourth place!)* in the competition, but because of the story reaching us through our television sets. I was there. Not in Italy, but on my sofa, watching television, the prism through which all significant sport now passes, and is given meaning.

Don't take my word for it. Simon Barnes, who has reported for *The Times* from pretty well every sporting arena worthy of mention, recognises in his book, *The Meaning of Sport*, the inadequacy of simply being there. He describes the trip in an open-topped bus by England's World Cup-winning rugby union team in 2003, through crowds ten-deep on London's streets, an estimated three-quarters of a million lining the route, some hanging from windows, shinning up lampposts, crowding onto balconies:

'It struck me,' writes Barnes, 'that I had no understanding of the event I had just covered, not until that bus-ride. How could I have understood how much it mattered, when I was stranded out there in Sydney watching Jonny Wilkinson make the winning drop-goal? The real event happened in England, on television, where everybody surfed the wave of rising hope.'

I surfed that wave, and I am a rugby league man, a former militant. But that is what television does. It is the single most powerful homogenising, democratising force in British society. The former prime minister John Major talked about the classless society; ITV created it. Guinness and Gillette, and all the other advertisers and sponsors flinging their money at rugby, demanded nothing less. Of course, one World Cup did not do it. The barriers eroded over time, but 2003 was rugby's Berlin Wall moment.

Unless you were brought up in a rugby league area in the North of England, you can have no idea of the hatred for the other code. My father and all my uncles were league men, wavering between Salford and Swinton, but staunchly Swinton when they first started taking me to matches in the late 1950s. We spurned rugby union as you would a rabid dog, and the feeling was mutual.

It was not just the apartheid; the Welsh league converts ostracised in their home towns just for wanting to earn a few bob from their talents, the stories of chaps who had played a little RL in the armed forces being barred from playing RU, the hypocrisy of the supposedly amateur union guys getting soft jobs and fivers in their boots. Not just that, not just the history either, but the way the fifteen-a-side game was presented to the public by the BBC: proper previews, the match in full (rugby league matches were restricted to second-half only in the 1970s and 1980s) and commentators who took it seriously, unlike our man Eddie Waring, undoubtedly a rugby league aficionado, but one who we always felt was having a laugh.

Their commentators seemed like poets to us: mellifluous Cliff Morgan, the schoolmasterly Scotsman Bill McLaren, with his endearing chuckle at transgressors as if they were errant pupils and, just to really put us in our place, a chap with a hyphen, the former England fly-half Nigel Starmer-Smith. Huddled in our post-industrial mining and mill towns, we were the outcasts of rugby.

The joke was that their game was really rather poor compared to ours. We ran the ball out of defence, using the three-quarters and mobile second-row forwards – and Swinton were the best team in the league at this – while they just put the boot to it. They didn't even have a league championship, for goodness' sake. At international level, and in Wales and parts of Scotland, it was taken seriously enough, but round our way, club rugby was more to do with the beer and sticking your arse out of the minibus windows on the drive home.

But once rugby union went professional in 1995, and had to compete on the open market for TV time and sponsors' money, they took the best bits from our game and a little from American football, invented some decent competitions like the Heineken Cup, and now have a pretty good TV product which I am happy to settle down on my sofa to watch. No hard feelings.

Let me tell you about my sofa, because home comforts cannot be discounted as a factor in the onward march of sport on television. Any historian of the cinema will tell you that the years of decline for the suburban Roxys and Regals coincided with the growth of affordable, comfortable furniture. We are all familiar with those archive photos of 1970s and 1980s families on their G-Plan sofas, coal-effect fires blazing away, watching Morecambe and Wise on TV, while the wind whistled round their local picture houses standing forlorn and unloved, awaiting the wrecker's ball, or conversion into bingo halls. It is a simple equation really. When our homes were shit-holes with the only comfortable chairs in the front parlour for Sunday best, we went out. Once we had invested our money in decent carpets and furniture, not being there – anywhere – became an attractive option.

My sofa now is called a Mitford. It is 'custom-made and hand crafted' according to its CV, made of 'fully seasoned beech and hardwoods from managed sources'. The 'managed sources' are important to me. I should not like to think any poor trees had suffered, just so I could loll on the Mitford watching the Champions League. Its cushions are 'Oriental duck feather pads' (something I am sure I ordered once in a Chinese restaurant). From the heart of this Mitford I make notes on televised sport, mocking its excesses, but marvelling at its amoeba-like growth. Ten-pin bowling? Fishomania (a whole day of competitive fishing from a lake near Doncaster)? Who would have thought it?

Enquiries of John Sankey, quality furniture manufacturer of Long Eaton, Derbyshire, have so far failed to reveal which Mitford my sofa is named after. I like to think Jessica, who was on the side of the rebels in the Spanish Civil War, like my dad and his mates, or Pamela, the Mitford nobody has heard of. (Just as the Monkees had their Peter Tork, and the Magnificent Seven its Brad Dexter, the Mitford sisters had their Pamela, the one who married a businessman and led a quiet life in the country-side as Mrs Derek Jackson.) I hope it is not named for Unity or Diana who – literally and metaphorically – got into bed with the Nazis.

Although I suppose I should thank the Nazis for starting it all, because it was Hitler – now there is a name you probably weren't expect-ing to crop up in a light-hearted romp through the history of sport on TV – yes, Hitler, or one of his smarter henchmen at least, who realised before anybody else that sport and television was a union devoutly to be desired, a marriage made in heaven, or possibly the opposite place in the Führer's case.

The Nazis saw the union as the perfect instrument to promote their twisted ideology – and so the Berlin Olympics of 1936 became the world's first live television broadcast of a sporting event. According to *Television and Shortwave World* magazine, as many as 150,000 viewers in twenty-eight viewing rooms throughout Berlin watched the Games. Seventy-two hours of live transmission, says the magazine, went over the airwaves to 'Public Television Offices' in Berlin and Potsdam. An eight-page booklet trumpeted Germany's achievements in this field, claiming regular transmissions since 1929, with a new system developed in 1934 'attaining remarkable picture quality'. But, as the literature is branded with a swastika, the claims may be mildly gilded. Nevertheless, as BBC cameras did not pitch up at Wimbledon to bring Britain its first televised sport until 21 June 1937, it is difficult to escape the conclusion that the Germans were slightly ahead of us, a position we have had to accept in international football tournaments – with one or two notable exceptions – pretty well ever since.

The final sentence of the Berlin Olympics booklet notes perceptively: 'From these initial stages of television in broadcasting and telephony, there is growing up a cultural development that promises to be of unsus-pected importance to the progress of mankind.' Say what you like about the Nazis, we have to hand it to them on the Volkswagen, the autobahns, and on recognising the huge impact of sport on TV, although I am not sure the Third Reich foresaw, as part of mankind's progress, my watching rugby league live from Australia while still in my pyjamas on a Saturday morning, or a heavyweight boxing champion trousering $137.5 million for lending his name to a device for grilling turkey steaks, or indeed *A Hundred Great Goalkeeping Gaffes* on Blu-Ray.

Those first television pictures of the 1936 Games were not available outside Germany, but Leni Riefenstahl's groundbreaking official film *Olympia* was, and seemed to achieve everything Hitler might have wanted in propaganda terms. Not only that, but it pioneered techniques now common in the filming, and televising, of sport: using close-ups to illustrate the joy of athletic triumph, and quick cutting to accentuate the drama. The genius of the Führer's favourite film-maker helped present the host nation in the best possible light, to which purpose normal rules of book-keeping and budgetary control were also set aside, as has been the case at more or less every subsequent Olympics. Ticket revenues at the Berlin games were said to be 7.5 million Reichsmarks, generating a profit of around one million marks. But the official budget did not include outlays by the city of Berlin (16.5 million marks) or the German national government, which did not make its costs public but is estimated to have spent 130 million marks (about £6 million), mostly on capital projects. Look out for similar creative accounting when the cost of the 2012 games is finally totted up.

Michael Winner, the director of films as varied as *Death Wish* and *Death Wish 2*, once described film-making as 'painting with money', and you could say the same about the Olympics. 'The largest single withdrawal on the world's physical, mental and economic resources, and it produces nothing but two weeks of television,' as the scabrous TV critic A.A. Gill wrote in the *Sunday Times*.

The Berlin Games were undoubtedly the template, providing a chilling portent of what was to come in Germany, with the Ministry of the Interior authorising the arrest of all Gypsies in the German capital and their detention in a special camp. Scandalous of course, but not radically different from the kind of clean-up operations that have been going on at international tournaments ever since, most recently at the 2010 Commonwealth Games in Delhi, where 400,000 slum dwellers' homes were demolished in time for the world to watch the opening ceremony.

So, the ground rules for big-time international sport – especially the manicuring of the host country for the benefit of a watching world – were set in Berlin. But because of the other big fixture a few years later that engulfed in flames much of the world, especially Europe, the baton was not really picked up until Rome 1960: *The Olympics That Changed the World*, according to the title of a book by the Pulitzer Prize-winning American author David Maraniss.

After the war, the European nations, broke and exhausted from the conflict (I recommend one of the post-war Italian neo-realist classics like *Rome, Open City* or *Bicycle Thieves* if you want to know exactly how broke and exhausted), had neither the money nor the appetite for anything very grandiose in the way of international competition, and so tended to look inward. That was the world into which I was born, and is, to all intents and purposes, where this story begins.

Due credit has to be granted to the pioneers of the 1930s and 1940s, and to the major figures of the radio era, who established a style of sports commentary and an ethos of outside broadcasting their television heirs were happy to follow. However, it is clear many of the crucial developments in sport on television took place in the two decades following the end of the Second World War – slightly earlier in the US, where the war had not had such a shattering effect – and mostly at Britain's uniquely financed BBC.

Because the BBC is neither a state broadcaster nor dependent on advertising income, a spirit of experimentation was, if not encouraged, at least tolerated, and the frequent cock-ups were rarely job threatening. Into this culture arrived a remarkable cadre of men, mostly newly demobilised Royal Air Force veterans, who proceeded to trade on the wartime *esprit de corps* to bring to the nascent TV audience a rich diet of broadcast sport.

Chief among their number was Peter Dimmock, who joined the BBC in 1946, as the organisation resumed broadcasting after the war. One of his first tasks in fact, as the newly appointed Assistant Head of Outside Broadcasts, was to lie on the pavement outside the BBC's headquarters at London's Alexandra Palace out of vision in order to cue in announcer Jasmin Bligh welcoming viewers back 'after the short interruption'. With the sure touch the BBC has traditionally shown at great moments in the life of the nation, Bligh announced that the Mickey Mouse cartoon, *Mickey's Gala Premiere*, that had been showing when the BBC's television service was peremptorily shut down at noon on 1 September 1939, was to be shown again.

But the young man lying at Bligh's feet was convinced there were more exciting ways to unite the nation than through the medium of Mickey Mouse, as he told me when I spent a day with him at his home in Norfolk. Dimmock, was already past ninety but with razor-sharp recall, bolstered by scrapbooks full of newspaper cuttings, TV schedules and the like, confirming his memories of what has to be regarded as a golden age for the BBC.

Sadly, some of Dimmock's predecessors, like Lord Reith, the stern, founder of the BBC, and Dimmock's former boss, the magnificently named Seymour Joly de Lotbinière ('Lobby' for short) who laid down many of the ground rules for sports commentary, are no longer around to share tales of the very early days. But we have their memoirs and the sheaves of papers dutifully collected at the Corporation's written archives in Caversham, relating to their decisions, the BBC being an organisation where kicking an idea around the ballpark, running it up the flagpole and so on, has never been quite as popular as getting it down on paper and distributing it to myriad people hiding behind impenetrable collections of initials.

I have before me a memo from Dimmock to Lotbinière (C.Tel – Controller, Television, one supposes) dated 10 October 1950, discussing something called Operation Pegasus, an abortive experiment in producing pictures from the air, which Dimmock was keen to persevere with.

Copied into the correspondence are S.S.E.Tel., H.Tel.P., H.O.B., A.H.P.I.D., and E.i.C.Tel.O.B.s.

I have no idea who these people are, but my experience is that memos – emails nowadays – are something of a fetish at the BBC. As anyone who has ever worked for the organisation will tell you, office politics is its main business, with broadcasting a distant second. That said, the BBC is a magnificent broadcaster, regularly topping polls as one of the most trusted and respected institutions in Britain, as befits an organisation that helped keep resistance alive when Europe cowered under the Nazi jackboot, and later produced *Fawlty Towers* and *Strictly Come Dancing*.

Valued or not, the BBC is going through a crisis as I write this. The BBC is always going through a crisis. I have worked for it as a freelancer on and off for more than twenty-five years, and I cannot remember a time when one or another of its services was not under threat. On the day I presented my first show for Radio Two around 1985, I picked up a copy of *The Times*, and there on the front page was an item about something called 'the Black Spot Committee' looking for savings, and recommending the closure of the very network on which I was broad-casting. Its contention was that Radio Two was not providing a public service, although I should have said keeping me off the streets, present-ing what we used to call 'a lively blend of music and chat', was public service enough.

Radio Two, as we know, survived and flourished, and the BBC, as is its custom, reverted to the old Navajo Indian trick of arranging another round of committees, meetings, and lunches, setting up an initiative or two, and then doing nothing.

This, though, is no longer an option, as the Formula One story demonstrates. In 2008, the BBC signed a £200 million five-year deal to televise the sport, but by 2011 it was finding it difficult to justify that expense in a climate of cuts in public services. The Corporation agreed, therefore, to relinquish the last two years of its exclusive deal and share coverage with Sky, halving the cost to the licence payer, but also losing half the races. Enthusiasts, who generally enjoyed the BBC coverage, and had become accustomed to free-to-air motor racing, cried into their Castrol GTX, but to Formula One agnostics it made sense. The BBC would now be paying £20 million a year for the sport rather than £40 million. If, as prime minister David Cameron, maintained, we were 'all in it together,' the BBC needed to show it was sharing the pain.

By contrast, in the immediate post-war years, a nation hungry for entertainment (cinema attendances and crowds at sporting events were never higher than in the late 1940s) was generally happy for the BBC to fix its own terms of reference. Not that the corporation was immune from criticism in those days, but it was rarely more than benign satire from radio comedians like Tommy Handley and Arthur Askey, gently sending up the management's prudery, its frosty attitude to its talent, and a tendency to act like a branch of the civil service.

But this is not a book about the BBC, which may already be one of the most written-about organisations ever, so forgive me if I miss one or two of its bouts of navel-gazing. This is primarily a book about the joy of not being there, and the work that people like Dimmock and his successors at the BBC did to make that the rich, fascinating, and funny experience it continues to be.

Dimmock was convinced that the future of television depended on sport. His first job was as a horse racing journalist with the Press Association, and he sensed the drama, passion, and human interest of sport unfolding live before your eyes, would cost fortunes if you were to ask producers, directors and writers to create it in a studio. Dimmock was a visionary, dedicated to the 'progress' and 'cultural development' that started at the Berlin Olympics, but came to a full stop for the hostilities.

Not everyone, however, viewed the development of television so positively. A leader in *The Times* on 21 February 1953, just two months before sport on TV started properly, warned those running television that it did not expect screens to be filled with mere harmless diversions. Radio was still the dominant medium, but as TV licences in Britain approached the two million mark, *The Times* leader fulminated:

'Nothing would be easier than to go ahead seeking to tickle the palate of the big battalions. Nothing would be more fatal. If television were conducted with the aim of amusing the largest possible audience at all hours, it would be a Trojan horse dragged within the home and spreading ruin among the values which make national life alert, sane, and precious. A passive approach to their responsibilities by those in charge of television would create, as it appears to be in danger of creating in America, a generation that glues its eyes to the screen while its wits go wool-gathering.'

Well, here is something for irony fans. With commercial television waiting in the wings in the UK, this leader appears to be nothing more or less than a rather po-faced warning from *The Times* to the 'big battalions' of commerce that the British public expected something more from its telly than *Double Your Money* and *I Love Lucy*. That would be the same *Times* that was sold just over a decade later to the Canadian press magnate Roy Thomson, who described a commercial TV franchise as 'a licence to print money', and was gleefully and profitably helping wits go wool-gathering with a diet of lame-brained quiz shows and undemanding sitcoms on his Scottish Television. The same Roy Thomson, incidentally, whose son later sold *The Times* to Rupert Murdoch, who … well, you get the picture.

At the BBC, meanwhile, the aim – even before the big battalions entered the fray – was to consummate the marriage between sport and television. Not that this union was what you would call love at first sight. The two circled each other warily for a while for practical reasons as much as anything; sport anxious the sofa-bound might spurn the live product, and TV still not entirely convinced that sport was its business, and in any case lacking the technology and the screen time to show much of it.

But they got together, and stayed together, for the sake of the money, and now you cannot imagine one without the other. Sure, they argue and haggle like any old couple, but nevertheless are indivisible, like a pair of oldies sitting in a teashop finishing each other's sentences.

There is sport all over the television these days – as non-believers will readily testify – much of it sold to satellite TV to be mainlined by hopeless addicts, but with plenty of scraps left for the terrestrial channels to fight over. And an interesting recent development is that even the prime-time stuff that is not supposed to be sport looks like sport: competitive cookery, dancing, singing, antique hunting, even competitive baking. The argot of the commentary box, meanwhile, has become the lingua franca of TV: 'she really nailed that boeuf en croute,' 'this is the big one', 'I'm going to give this Whitney Houston song 110 percent'.

This is a world away from the climate into which Dimmock walked. TV in those days was mostly run by chaps in dinner jackets, who knew how to handle a cigarette holder, and in some cases had read Ibsen. They deigned to point their cameras at muddied oafs and flannelled fools – at least until the light began to fade – but only considered a sporting event truly significant if it boasted royal patronage. And the people involved in broadcast sport knew to come in via the tradesmen's entrance, and kindly bang the mud off their boots first. Within a couple of decades, though, Dimmock and his chums in sports broadcasting were having the last laugh. Producers like Paul Fox, and Bryan 'Ginger' Cowgill from Clitheroe in Lancashire – who, at twenty-eight years old, had never even been to London before his BBC interview in 1955, let alone attended first nights at Covent Garden – bagged the big jobs in TV, while presenters like Frank Bough and Eddie Waring tripped lightly over into mainstream entertainment shows.*

And once they had vaulted the barriers and kicked down the doors at Television Centre, the people who played sport themselves got their turn in front of the camera. Scarcely an eyebrow is raised these days when the former England international striker Gary Lineker, or the 1976 French Open tennis winner Sue Barker, pops up in prime time. Come to think of it, becoming a moderately decent tennis professional in Britain

---

* Cowgill, a future Head of Sport and Controller of BBC1, was described by John Motson, one of his commentators, as 'a television storm trooper', ruthless with his staff when they fell below his high standards.

is probably a more effective route into the media than any BBC training scheme. Ask Andrew Castle and Annabel Croft.

What follows is the story of how it happened: how sport ate your TV, and how in a reciprocal arrangement, television feasted on the flesh of almost any sporting endeavour you care to mention – from English Premier League football to the Eskimo Olympics, often adding garnishes and flourishes, sometimes radically altering the flavour. And I shall tell it from the perfect vantage point, the Mitford in my living room because, as we have established, that is where I was when most of it happened. I suspect your sporting life might be similar.

Let's be honest, very few of us get to attend a World Cup or an Olympics. I have never been to either, nor to the European Athletics Championships, the Open golf, Six Nations rugby union, the Commonwealth Games or even the World Professional Darts Championships. I have been to some cup finals – both football and rugby league – to Wimbledon once or twice, the odd Test match and a game at Euro '96 when the tournament was held in England, but my default position for big sporting events is to be not among those present.

Successive television receivers can bear witness to the great sporting occasions I have failed to attend: from my parents' walnut veneer cabinet-style sets, sitting in the corner of the room pretending not to be anything as common as a television, via the eccentric equipment in shared student flats in Glasgow requiring one or other of the tenants to hold a twin-pronged space alien-style indoor aerial aloft so we could watch the FA Cup final through a snow storm, to my current Sky Plus High Definition 3D job.

My memories – in common with almost everybody else's – of the greatest moments in sport come filtered through the cathode ray tube, and its flatter, more technologically elaborate successors. Of all the sports books jostling for space on the shelves, this, therefore, is the one that most accurately reflects Britain's sporting life. Here is sport, as most of us know it. It is the authentic sporting life of the common man and woman: the sofa, the snacks, the slo-mo.

TWO

WHERE'S THE BALL?

The role Scotland has played in shaping the world we live in is sometimes undervalued. Not by the Scots, obviously. They have the opposite tendency, and make sure due recognition is granted to two Scots who helped pave the way for the on-screen riches we sports fans enjoy today.

Firstly, let's hear it for John Logie Baird who, despite competing claims, is generally considered to have transmitted the first television pictures. That was what we were told at school in the 1960s anyway, leading to the popular (and then topical) joke: 'If Logie Baird invented telly, where was Boo Boo?' Terrible playground stuff, I know, and I only repeat it to emphasise that ours was the first generation to whose lives television was central, so it naturally informed our childish humour. There were Lone Ranger and Batman jokes too.

Baird, born in Helensburgh, Dumbartonshire, in 1888, was, it should be said, just one of a number of scientists, techno-buffs and in some cases just bonkers inventors conducting experiments in the transmission of images via radio waves in the 1920s. But it is generally accepted that television started on 2 October 1925 when Baird successfully transmitted what is believed to be the world's first television picture. It was the head of a ventriloquist's dummy called Stooky Bill, the model, unkind wags might suggest, for any number of future sports presenters (insert chosen names here).

Nowadays, we would probably see the pasty-faced Baird, who was dogged by ill health all his life, as something of a geek or an anorak. But he was persistent and talented, and, despite setbacks that would have thwarted lesser men, had an unshakeable belief in the possibility of television. He is said to have built his first working TV set out of an old hatbox, some darning needles, a few bicycle light lenses, a used tea chest, and sealing wax and glue – with the wireless gubbins inside it, I am assuming.

For his successful test Baird was unable to use a human because the lights illuminating the subject generated too much heat: eventually the dummy's hair became singed, and his painted face cracked in the high temperatures. (Having sweated under the lights on one or two TV discussion shows, I should say this is an issue that has not entirely been sorted out.) Nonetheless it was a landmark, and Baird told in his memoirs, *Television and Me*, how he visited the *Daily Express* in a state of great excitement to tell the paper about the device he had invented for 'seeing by wireless'. He recalls speaking to the editor and being promised 'a first-class show on the front page', following which not a word appeared in the paper. Years later Baird found out why, when he met the chap he had spoken to at the *Express*, who was not the editor at all but a messenger who had been instructed to go down to reception and 'get rid of a lunatic'. One of the assistant editors had warned him: 'He says he's got a machine for seeing by wireless. Watch him carefully, he may have a razor hidden', a story that neatly encapsulates the fear and suspicion that would inform the press's attitude to new technology for most of the century.

Baird's demonstration took place at his laboratory at 22 Frith Street in Soho. The event is commemorated by a blue plaque above the front door of the Bar Italia, occupiers of the property since 1949, and coincidentally a popular venue for watching Italian Serie A football on a big screen – and also for TV reporters doing colour pieces with Italian expats on their nation's progress in World Cups and European competitions.

As it happens, the site is also little more than a crostini's length away from the Groucho Club in Dean Street, a members' club much favoured by media types, and often a venue for meetings between TV executives and agents representing sports broadcasters, so I think we can claim to have discovered the true spiritual home of sport on television. Those few dozen square yards in Central London really ought to have some way of celebrating its role in history, maybe an annual procession of young men in fashionable trousers (as opposed to the daily one you can see any time) tapping away on BlackBerries and iPhones.

Baird was far from being alone in his enthusiasm for television in the 1920s and 1930s, but there was no great clamour for it from the general public, because radio had only just got going, which brings us to our second epoch-making Scotsman, the man who built the BBC, John Reith. I referred to Reith in the previous chapter as 'stern', and must confess to having taken the lazy writer's route by reaching for *Roget's Thesaurus* to find an alternative description for him here. Amazingly, virtually all of the hundreds of words I found seemed to fit, so take your pick from these: harsh, merciless, lordly, domineering, unforgiving, austere, puritanical, unsparing, despotic, exacting. He was all these, but he was also the man who founded the greatest broadcasting organisation in the world – the Hypocrite Who Built the BBC, according to a headline in the *Daily Mail*.

It seems a little below the belt for the *Mail* to be having a go at the BBC from beyond its founding father's grave, but as the headline appears above a review of the coruscating memoir *My Father: Reith of the BBC* by Reith's daughter Marista Leishman, it appears to be more than fair comment. Frances Hardy's review of the book will have more than chimed in with *Mail* attitudes. In fact, it will have rung a whole fire station of bells at a newspaper that can be as moralising and unsparing as Reith himself.

'Publicly, he abhorred infidelity; but privately, he enjoyed relationships with a series of malleable young women – and once, while in his twenties, even had an intimate liaison with a man,' wrote Hardy. If Leishman were the only source for this, one might be prepared to cut Reith a little slack, but Reith's own diaries, which he kept for sixty years, confirm that the director general's private life fell well below the standards of the, er, Reithian BBC, not to mention the present-day *Daily Mail*.

There is, though, total agreement that even if Reith was austere, egotistical and hypocritical, he was a brilliant man, whose intelligence and application transformed the British Broadcasting Company, a commercial operation with a staff of four which he joined as general manager in 1922, into the Corporation he left in July 1938, employing thousands and boasting a monopoly of radio in Britain, and a world lead in television.

A great symphony orchestra, the Proms, the *Radio Times*, the *Listener*, children's programmes, features, sport, and variety … they all flourished under Reith's stewardship. His other great gift to the BBC was a doughty independence, nowhere better demonstrated than during Britain's General Strike in 1926, when he refused to allow ministers, including Winston Churchill, to use the BBC as a government mouthpiece, and turned down the Archbishop of Canterbury's request to appeal for an end to the strike. The BBC's independence is constantly under threat, and some director generals have been less diligent than Reith in defending it.

But Reith may also have bequeathed the BBC a certain arrogance. His open flaunting of young female companions (one former colleague, Leonard Miall, recalled that he kept a picture of his 'god-daughter' on his desk, although it was hurriedly removed when the *Listener* came to photograph him) hints at a belief in untouchability. Many years ago I saw an Italian film, *Investigation of a Citizen Above Suspicion*, in which the head of the police's homicide squad murders his mistress and then leaves clues all over the place, to test his theory that, as the movie's tagline goes, 'when you are a big man in a big city, you can get away with murder'. The film came to mind for the first time in years when I was reading about Reith.

Could it be that alongside the BBC's righteous and universally respected independence, Reith's vanity, his overweening bumptiousness, his belief in the corporation's innate superiority, also persisted long past his reign, right down to the time in the 1980s and 1990s when the BBC began to lose – to its own executives' evident surprise – its sports rights to supposedly lesser broadcasters, leaving its once mighty *Grandstand* an empty hulk?

But we are getting ahead of ourselves. Long before the television era, the appetite for broadcast sport was established through radio and newsreels and, as luck would have it, radio is my specialist subject, having broadcast on it for thirty years, both for the BBC and in the private sector. In my view, we have never got radio right in Britain, complicating unnecessarily what is essentially a simple and very cheap medium, saddling it with all sorts of restrictions, meaning British radio sport has lagged behind the Americans.

Chronologically, that is certainly true. What is generally credited as the first broadcast of a sporting event was on 11 April 1921, when KDKA in Pittsburgh, Pennsylvania, a station owned by the electrics company Westinghouse, broadcast a ten-round featherweight boxing match between Johnny Dundee (known, rather charmingly, as the 'Scotch Wop') and Johnny Ray. This heralded a frenzy of activity, as stations owned by Westinghouse's competitors – General Electric, American Telephone and Telegraph (AT&T), and Radio Corporation of America (RCA) – scrambled to keep up.

Details of the Scotch Wop's fight were simply telephoned in from Pittsburgh's Motor Square Gardens, and then recreated in the studio. But within a few months KDKA was doing a proper outside broadcast, a baseball match between the Pittsburgh Pirates and the Philadelphia Phillies, described live from Forbes Field using what was little more than a converted telephone. (Competition drove radio in the United States, and continues to do so. In 2011, all-sports radio, with 673 stations, was the fourth most popular format in the US, behind only country music, news/talk and Spanish language. In Britain there is one dedicated sports radio station, Talksport.)

So while America raced ahead, the Post Office, who laid down the rules for Reith's British Broadcasting Company, forbade live commentaries on sport in order to protect the newspaper industry. The tradition of British broadcast protectionism was born. A good example: when I was looking through the *Daily Express* archives for coverage of England's World Cup triumph in 1966 I happened across a piece about government plans to close down the pirate radio ships, whose shows were enjoyed by me and lots of other teenagers. The Postmaster General's Bill, said to be a 'foolproof' plan to force the radio stations off the air, mentioned prison sentences of up to two years for anyone working on the ships.

Now, while throwing disc jockeys in jail is a policy that would not be without popular support, nobody really believed the government's arguments about the broadcasts being a danger to shipping, and this particular sledgehammer tied our public service broadcaster in all sorts of knots, forcing it to try and replace what the pirates had offered. As a result, licence payers are paying a good deal more than we should to listen to pop records on Radios One and Two: the market is skewed against commercial radio, and local radio, which should be run locally, is controlled centrally and expensively from the BBC in London.

Lord Reith would probably revolve in his grave at the mere sound of Radio One. In 1937 he wrote to the editor of the *Listener* complaining that it was publicising jazz music: 'Jazz in its place is all right,' wrote Reith, 'but do you not agree that it has got altogether out of its place ... and that to some extent anyhow it is degrading?'

He knew his own mind all right, and was not about to be dictated to by the Post Office when he was marking out territory for his British Broadcasting Company in the 1920s. 'Reith had his own vision of what was worthy of transmission,' wrote the radio historian Dick Booth. 'He was not a great sports enthusiast, but he wanted the BBC to broadcast the big events of contemporary life ... Reith understood the unique quality of radio when compared to previous means of communication, that it went directly into the heart of people's homes.' 'Not even left like milk on the doorstep', as Reith himself put it.

On 15 January 1927, shortly after the British Broadcasting Company Limited was wound up, and became the British Broadcasting Corporation we know today, a rugby union international between England and Wales became the first sports event broadcast in Britain, with Captain Henry Blythe Thornhill 'Teddy' Wakelam as commentator. A week later Wakelam commentated on the first football match on British radio:

Arsenal v. Sheffield United at Highbury. It is widely believed the phrase 'back to square one' has its origins in that commentary, as the *Radio Times* printed a grid of a football pitch divided into eight numbered squares so the audience would be aware of the ball's location, 'back to square one' meaning the game was to be restarted with a goal kick. However, nowhere in the surviving recordings of the commentary does the phrase occur, so it is possibly a handy, but fanciful, theory.

Teddy Wakelam also commentated on cricket and Wimbledon and non-sporting events like the Tidworth Tattoo, but as an ex-Harlequins player, rugger was his speciality. He was undoubtedly the first star of the commentary box, attracting admiration and criticism in roughly equal measure, much as today's sports broadcasters do. The *Manchester Guardian*, for instance, felt Wakelam did not succeed in extracting 'the essence of the game', although this prompted a listener's letter declaring the broadcast 'an unqualified success'.

But Wakelam could not do it all, and de Lotbinière, who was Director of Outside Broadcasts, set about training the staff the BBC already had in the art of commentary, and recruiting new ones, as a document in the BBC archives, *Note to Applicants for General Commentary Work*, written by de Lotbinière in March 1937 illustrates.

Thirty-two years before the BBC auditioned four hundred people for a commentators' competition on *Sportsnight With Coleman*, it was clear half the nation thought itself qualified to describe a football match. So much so that Lobby felt constrained to write: 'Applications from would-be commentators are so numerous that it is not possible to arrange a test for everyone who applies, and those who live far from London are advised that they should wait to apply for an interview until they are coming to London for some other purpose.' Reading through Lobby's memos, it is remarkable how many arguments still raging today about sports commentary were raised by him in the 1930s. For his early outside broadcasts, he looked for experts in the sport or event that was being covered but, writing in the 1939 BBC Handbook, he rather cuttingly spurned this strategy: 'In arranging, for example, a circus broadcast,' wrote Lobby, 'it has been found more satisfactory to employ a regular commentator who can learn about circuses than to search amongst the clowns for someone with the requisite natural abilities and then teach them commentary technique.'

He was a particular admirer of Lieutenant Commander Tommy Woodroffe, whose horse-racing commentaries he praised at a meeting in December. Woodroffe, a staff member, had taken over from racing experts, providing, according to Lobby, 'better commentaries than we have done for the past ten years.'

Ironically, though, Lobby's reservations about using specialists as commentators were reinforced by his favourite. Commentating on the Spithead Review of 1937 from his old ship HMS *Nelson* after enjoying a reunion with former colleagues, Woodroffe was quite audibly intoxicated. He was, in fact, as drunk as three men, as a friend of mine likes to say. He is not the only broadcaster to appear before the mike while in his cups, but his efforts remain the gold standard. All these years later, should you google Woodroffe, you will find countless sites offering audio of the infamous commentary, which mostly consists of slurred repetition of the phrase 'The fleet's lit up,' when clearly it was the Lieutenant Commander himself who was lit up. Reith suspended him for a week.

Despite this setback, the Director of Outside Broadcasts' thoughts on commentary technique were considered no less valuable, and are recorded in numerous documents. In December 1938, under the heading *The Evolution of Technique*, he circulated a memo to producers, insisting a commentary should comprise 'scene setting, a description of the action, general associative material that may be historic or personal, and an assessment of the significance of the occasion. All these ingredients have to be woven into a single pattern, and must not come in successive slabs.'

Even the revered cricket commentator John Arlott had to conform. David Rayvern Allen, Arlott's biographer, noted that, by the end of the 1947 season, 'John had distilled the essentials of commentary into what was to become, eventually, almost his own art form. These essentials had been handed down to all commentary teams like tablets of stone by the imposing

Lobby.' (Lobby, like Reith, had extraordinary physical presence, being six foot seven inches tall, unusual height possibly being the secret of success at the early BBC.) Many of the commentators Lotbinière either appointed or nurtured became household names, including John Snagge, now remembered chiefly as the voice of the *Dad's Army* titles, boxing commentator W. Barrington Dalby, and the aforementioned Tommy Woodroffe. The one I remember best is Raymond Glendenning, who must have still been doing football commentaries when I was growing up in the 1950s.

What I recall most about Glendenning was that he irritated beyond measure my father, who thought him a pompous windbag. So I was pleased to find evidence in the archives that my dad was not alone. A producer on the Light Programme, John McMillan, sent at least two complaints to Lobby about Glendenning overrunning his allotted time: 'At about 5.05pm today Raymond Glendenning came through from Wimbledon advising that we go over for one minute because he had an exciting flash,' McMillan wrote, concluding, 'After seven minutes we decided to get out.' A further memo from McMillan complains, 'Raymond Glendenning took 2 minutes 38 seconds exactly to sign off. There was no particular reason why he need have summed up for so long ... What steps can be taken to impress your and our requirements upon him for all time?'

Fancy that, commentators not knowing when to shut up. And bless the BBC for lovingly preserving the minutiae of sixty-year-old rows in its archives. In typical BBC-style, the anti-Glendenning memos were followed by a personal letter to the commentator from T.W. Chalmers, Acting Controller, Light Programme, beginning 'My Dear Raymond,' and praising the commentator for his work at the 1948 FA Cup final, in the cause, I suspect, of damping down inter-departmental rivalries. Glendenning was clearly a popular figure with listeners – other than my dad. I have the *Raymond Glendenning Book of Sport for Boys* for 1950, the introduction for which starts: 'Hullo there! I wonder what you look like – you who are just opening this book. Have you got fair hair or dark? Blue eyes or brown? Are you tall for your age or are you medium size and sturdy?' Our hero then goes on to describe himself – 'My waistline's a bit bigger than I'd like it to be, but when you get to forty you know you've got to expect that' – as if this were some 1950s dating site. You have to have some sort of rapport with your public to get away with discussing what these days would be termed body image issues.

Away from the wireless, the other chief outlet for sports coverage in the pre-television age was the cinema newsreel, whose style has now been parodied to death, but was at one time an important source of news and sport for the average Briton. Until the early 1960s, most cinemas used to change their programme in the middle of the week – except for one big screen in town which might show *South Pacific* or *My Fair Lady* for three years – and twice-a-week attendance at the local picture house was the norm. The newsreels conformed to this rhythm, producing two different editions a week, so the midweek changeover, when a brief glimpse of Saturday's FA Cup final might be included, became an important appointment for football fans. The coverage usually concentrated on the 'human interest' angle of the match. There were brief sequences of goalkeepers flapping at the ball or wizards of the dribble. But these had to fight for space against shots of attending royals, and cheery flat-capped members of the lower orders rattling their rattles on the terraces.

Mind you, the newsreel companies, arriving and disappearing with dizzying regularity in the medium's golden age in the 1930s and 1940s, fought tooth and nail for the best sports and news stories. It was a cutthroat business with a kind of gold rush morality to it, best depicted in a 1978 Australian film, *Newsfront*, which shows newsreel reporters in early 1950s Australia metaphorically selling their grandmothers for a story, and it was much the same over here. But, as television ownership in Britain grew exponentially through the 1950s, the frustration of seeing the brief blast of bombast that passed for FA Cup final coverage at the cinema acted merely to sharpen the appetite for a more detailed version, playing into television's hands.

By the way, I hope you spotted my tribute to the newsreel age, the 'brief blast of bombast'. When I was growing up, there was still the odd fringe player about, but primarily newsreels meant Pathé News or British Movietone, both characterised by their cheesy background music and even cheesier commentaries unhealthily reliant on alliteration. I recently saw a British Movietone newsreel from the 1960s about storms in Blackpool, the commentary for which began, 'Behold Blackpool, buffeted by boisterous blasts, bashed and blasted by bursting billows. What wicked wet weekend weather!' And so on.

The voice of British Movietone news was Leslie Mitchell, who had the distinction of being the continuity announcer both when the BBC's TV service began, on 2 November 1936, and at the start of ITV, making the announcements on the first day of broadcasting for Associated-Rediffusion on 22 September 1955. His counterpart at Pathé was Bob Danvers-Walker, who was also prominent in the early days of commercial television as the announcer on the quiz show *Take Your Pick*, a Friday night ratings winner for ITV in its early days. Danvers-Walker's were the dark brown tones advising contestants they might win 'a lovely lounge suite'. As previously mentioned, the coming of the television age, and especially the addition of a second channel, did foment the growing interest in soft furnishings.

Overall, the contribution of newsreels to sport on TV should not be underestimated. News on the BBC in the 1950s tried to marry Reithian values to the newsreels' breezy style, and in fact its first 'in-vision' news programme (as opposed to a sound bulletin, illustrated with stills), at 7.30pm on 5 July 1954, was called *News and Newsreel*, presented by Richard Baker. In addition, as the days of cinema newsreels appeared numbered, many of their people defected to TV, notably Paul Fox, who in 1950 left his job as a scriptwriter for Pathé to take a similar job at the BBC.* In its heyday, the newsreel provided what these days would be called 'added value' for cinemagoers, especially during wartime when it kept audiences in touch with events – on a highly selective basis – and its chirpy cheerleading was what the nation demanded. After the war newsreels became more sources of entertainment than information.

---

* Amazingly, Pathé limped on until 1970, and British Movietone until 1979.

Most cities had news theatres in the 1960s. There were two in my native Manchester, one at each end of Oxford Road – where you could see newsreels alongside cartoons and short comedy films. The newsreels washed over me, frankly. The vanilla-flavoured library music, and mannered voice-overs that accompanied all of them made them all merge into one. I don't think I can recall a single minute of newsreel I saw in the Manchester News Theatre or the Tatler, although I remember vividly a Charlie Chaplin short I watched when I was about ten, in which Charlie was strap-hanging on a crowded bus, got bumped out of the back of the vehicle, and ended up in a deli, hanging onto a salami.

The latest Gaumont British News and British Movietone newsreels were shown on TV when it first started in 1936, but without generating any great enthusiasm for the new medium. Why would they, when you could go out and view the footage on the big screen? Even in Germany, with the Olympics as a TV showcase, there was little evidence of a rush of Teutonic early adopters. Perhaps it was its sheer implausibility in the 1920s and 1930s that stifled TV's development. I suspect even those who had heard of television thought of it as too outlandish to contemplate, rather as we might think today of time travel, or reasonably priced Japanese food.

Nor did many sixpences, I warrant, go on purchasing the report of the British government's Television Committee, published by the Stationery Office in 1935. In fairness, sixpence was a lot of money in those days, as illustrated by a popular song parents of the era used to croon to their children, which went, 'I've got sixpence, jolly jolly sixpence, sixpence to last me all my life, I've got tuppence to spend, and tuppence to lend, and tuppence to send home to my wife.' Clearly, the report of the Television Committee was not a priority purchase if popular song is to be believed. It got a glowing review in *The Times* however, on 1 February 1935, bylined significantly 'From Our Wireless Correspondent'.

'Formed in May of last year, the Committee, under the chairmanship of Lord Selsdon, has, in just over six months' time, made a most careful examination of the development of television in

England, America, and Germany, and been able to formulate proposals for its further exploitation in this country that are both reasonable and practicable. The report itself, though dealing with complicated electrical matters, is not severely technical, and gives the general reader a most comprehensive and informative account of the problems of television as well as the result of present-day efforts at their solution.'

A rattling good read, then. The BBC's Director of Television at the time – its first – was Gerald Cock, an adventurer who, after a public school education, left Britain in 1909, aged twenty-two, to travel around North America, where he took work where he could find it, often in unlikely fields for a middle-class young Englishman: as a rancher, a gold miner, and even as an extra in Hollywood films.

Cock returned home in 1915 to serve with the Royal Engineers in France and Belgium, rising to the rank of captain, and worked in various jobs in London before joining the BBC as Director of Outside Broadcasts in 1925. Cock's military background together with his varied and colourful employment history left him uniquely qualified for this post. As an army officer, he would have been comfortable with the BBC's rigid hierarchy, perfectly happy to turn up for meetings suited and booted; but also out in the field, competing with newspapers on behalf of the wireless audience for coverage of important news stories. I like to picture him as a buccaneering figure, prepared to bend a rule or two to make wireless.

Because of his enthusiasm for new broadcasting techniques, Cock was made Director of Television in 1935, his target to establish from scratch the world's very first regular service, ready for launch in November 1936. As it turned out, the date was brought forward in order to demonstrate TV at the Radiolympia exhibition in 1936, a crucial engagement. As is the case with digital radio nowadays, getting the equipment out there and widely accepted was vital for your fledgling technology to take wing. Get it wrong, and you remain grounded, as my collection of laser discs will testify.

According to the Television Committee, the price of 'a receiving set capable of producing a picture, 5 inches by 6 inches, with the accompanying sound transmission would be from £50 to £90, but it is reasonable to assume that, in mass production, this price could be substantially reduced'.

What the committee said about programmes mirrored Cock's thinking. Together they were matchmakers for the soon-to-be consummated marriage between sport and television. 'No doubt the televising of sporting and other public events will have a wide appeal, and will add considerably to the attractiveness of the service,' declared the committee's report, 'We regard such transmissions as a desirable part of a public television service, and it is essential that the British Broadcasting Corporation should have complete freedom for the televising of such scenes, with appropriate sound accompaniment, at any time of day.'

And so it was that on Monday 21 June 1937 a tiny number of viewers – thought to be around 2,000 of London's most moneyed and curious – heard a BBC television announcer declare: 'Ladies and Gentlemen. Everyone knows that the lawn tennis championship meeting is taking place at Wimbledon over the next two weeks, starting today. By the courtesy of the All England Lawn Tennis Club we've been able to make arrangements to televise matches in the Centre Court throughout the fortnight. For the first time, anywhere in the world, then, television will bring into viewers' homes pictures of outstanding international events at the exact moment they are taking place, without the aid of an intermediate link of special cable. It's a great experiment.'

The *Daily Express*, then Britain's best selling newspaper, in a volte-face from the John Logie Baird days, was terribly excited about the experiment. In a front-page story the Thursday before the broadcast, they hailed the test transmissions an 'unprecedented success'. 'Cigarette smoke was visible,' gushed the report. 'An Alsatian dog was seen running about. When actual play begins, I am told viewers will be able to see the ball.'

Unfortunately, that brave prediction proved slightly wide of the mark. There was some interference on the day, and that pesky ball got lost in the ensuing snowstorm. Not that the television critic of the *Listener*, the

BBC's in-house intellectual magazine, was unduly concerned: 'As in the news films, it has seldom been possible to watch the progress of the ball itself,' he wrote. 'But the strokes and the movements on the court have all been so clearly visible that the absence of the ball has hardly seemed to trouble the viewers.' Those of us born too late to enjoy this ball-less tennis had to wait until 1966 for Michelangelo Antonioni to recreate the surreal experience in his film *Blow Up*.

There were three BBC vans at the All England Club, one containing camera and scanner, another housing the transmitter, and the third containing a generator. Freddie Grisewood commentated. A highlight for the select band of viewers was when the camera swung around to catch the entrance into the Royal Box of Queen Mary, who was probably personally known to most of them anyway.

A fairly routine afternoon's work for Britain's own Bunny Austin – a three sets to one first round victory over Irish challenger George Lyttle-ton Rogers – was an event of far-reaching importance for Cock and the BBC. It was Cock's assiduous courting of the All England Club secretary that had pulled off the coup, and now he set his cap at some of the tougher nuts in the sporting world, representing football and cricket.

According to Professor Steven Barnett in his book *Games and Sets*, Cock wrote to Stanley Rous, Secretary of the Football Association, with proposals to televise the following year's England-Scotland international and FA Cup final. Rous was a great supporter of television but the FA council was fearful of the harmful effect live coverage might have on attendances at some of the less significant matches taking place at the same time, a stance the FA and some other sporting bodies adhered to for several decades. 'Here is the beginning of a great new industry, the progress of which depends to a great extent on the co-operation of institutions such as the Football Association,' Cock pleaded, finally being given the go-ahead by Rous to televise the international, and Huddersfield Town v. Preston North End in the FA Cup final a fortnight later.

The first televised final was to be a royal occasion, and Arthur Elvin, the managing director of Wembley Stadium, wrote to the BBC asking for a 'television receiver' to be made available in the Royal Retiring Room: 'I think that their Majesties are likely to be most interested to see the Machine in the Room when they arrive,' he predicted.

That same year, 1938, the Machine also carried the first televised Boat Race (2 April), Test Match cricket (24 June), and Neville Chamberlain doing his hilarious 'Peace in Our Time' routine on arrival at Heston Airport on 30 September. Commentary on all the TV outside broadcasts in those early days was taken directly from radio, which did not seem to affect the enjoyment of a small but appreciative audience, whose sense of wonder overcame the raw, single-camera coverage.

There was, in that brief hiatus before Chamberlain was proved so disastrously wrong, what we would call a real buzz around television. Had its arrival not pre-dated that of the office water cooler by at least half a century, the medium itself rather than anything on it would have warranted a water cooler moment.

By the early months of 1939, 23,000 licences had been sold, and programmes were being broadcast seven days a week from Alexandra Palace, dubbed Ally Pally, a name invented, say some sources, by one of its denizens, the popular musical comedy performer Gracie Fields. That jokey nickname suggests to me that BBC TV was moving out of its experimental phase and on its way to becoming the nation's Auntie. The TV manufacturers certainly sensed big things on the horizon, and coined its own slogan, 'You Can't Shut Your Eyes To It'.

But on 1 September 1939, there was no choice. The screens went blank. Many of the technical and engineering staff were recruited for the war effort to work on the radar programme, and Cock, with no television service to run, was sent off to be the BBC's North American representative.

While in the US, where TV continued throughout the war, Cock was able to see some of the latest developments, information he used in compiling a report that paved the way for the return of the British service in 1946. But even then a war-ravaged Britain was not yet quite ready to take John Logie Baird's invention to its bosom. Radio, stronger than ever, was still king.

THREE

INTO THE LIGHT

Maybe it is because we in Britain are naturally curmudgeonly, but in the post-war years television, arguably the greatest invention of the twentieth century – notwithstanding the Breville sandwich toaster – was given the kind of grudging welcome back one might afford a neighbour returning home after completing his prison sentence for setting fire to your dustbin.

The general attitude, within and without the BBC, seems to have been that television could kindly sit in the corner and behave itself, we were quite happy with the wireless, thank you very much. Television was considered an irrelevance in the post-war world of rubble and rationing. Radio, after all, had helped win the war, not just through the BBC's broadcasts to embattled continental Europe, but by raising spirits at home with jolly catchphrase-based comedy shows like Tommy Handley's *It's That Man Again* (universally known as *ITMA)*, which kept folk cheerfully parroting 'Can I do you now, Sir?', 'After you, Claude', and 'TTFN' even as the bombs rained down.*

An indicator of the relative positions of the two media is the 1948 Christmas Day radio and TV schedule. All the marquee shows – as they

---

* This may be the origin of the virulent catchphrase epidemic that occasionally afflicts Britain. At any one time half the nation will be going round saying, 'Simples', 'You are the weakest link', or, 'Suits you, Sir.' The problem is that people persist in using such phrases long after the tiny trace of humour once present has been sucked dry, leaving not so much a rotting husk as musty powder.

almost certainly would not have been called at the time – were on the BBC's main radio network, the Home Service: *Gracie Fields' Christmas Party* was on at lunchtime, followed by the aforementioned *Tommy Handley's Christmas*, a programme called *Good Neighbours*, Christmas reports from around the world, narrated by the film star Robert Donat, and then King George VI's Christmas message to the nation. The best television could offer was *A Visit to Dr Barnardo's Homes*, a production of *Alice's Adventures in Wonderland* from 1946 starring Vivian Pickles, and a cinema newsreel.

It was hardly surprising television had a somewhat threadbare look to it given its budget compared to radio. In 1947–48, TV accounted for less than one-tenth of total BBC expenditure, and even in 1950 its budget was still only half that of the Home Service. Nor need you look far for the reason. According to the broadcasting historian Andrew Crissell, the post-war director general, William Haley shared the 'misunderstanding and dislike of television' of his predecessor, John Reith, who before the war had proposed 'integrating' radio and television.

Haley and Reith may have been reading the public mood accurately. Two short paragraphs in the *Daily Express* of 20 June 1947 give a fair idea of the general indifference. The paper reports a car park dispute between the BBC and the trustees of Alexandra Palace, which ended with the telly people being ordered to shift their outside broadcast vans. 'Outside programmes, including racing at Sandown, will be affected, but they are only one-twelfth of the total time,' said the *Express*. 'Studio programmes will fill the gap.' The fact that a car park attendant's 'you can't park that there 'ere' could take BBC TV's sport off the air was not deemed worthy of comment.

Radio, meanwhile, was enjoying a golden age. In the late 1940s and early 1950s, long-running programmes like *Woman's Hour* and *Any Questions* started, as did the popular soap operas, *The Archers* and *Mrs Dale's Diary*, and crowd-pleasers like *Dick Barton – Special Agent* and *Journey Into Space*, while groundbreaking drama like Dylan Thomas's *Under Milk Wood* enhanced radio's prestige. They could park where they wanted.

Within the BBC, snobbery clearly played a part. The pioneering broadcasting executive Grace Wyndham Goldie, who was also the *Listener*'s first television reviewer, said the essentially bookish souls at the BBC* felt television was intrinsically lowbrow, like music hall or the pictures, which had not yet become 'cinema', and thus a suitable subject for high-flown analysis. 'Their speciality was the use of words; they had no knowledge of how to present either entertainment or information in vision,' Wyndham Goldie wrote of her cohorts. 'They were afraid the high purposes of the corporation would be trivialised by the influence of those concerned with what could be transmitted in visual terms.'

There was little sign, then, of a wind of change blowing through the BBC, but a slight breeze was wafting over from producer Angus Mackay's sports news department, home of the longest running sports radio programme in the world, *Sports Report*, which started on the Light Programme in January 1948, and remains a mainstay of sports radio sixty-odd years later, still using the same theme tune.

Its signature tune is 'Out of the Blue', composed by Hubert Bath, who wrote incidental music for a number of films, including Hitchcock's *The 39 Steps*, and died in 1945, too soon to enjoy the glow of pride – or indeed the royalties – after Mackay grabbed an album of library music from the shelf, and chose Bath's track to introduce his new programme. The most potent theme tunes evoke a Proustian rush: if I hear the theme to the Sunday night BBC series *Dr Finlay's Casebook*, I am immediately back in the 1960s finishing off homework and packing up books for the start of the school week. But 'Out of the Blue' is extraordinary in that it is evocative to sports fans of several different eras. Is there a sports lover of any age alive in Britain today whose father did not da-dum-da-dum-da-dum-da-dum along with the music, while waiting for the football results? I doubt it.

But Mackay had an influence on TV too. He gave a start to a number of presenters, like Eamonn Andrews, Jim Rosenthal, jack-of-all-trades at

---

* I picture them as characters from Kingsley Amis's *Lucky Jim*: bluestockings or their male equivalents, who I guess you would call corduroys or tweed jackets.

commercial TV, and Desmond Lynam, plucked by Mackay from BBC Radio Brighton. Lynam went on to anchor more or less everything in sport there was to anchor for at least two decades, and established a laid-back style many have striven to replicate without quite succeeding.

Mackay had a reputation as a hard case, well earned according to Lynam. Des says he was present when one of the contributors to *Sports Report*, the outspoken J.L. (Jim) Manning of the *Daily Mail*, failed to make it. 'I overheard Angus on the phone with Jim's wife, who was explaining that Jim was in hospital in intensive care after suffering a heart attack, and Angus was expressing sympathy, saying "all our thoughts are with Jim", "anything we can do to help, of course we will", "love to all the family", and so on, at which he put the phone down, and, without a pause, shouted to the team, "We've got a problem. Manning's fucking let us down."'

If Mackay's chosen theme tune was pure 1940s, he was clearly not, and neither was the somewhat breathless tone of his programme, which went against the grain of the BBC at the time. It must have influenced TV sports magazines like *Sportsview* and *Grandstand*, waiting just around the corner. A key figure in both those programmes was Peter Dimmock, who we last met lying on the ground outside Alexandra Palace, cueing in television's rebirth after the war. Dimmock was one of a number of young men, mostly fresh from the forces, excited by the possibilities of the new medium, and undaunted by its lack of resources. Having recently survived active service, they were not about to be thrown off course by having to make do and mend, nor by BBC internal politics.

Dimmock's wartime service was arguably perfect preparation for the BBC. After transferring from the Territorial Army to the Royal Air Force, he qualified as a pilot, and later a flying instructor with the rank of flight lieutenant. In the latter days of the war he was appointed as a staff officer at the Air Ministry, where he will have gained valuable experience shuffling pieces of paper around. After a brief period working as a journalist with the Press Association, he joined the BBC in 1946. His interview was a carve-up. 'The chaps on the board were all like me, ex-RAF men,' Dimmock told me, 'Four candidates were after two jobs, and two of us were RAF; myself and a chap called Keith Rogers, ex-radar. Guess who got the jobs?'

I visited Dimmock at his rather grand house near Wells-Next-the-Sea in Norfolk with its orchard in the garden, and an outdoor swimming pool. He lives there with his second wife Christabel who he married after the death of his first wife, the TV reporter Polly Elwes.

Speak to any BBC veteran who worked with Dimmock, and it will not be long before the word 'charm' crops up. I remembered him chiefly as the presenter of *Sportsview* in the late 1950s. With a neatly clipped moustache matching his vocals, his politeness to interviewees, and generally smooth delivery, he was quite patently officer class. I knew little about his career behind the scenes, but it seems the unflappability and gentlemanly competence, which came through on-screen, served him well off it.

Paul Fox (Parachute Regiment, 1943–46), the former newsreel scriptwriter who edited *Sportsview*, and later became Controller of BBC1, describes Dimmock as a 'terrific operator, and a very good boss. He was 6 foot 2, good-looking, he had style, and everyone had seen him on-screen, and in those days that meant something.'

And the style did not fade. He shuffled a little stiffly to the front door to welcome me, solicitous about my journey to Norfolk's backwoods and, despite the fact he now walks with a stick, he insisted on going round the house hunting out albums of newspaper cuttings for me, and apologising in advance – unnecessarily – for memory failure. 'At my age I forget everything very quickly,' he tells me, 'I have to remember to take these bloody pills too, which is frankly boring.'

Dimmock was in charge of televising the 1948 Olympics, including the opening ceremony, which he describes as follows: 'The teams all came into Wembley, lined up, then we had all the speeches, then they all marched out.' Austere opening or not, the 1948 games were crucial to the development of TV in Britain.

An article previewing the games in the *Radio Times*, written by Dimmock's boss Ian Orr-Ewing, is positively gushing, at a time when the magazine usually lived up to its name and barely mentioned the upstart alternative. 'The 1948 Olympic Games provides television with one of its greatest opportunities; an opportunity which has been whole-heartedly seized,' writes Orr-Ewing. 'Live television will cover all the main events at Wembley, where one unit is being installed in the stadium and another in the Empire Pool.'

The *Radio Times* marvelled at the 'average of three and a half hours a day' of coverage planned, alongside one-and-a-half hours of the usual studio-based programmes. 'From correspondence received,' Orr-Ewing concluded, 'it is clear that a large percentage of viewers still try to see all programmes televised. It is hoped that this habit will not persist during the period of the Olympic Games or viewers will be easily recognised on the streets of London by their pallid appearance!' (This is the first known sighting of television's traditional 'Don't try this at home' warning.)

The difference in tone between the 1948 games and those of 2012 was starkly illustrated by prime minister Clement Attlee's welcome message: 'May the weather be fine, the events well contested, and may records be broken,' delivered as if it were a warning to be wary of chip pan fires. No wonder Churchill used to tease Attlee about his lack of charisma, calling him 'a sheep in sheep's clothing' and 'a modest man with much to be modest about.' By the 1966 World Cup, thanks mostly to television, politicians had become rather better at making hay when the sporting sun shone, not necessarily to the benefit of viewers.

But if Attlee got little out of the 1948 games, that was not true of television. Pictures were still only available in the London area, but despite the shrivelled post-war economy the number of licences jumped from 15,000 to 90,000, and significantly the press was beginning to tune in and take notice. A piece in the *Daily Express* on 17 August, shortly after the start of the Games, signalled TV's new status. John Macadam, a self-confessed TV sceptic, wrote: 'Last Thursday, the British television teams had their greatest day out – they sent seven-and-a-half hours of continuous sport right into the homes of viewers. Such Olympic successes have set the key for the months ahead. Whatever the failings of television as a medium for other entertainment, it really can do sport brilliantly.'

A companion piece in the paper noted that television 'has had a fight to work itself into the vocabularies and interests of ordinary people' but says the corner may have been turned, its evidence being the fact that cartoonists were latching on to it as a suitable subject for jokes. The example it prints from Osbert Lancaster shows a chap fully dressed for a day at the races, sitting on a shooting stick in front of the TV with a pair of binoculars, watching the horses. His wife is saying, 'Are you proposing to come in to lunch or do you expect me to bring you some sandwiches on the course?'

This new acceptance of the medium, and especially of the benefits of outside broadcasting, must have done Dimmock's career prospects no harm at all, although he credits the spirit within his department rather than any change of attitude among the corporate hierarchy for the success, 'We were jacks of all trades,' he told me, 'a lot of ex-forces people who had self-discipline. That's what made life so much easier for us all. We were all self-reliant. People were not bolshie at all. We used to work seven days a week really. I would put people on standby over the weekends, which used to annoy them, but they lived with it.

'In those early days, we were always doing firsts, like broadcasting from a submarine live, things like that. We got as much fun out of these projects as the viewers did, and in those days the viewer forgave us if we had breakdowns, which we frequently did. It was all part of the enjoyment and excitement of doing something for the first time.'

As well as organising Olympic coverage, Dimmock was also one of the commentators alongside yet another war veteran, Richard Dimbleby, who as the BBC's air correspondent had taken part in a raid on Berlin in a Lancaster bomber. 'We covered more or less everything at the games,' said Dimmock, 'Five or six hours a day usually, athletics and showjumping from the main stadium, and swimming from the Empire Pool next door. But I am not sure how many people watched it.'

It was 1949 before the Midlands came on air, and with the North having to wait a further year, progress on the sale of licences was still not spectacular. By the start of the 1950s there were still only 340,000 TV licence holders. And the outside broadcast department was still comically under-equipped, as Gerald Cock's successor as Director of Television, Maurice Gorham, recalled, 'I was running television in a country that could hardly afford it. Our equipment was hopelessly old-fashioned in design, the actual gear we used was mostly ten years old, and it was inadequately served. For instance, our outside broadcast unit still took to the road like a travelling circus with four enormous vans and thirty or forty men to operate it, while the Americans were using one small van and six to eight men.' And the fleet that housed this cumbersome, antiquated equipment had no base; it literally had not got a roof over its head.

'Throughout the cruel winter of 1946–47,' Gorham wrote, 'it could be seen standing on the parking space outside Alexandra Palace whilst its devoted engineers did all the maintenance work on the complicated equipment in the open, and sometimes in the snow.' In fact, a shortage of fuel that winter closed down the television service for a month – to no great consternation, it must be said. Despite all that, a newsreel piece just before the Olympics boasted about all the fine equipment the BBC was using at the games for the first time, including a compact trailer in which the control room staff would sit in comfort, 'instead of standing like they had to in the old vans.'

The engineers all came from the same source: just as Hitler's Olympics were televised by his *Reichspostzentralamt*, so the Post Office held sway in the BBC's engineering department, and they stuck to Post Office ways in the early days. 'For instance, they wouldn't let us use a microwave link; we had to have a cable, a Post Office cable. Well, this was crazy,' said Dimmock.

Orr-Ewing's newsreel piece, broadcast just before the 1948 games, boasted of the BBC's new equipment but failed to mention that the Corporation's new CPS Emitron cameras were less effective during the winter months. For instance, viewers would be lucky to see much more than half a rugby match. At around 4pm on a January afternoon, the Emitron would hoist the white flag, unable to cope with the poor light, and the holder of one of the new television licences might as well go and toast a crumpet or two, as coverage continued in sound only.

'The engineers quite understandably wanted only British-made equipment,' said Dimmock, 'I was always fighting with them, because I was trying to get us to buy the best. When the light was too low, our camera peeled off, it was like a white sheet coming across the screen. But I had seen an American camera called the Image Orthicon, which would continue to operate no matter how dim the light.

'They continued to resist it, though, so I hired a boxing ring, and put a candle in the middle of it, and I got Marconi, who had the rights for the Image Orthicon in this country, to bring one along. We gradually turned the lights down, down, and down until there was just the light from a single candle, and of course we still had a picture. Well, I said, "Come on boys, you can't argue, we've got to move forward, we've got to have this."'

The zoom camera was the next big step forward, enabling the shot which arguably secured the future of television in Britain. The Coronation of Queen Elizabeth was to take place at Westminster Abbey on 2 June 1953, keenly anticipated in a country that had had little to celebrate since winning the war.

While Germany's *wirtschaftswunder*, or economic miracle, was indeed working wonders, rebuilding our vanquished and shattered foe, big northern cities like Manchester and Liverpool were still scarred by bombsites and other reminders of the conflict. As late as 1959, I can remember picking up rubble left over from wartime bombing raids and pitching it at my mates from primary school, or playing hide-and-seek and collecting caterpillars in air-raid shelters. Until February 1953, sweets were still rationed; a coupon issued by the Orwellian Ministry of Food allowing British children no more than six ounces per week.

The Coronation of the young Queen was to lift the nation from this slough of despond although, if those in her inner circle had had their way, nobody would have been watching it. The Establishment, in the form of the Coronation Joint Executive Committee, chaired by the Duke of Norfolk, said the Coronation should not be broadcast live.

This august body decided that to have live television inside the Abbey would impose an intolerable emotional strain on the young Queen. The bright lights and the heat, the committee felt, could prove to be a disastrously heavy burden on a long exhausting day. Cameras would also, of course, deprive the privileged class of peers of the exclusive opportunity of witnessing at first hand the crowning of the new monarch. It was reported back to Dimmock that Churchill himself was dead set against it, feeling that television's intrusion would destroy the monarchy's mystique. The Cabinet agreed that no facilities should be provided for television inside the Abbey, noting that 'a cinematograph film was to be taken', as it was for George VI in 1937. This, it graciously decreed, could be shown on television later in the day.*

It is believed the Queen herself intervened to ask the Cabinet to reconsider. Enter young Dimmock to arrange a trial run designed to convince the Abbey authorities that the lighting level would not be oppressive, nor the cameras obtrusive. He demonstrated the discreet long-distance picture that was obtainable with a two-inch lens on the camera, but on the day he used a 12-inch lens and caught a close-up of the actual lowering of the crown onto the Queen's head. At the perfect moment, he cued his commentator Richard Dimbleby to mention Prince Charles, and cut to a charming image of the four-year-old prince in the royal box, watching his mother being crowned.

'The zoom camera made a heck of a difference,' Dimmock told me. 'I used it for the shot of the Queen processing out of the Abbey, and it was marvellous because, you see, I held her in close-up right the way down the aisle from the organ screen to the west door, and she was full screen all the time, while the music ... Well, I managed to persuade them to play "Land of Hope and Glory", and it was stunning, absolutely stunning.'

---

* It was not all bad news for the long-suffering British public. A Cabinet meeting two weeks later was told that the Ministry of Food would be raising the weekly meat ration from one shilling and ninepence (nearly 9p) to two shillings' worth (10p). 'And to think, we *won* the war!' as people used to like to say at the time.

A theme that will crop up repeatedly when we come to examine some of the great sports broadcasters will be the importance of preparation, how the best commentators are meticulous in their attention to detail before the mike is opened, and Dimmock's chosen voice, Richard Dimbleby was a prime example.

A number of stories have grown up around the Coronation broadcast. One is that the Queen's grandmother, the old Queen Mary, wanted cameras in the Abbey because she realised she would be too frail to attend. Dimmock's colleague Paul Fox says that Duke of Norfolk was just starting to waver when the Duke and Dimmock happened to go to the loo together. 'Peter stood next to the Duke and said, "Come on, Bernard, say yes."' Dimmock did not recall the incident, but if true, it is one of the great urinal stories. (The best I can offer is the time at Aintree on Grand National day when I found myself peeing next to Ken Barlow off *Coronation Street*.)

However it came about, the Coronation broadcast established the television age in Britain. In Leonard Miall's words: 'The combination of Dimmock's impeccable camera direction and Dimbleby's felicitous words, together with the pageantry of the scene and above all the bearing of the young Queen, assured a television triumph. The viewing audience that day was over twenty million, many watching in friends' houses or in public places.'

It was the first time the TV audience had beaten the radio audience and the number of licences began climbing steeply: up 50 per cent the next year. As Dimmock put it, 'When the Coronation was such a huge success, people not only started to buy sets, so the manufacturers were doing well, but secondly Broadcasting House had to increase the television budget, because we had been the paupers, you know. We said we've got to have money, we've got to buy modern equipment, we've simply got to move ahead now and make our television really good, and rather reluctantly they did stump up.'

An unintended consequence was that sporting authorities became more aware of the new medium, and began to fret that the prospect of watching top sport in the comfort of their own home – or what passed for comfort in the 1950s – might persuade people to forego the delights of cold and crumbling terraces.

Well before the Coronation, the 1950 Cup final between Liverpool and Arsenal had attracted a TV audience of around a million. In those days normal league matches were held on Cup final day, and there were definite signs that attendances had fallen. The BBC argued that bad weather was largely to blame and that there was not much difference in the areas that did have TV, London and Birmingham, and those that did not. But it did agree to show only the second half of the final in 1951. The Football Association said the 1952 final could be televised in full, but – small catch – a week later. The BBC decided not to show it at all, the last time Britain was denied full live coverage of the match.

If the Football League, always more militant against TV than their counterparts at the FA, had had their way, the 1953 final would not have been shown either, but the FA gave in on one condition: the BBC had to pay a thousand pounds for the rights. This was a new development. Until then there had been murmurings about rights payments, but all that was paid were 'facility fees'. 'Peanuts really,' said Dimmock, 'A hundred and fifty, two hundred pounds. I treated the BBC's money as if it was my own.'

As it turned out, the money paid for the 1953 Cup final may have been the best thousand pounds the BBC ever spent.

FOUR

THE MATTHEWS FACTOR

The 1953 FA Cup final, between Bolton Wanderers and Blackpool, changed everything. If you have ever wondered when the seeds were sown for the ludicrous, self-important, over-inflated all-consuming leviathan of a game (yes, despite everything you read and hear, it is just a game) we have today, it was on that first Saturday of May in 1953, the so-called 'Matthews Final'.

Football on TV started properly then, and then was pumped up and pumped up, to the extent that in February 2011 several newspapers led – the main story on the front page, most important thing in the world – with news of two chaps who don't even play football, but just talk about it on the telly, being sacked for some injudicious off-air badinage. I myself was on four separate media outlets discussing the sackings, on one occasion beating to air the BBC's Middle East specialist, who merely wanted to talk about the possible fall of two Arab governments.

Very rarely do those of us who fill the sports pages of newspapers, and airtime on radio and TV, stop to think football may not be quite as important as we keep making it out to be. It hit me particularly forcefully one night in the 1990s when I was presenting a regional evening radio show in the North of England. On busy football nights I used to take regular reports from the various matches in our region – as many as twenty sometimes – from Liverpool, Newcastle, Manchester United and so on, as well as the lower league fixtures at places like Fleetwood and Blyth Spartans.

I also used to book a studio guest, who on the night in question was the Liberal politician Michael Meadowcroft, who had just returned from a UN-sponsored trip to the former Yugoslavia to advise on the organisation of democratic elections. I was asking him about the prospects for the troubled region, and he launched into an explanation of how instability in that part of Europe could spell disaster for those of us in the West. 'This may be the most important issue in the world today,' he explained. 'I cannot stress strongly enough that if this opportunity for peace and democracy is not taken …' at which point I said, 'I am afraid I'm going to have to stop you there, Michael, there's been a goal at Worksop.'

I venture to suggest there was a time when world peace would have been considered more important than football – in the years immediately after the Second World War, for instance. Before the Matthews Final, a football match was just a football match, of huge interest, of course, in the towns the teams represented but not a matter of national moment.

Certainly, our national broadcaster made no great fuss of football. On the contrary. The fact that officer-class chaps were favoured at Orr-Ewing and Dimmock's pioneering, under-funded, outside broadcast department meant that the sports favoured by England's public schools, especially cricket and rugby union, loomed a little larger at the BBC than they did in the country as a whole. There was a degree of snobbery involved, fostered no doubt by the spirit of the first director general haunting the corridors of Broadcasting House. According to Dick Booth's book, *Talking of Sport*, Seymour de Lotbinière, who laid down the rules for the BBC's sports commentary, owned up to being infected: 'I may have concentrated mostly on the Oxford and Cambridge accents and backgrounds,' admitted Lobby, 'so that a Howard Marshall may have been preferred to a John Arlott.'

Before the Matthews Final cricketers were reckoned to be bigger names than footballers, at least at the BBC. Characters like Len Hutton, Alec Bedser, and Denis Compton meant more than any from the winter game.

Some idea of how central to the nation's conversation cricket was before the takeover by football can be gleaned from Alfred Hitchcock's

1938 film *The Lady Vanishes*. It seems perfectly natural in the movie to have the two comic characters on the train, Charters and Caldicott (Basil Radford and Naunton Wayne), quiz every English passenger they come across about the progress of the Test Match. English people would have been expected to know. Nowadays the question 'Do you know how United got on?' would be more likely, even in a first-class compartment.

Back in 1950, cricketers were household names. It was Denis Compton,* not Tommy Lawton or indeed Stanley Matthews, who was able to cash in on his fame, and earn a thousand pounds a year selling himself as the face of Brylcreem hair products. Not quite the millions that ex-international footballer Gary Lineker pockets for hawking potato crisps, but an indication of the cultural primacy of cricket.

The sport was a sure fire topic for comedians of the day, too, alongside staples like seaside landladies and British Railways pork pies – especially if the England team was playing poorly. The following is from a website collecting jokes of the 1940s: 'A batsman, scoring freely against a fast bowler, is handed a note. He reads it, frowns, and tells the umpire, "It's about my wife. She's seriously ill, and I need to get to her. Can you get the bowler to shorten his run-up?"'

No explanation needed. Cricket was as central to the English way of life as the weather. All that began to change after 2 May 1953. One hint came four days later when the influential cricket writer Neville Cardus wrote to *The Times* in despair about his own game. Here is his letter in full, because it is entertaining, what with the arbitrary Dickens reference and all, and because it recognises the shifting sporting sands:

'Sir,

In his brilliant report of the Cup Final, your Association Football Correspondent refers to "the game of the people" meaning Association football. A few years ago I would have contested the

---

* Also a footballer, good enough to play wartime internationals for England. But he played mainly to fill in the gaps between cricket seasons.

description "werry fierce". Nowadays I am not so sure. While the drama and heroism were going forward at Wembley on Saturday afternoon I went to Lord's for the first cricket there of the season. Play was not possible until 3.15. Then the players came into the field and in an hour twenty-odd runs were scored without a sign of a daring gesture, without a hint of personal relish.

And then, after an hour of what I can fairly call a creeping paralysis the players left the field – for tea. The small crowd looked on in silence. As I departed from the ground I felt pretty certain that I had been attending a decaying contemporary industry which, but for the artificial respiration applied from time to time by the Australians, would before long pass into the hands of the brokers, and gradually disappear, not greatly lamented, into profound oblivion.

Yours faithfully,

Neville Cardus,

112 Bickenhall Mansions, W1'

A number of points arise from Cardus's letter. Firstly, how genteel society must have been that a journalist could publish his home address in a newspaper; secondly, what tricks memory plays on us – I have visited numerous websites where fans reminisce about the 1953 final, and not one mentions any rain that day. 'Warm sun after heavy rain,' says *Wisden*, which was clearly disappointing for Cardus and the waiting hundreds at Lord's, but remarkably apposite for Wembley where, after the dark days of the war and the privations that followed, football was to enjoy its unforgettable day in the sun. Also, you cannot help admiring Cardus for smuggling in a letter about cricket under cover of a comment about *The Times'* football coverage.

In some ways, Cardus is merely marking the first stages of the interminably slow death of county cricket, for which artificial respiration later arrived in the form of the one-day game, but you also get the impression of the writer's regret at being in the wrong place at the wrong time. Cardus clearly felt history – and 'drama and heroism' – was happening elsewhere, and the rest of the nation was present. In this, he was spot on.

Two academics, Martin Johnes, and Gavin Mellor, who have researched the match, see it as only slightly less significant in television history than the Coronation a month later:

'Estimates at the television audience for the 1953 final were as high as twelve million, but were more often put at ten million. This was significantly less than the twenty million estimated to have watched the Coronation, but it was still a huge audience for the time. Those who did not have their own sets crammed into the houses of friends and neighbours. A cartoon in a Blackpool paper (the *West Lancashire Evening Gazette*) showed a man asking his neighbours if he could watch the game at their house: "I can't get near *mine*," he is saying, "for unexpected visitors."'

There was a sense in which the match was part of a year of great national celebration; Elizabeth II was crowned, Everest was conquered, and for the first time since 1933 – *pace* Cardus – England even won the Ashes. But the story surrounding the 1953 final was unbeatable.

The match was universally believed to be a last shot at a cup-winner's medal for Blackpool's mesmeric thirty-eight-year-old right-winger Stanley Matthews, nicknamed Wizard of the Dribble for his ability to shimmy past defenders at speed without losing control of the ball.

Emerging from the grime and poverty of the Potteries, Matthews signed for his local club Stoke City as a seventeen-year-old in 1932. In 1947, after years of being underpaid – in fairness, all footballers were then – and undervalued for his loyalty, he moved to struggling Blackpool and revived their fortunes. He helped them reach the FA Cup final, then the pinnacle of British football, in 1948, where they were defeated 4–2 by Manchester United. In 1951, with Matthews now thirty-six, Blackpool reached the final again, and were beaten 2-0 by Newcastle United. At thirty-eight years old was this working-class hero to be a three-time loser?

Matthews, though, was not a working-class hero in the way that later models like George Best, Alex Higgins, or John Lennon were – dragging themselves out of the backwoods and boondocks and using their talents to cock a snook at the establishment, to tell polite society what it could do with its polite society, sticking it to the man, as the modern idiom has it (or so my children tell me). Britain may not yet have been ready for that.

Matthews was the chap on the shop floor who did not make a fuss but got the job done, the kind of chap that had won the war for us. Arthur Hopcraft, in his famous book *The Football Man*, had Matthews about right:

> He was the opposite of glamorous: a non-drinker, non-smoker, careful with his money. He had a habitual little cough. He was representative of his age and his class, brought up among thrift and the ever-looming threat of dole and debt.
>
> We were always afraid for Matthews, the non-athlete; the sadly impassive face, with its high cheekbones, pale lips and hooded eyes, had a lot of pain in it, the deep hurt that came from prolonged effort and the certainty of more blows … For as long as he was one of the world's fleetest movers he never had exuberance.

So what happened to him on 2 May? More hurt? Or redemption? For the first hour the final had all the hallmarks of a stinker: Lofthouse scored a soft goal from distance for Bolton after seventy-five seconds, the ball bouncing over Blackpool goalkeeper Farm's outstretched arm, Mortensen equalised for Blackpool with the first of his three goals, though it actually took what nowadays would be termed a wicked deflection (is there any other sort?) and should have been credited (or debited) as an own goal to Bolton's Hassall. A mix-up between Farm and his defender Moir gifted Bolton a second. Ten minutes into the second half Bolton appeared to have the game wrapped up when half-back Bell, despite carrying an injury, headed a third. But it was a match notable more for its calamities than the beauty of the football.

Indeed, the TV commentator Kenneth Wolstenholme felt obliged to apologise for the misplaced passes and the general dullness of the spectacle, ascribing it to the wind, and the lushness of the Wembley pitch. (Wolstenholme was obsessed with the Wembley turf. His default position as a final kicked off was to give us chapter and verse on the state of the grass – invariably lush – on whether the players were taking any special stud-related measures to account for it, and how they were coping with the unusual eventuality of playing on a grass-covered surface. Pretty well anything untoward that took place during a match was blamed by Wolstenholme on the Wembley surface.)

For the best part of an hour-and-a-quarter it was that kind of final, one during which your thoughts are encouraged to drift. But with Bolton 3–1 up, and carrying a number of injuries, Matthews took over. One of his many menacing right-wing crosses not dealt with by the tiring and injury-stricken Bolton defence led to Stan Mortensen scrambling a goal at the far post, and Mortensen also scored the equaliser in the last minute of normal time with a powerfully struck free kick.

Injury time now, and *The Times'* Geoffrey Green in what Cardus called his 'brilliant' report, described the climax thus:

'With the last minute already ticking away, the ball again went out to Matthews. He beat one man on the inside, swerved past another on the outside, and weaved his incredible passage in towards the by-line. As Barrass came across from the middle to challenge, over came a perfect centre. Perry, moving into the centre, flashed it home, and with only seconds left the incredible had happened.

Blackpool had won 4–3 at the very last breath. People were all but crying in their emotion. The press box itself was a bedlam as papers and pencils flew in all directions. The crowd was on its feet, cheering hysterically. And there as a last sight was Matthews being chaired off the field by his colleagues, shoulder high with his captain, Johnston, each of them with a hand on the Cup. Nothing like that had ever happened before. I doubt if it will ever happen again. That was the "Matthews Final."'

And it has been the 'Matthews Final' ever since even though Mortensen scored a hat-trick. When Mortensen died in 1991, some cruel joker suggested his burial would probably be known as 'the Matthews Funeral'.

If TV viewers needed to take a deep breath after the drama of the match there was plenty of opportunity. Coverage from Wembley finished at 4.50, in time for children's television, and there was no highlights programme later. The big show that Saturday evening was a party political broadcast, from 8.30 to 8.50, entitled 'Housing – A Progress Report by Mr Harold Macmillan', followed by something called *Looking at Animals*. From this we can see how crucial sport was to television in those early days. I can't imagine there were would have been too many people laying out £66 10s on the new Murphy V210 to look at animals and Mr Harold Macmillan.

Nor could Peter Dimmock, although he conceded that sport on its own was not the complete answer, 'Sport was terribly important to the BBC,' Dimmock told me. 'It was 60 per cent of our outside broadcasts, and it delivered good viewing figures, but especially if there was any sort of royal involvement. We would always get an extra 20 per cent if a Royal was present. People would switch on just to watch a member of the Royal Family.'

In that respect, the 1953 final hit the jackpot. Queen Elizabeth was there – the first reigning monarch to attend a Wembley cup final – with the Duke of Edinburgh. As that *Times* report put it: 'It will live with the countless multitude that viewed it second-hand upon the magic screen of television … not only because of its highly colourful and emotional climax … but because here, in the presence of the Queen and the Duke of Edinburgh, the game of football, the game of the people, was crowned with all felicity in this year of Coronation and national rejoicing.'

It was undoubtedly a watershed. Looking at the fixtures for that weekend, I see there was a First Division match, Portsmouth v. Middlesbrough, kicking off concurrently with the Cup final. This would soon become unthinkable and would remain so for more than half a century. By Cup final day 1954, there were only Third Division matches scheduled, at Norwich, Ipswich, and Shrewsbury, all starting at 6.30. By 1956, second-top billing was taken by the Glasgow Charity Cup. The Cup final on TV was now enshrined in the national calendar.

Incidentally, the *Light Programme*, then the main network for radio sport, did not even carry the first half of the 1953 final, picking the match up after half-time, after coverage of the touring Australian cricket team at Leicestershire and a county match between Hampshire and Essex. The start of the cricket season would not eclipse the climax of football's much longer.

FIVE

AN AFTERNOON WITH AUNTIE ROSIE

One of the ironies of the 1953 final was that the new television audience that had bought sets in order to watch the ruling classes crown their Queen in Westminster Abbey, were now celebrating one of their own; and the zoom lenses that Dimmock had wheedled out of the BBC for the Coronation were put to use to emphasise the Matthews story.

As Johnes and Mellor wrote, 'From the opening minutes of the game, commentator Kenneth Wolstenholme continually constructed the final as "the great maestro's" last chance to win the FA Cup. The filming and editing of the match was also instructive as it frequently presented Matthews in close-up. At the moment of Blackpool's fourth and winning goal (scored by Bill Perry), Wolstenholme shouted, "There's the man Matthews. He's done it at last."'

The Matthews Final created the template for TV coverage of football. Whether it is Sky Sports with twenty or thirty highly portable cameras flitting around between sixty-odd camera positions in Wembley Stadium or the boys of '53 with four cameras in fixed positions, the principle is the same: focus on the main characters, as in a drama, and use the close-ups to follow the story through them.

'Television, in its portrayal of football, has a tendency to focus on, and isolate, players on the screen in an attempt to create a sense of visual/

dramatic impact and increase the "human" element,' wrote Charles Barr in a 1975 study for the British Film Institute. 'However, in doing so the viewer is presented with a selective and limited view that deprives them of a perception of the game as a whole and hence its pattern and tactics.' If you agree, the Matthews Final was where it all started.

Watching the 1953 final now, I am struck not just by the camera's adherence to Matthews despite the obvious difficulty it often has following the ball into the corners of the pitch, but also by what we today would call the minimalist nature of the commentary. Each goal was greeted by a short silence, a surprised gasp, and then an exclamation on the lines of, 'Oh, it's a goal, yes, it's a goal,' as if the possibility of a goal being scored were an extraordinary eventuality with which the commentator had just not reckoned. Yet, just as with his famous valedictory words at the 1966 World Cup final, Kenneth Wolstenholme found *les mots justes* for Matthews as the match neared its climax, 'Now here's a man who's really fighting for his cup medal. Can he score the winning goal now?'

These were the 'avuncular, crisply articulated tones, redolent of the comfortable armchair and a good pipe' that the *Daily Telegraph* noted in its 2002 obituary. Wolstenholme was not, you would have thought, someone who might speak to the depths of a young Jewish boy in Manchester. But, armchair and pipe or not, he was the voice of football for us products of the post-war baby boom, a presence in the BBC commentary box at every FA Cup final from 1949 to 1971, whose voice is as familiar to me today as my late father's. I expect that holds true for most of us brought up in that era.

Cup final day in those Wolstenholme years was a great national festival in Britain, second only to Christmas in terms of families gathering together for a common purpose. Town centres were more or less empty. Deserting the hearth on Cup final afternoon was the act of an eccentric or a refusenik. Even people with little interest in football – women, as they were known then – would be aware of the participants, especially if either was a local team. For a small boy, the excitement was palpable. The 1950s and 1960s were not just the Wolstenholme years, but the era of 'jumpers for goalposts', another phrase – like Wolstenholme's own 'They think it's all over' – later adopted ironically by TV comedy.

The ritual for a youngster on FA Cup final morning – in Lichfield Drive, Prestwich, as in the rest of the country – was to fill the hours before kick-off with a marathon game of street football, usually played out under the banners of the participants in the match to come. Boys would join the game as they emerged from sleep, paper rounds, or chores, the cast constantly changing as participants were called in for a hurried lunch, and then re-emerged: rather like the interchange system in modern-day rugby league.

The game continued until 2.15 pm when TV coverage of the Cup final began with 'How They Got There', a by no means complete record of the road to the final, merely a brief film of those matches at which cameras had been present. At 2.30pm, TV showed something called 'Community Singing'.

This was not a popular feature for younger members of the audience. Some of us were becoming dimly aware of skiffle and rock 'n' roll, and so were less than thrilled by a full fifteen minutes of adult males singing hymns and popular uplifting standards, as the camera panned over serried ranks of flat caps and trilby hats. (I believe there may have been a legal requirement in those immediate post-war years to wear some form of working-class headgear to gain entry to Wembley.) For light relief, if a Lancashire team was in the final, they would sing 'She's A Lassie From Lancashire', and if Leeds United or Sheffield Wednesday were there, 'On Ilkla Moor Baht 'At', waving around their song sheets, provided at every final by the *Daily Express*. At the end of each song, the crowd would rotate their wooden rattles which made an ear-splitting sound not unlike ack-ack fire, as the thin wooden prongs hit the rattle's teeth, many of which were in a better condition than those of the spectators wielding them.

To make matters worse, the adult audience at home, with recent memories of closing ranks around Mr Churchill and our fighting forces, digging for victory and so on, saw this sequence as some kind of extension of the wartime spirit, and felt obliged to provide tuneless accompaniment. My dad did anyway, while Mum took advantage of the hiatus to administer Germolene to grazes, and rub vigorously at my grubby face with a spit-moistened handkerchief.

'Community Singing' was typical of the kind of thing foisted upon us by adults in those days, like the mince and potatoes you had to eat at school dinners before you were allowed sponge pudding and custard. But TV was like that then, every morsel of light entertainment leavened by a lump of something perceived to be good for you. The days of instant unalloyed pleasure were some decades in the future.

It was an adult world and no mistake on Saturday 4 May 1957, when Manchester United met Aston Villa in the FA Cup final, the first one I remember watching, our house having been recently blessed with its first television set. My parents, a pair of old lefties with little time for the Royals, had resisted the national rush to get tooled up for the Coronation, and also failed to join the second wave of TV ownership at the launch of the commercial channel in 1955, because my mum was rather sniffy about the whole idea of adverts on TV. Frankly, I think she would have been happier in East Germany. Eventually, though, the siren call of *Hancock's Half Hour* and *Wagon Train* could no longer be resisted.

I was, of course, thoroughly excited by our reluctant entry into the television age, but looking at a copy of the *Radio Times* from 1958, and seeing what was on offer for younger viewers, I can't imagine why. On Sunday 1 June, for instance, children's television began at 5pm with *Wonders of the Sea – How Do Fish Swim?* billed as a fascinating study of the different methods of movement used by the many creatures of the deep in order to survive in their strange surroundings below the water's surface. This was followed at 5.25 by *La Compagnie des Marottes*, the famous French hand-puppet company featuring 'Papotin' the incorrigible compère. However incorrigible Papotin was I cannot recall him as much of a counter-attraction to collecting caterpillars and putting them in matchboxes.

A consequence of our late adoption was that our ultra-modern seventeen-inch Ferguson (ultra-modern, a favoured description, in those early days of consumerism, of everything from Formica table tops to chrome ashtrays on long legs, simply meant 'new') boasted an inch or two more of flickering black-and-white images than most of the equipment in the immediate vicinity, so we hosted some of our United-supporting neighbours who wanted a slightly better view of the action. Indulge me on the cast list because I think it has a bearing on our attitude to TV sport, and especially to Wolstenholme and his fellow broadcasters in the 1950s and 1960s.

Round the TV, then, that Saturday in May 1957, in time for the presentation of the teams to the Duke of Edinburgh at 2.55pm, were my uncle Maurice (not really my uncle), his wife Esther, my uncle Jack and auntie Rosie, also *faux* relatives, (in 1950s working-class Manchester, most kids had stand-in uncles and aunts, a hangover from the war years and the post-war austerity, when it was customary to leave children with a trusted neighbour while parents were out trying to earn a shilling), and my friend Frankie Hargreaves, a slightly older boy from up the street, a single-parent child, something of a rarity in those days, who we looked after while his mum went to work in the telephone exchange.

There was a touch of George Burns and Gracie Allen – the joy of whose imported comedy show we would shortly encounter – about Maurice and Esther. She was a small woman with hair and lips both an unfeasibly vivid shade of red, who seemed to enter a room in a typhoon of face powder, and did most of the talking, while he smoked a big cigar. Uncle Jack was a small dapper character, rarely seen without a suit and impeccably knotted tie, with hair brilliantined, and a military shine on his black brogues, a slighter version of Wolstenholme himself as it happens. Auntie Rosie was bigger than him in a seaside postcard kind of way, rosy-cheeked and jolly, my favourite locum relative.

When I picture the scene in our suburban Manchester living room, it seems odd now to think of the men, who were in their early forties, wearing suits and ties – you could have sliced fresh bread with the creases ironed into Jack's trousers – and their wives in full make-up. But this, I suppose, was an era before leisure wear. How else were you supposed to dress at the weekend? Rich people in big houses in the countryside might have had casual clothes in which to relax – wellies and tweed – but not ordinary folk in the North. For most of the nation, the fifteen to twenty years following the Second World War constituted a buttoned-up era, literally and metaphorically, for which Wolstenholme's straightforward unfussy commentary was perfectly suited, in the same way that the florid, fevered tones of Jonathan Pearce or Clive Tyldesley seem to chime in with today's excitable, emotionally incontinent, times.

Those present that Saturday were all fans of Manchester United, but not in the obsessive way that people support football nowadays. The males went to most of the home matches but in those days you could just turn up and walk in, so following a team was not the major commitment it is now, which might go some way towards explaining their reaction to the disappointment that followed.

The crucial incident in the match involved the Aston Villa forward Peter McParland bundling Manchester United goalkeeper Ray Wood into the net in scoring Villa's first goal after six minutes, knocking the goalie unconscious and leaving him with a broken cheekbone. No substitutes were allowed then, so United defender Jackie Blanchflower had to put on the goalkeeping gloves for the rest of the match while Wood limped forlornly – and one guesses fairly painfully – along the wing. Even within the rules of the game as they were then interpreted, with numerous variations on the shoulder charge accepted as entirely legitimate, McParland's actions clearly constituted a foul. The legitimate charge, shoulder-to-shoulder, is unlikely to cause a broken cheekbone.

This, it ought to be said, was no ordinary Manchester United side forced to play for eighty-four minutes without a goalkeeper. They were considered near-certainties to win the League and Cup Double, last achieved by Aston Villa themselves in 1897. 'The precocious qualities of this young United team, their high levels of technique, their passing and movement and above all their capacity to entertain has enthralled the nation,' cooed the *Guardian*. As I recall it, Kenneth Wolstenholme's verdict on the hugely controversial incident, which arguably denied the most famous team in English football history its birthright, went something like, 'Ooh, it's a goal. Yes, it's a goal'. I remember him reporting that McParland's assault was 'a fair shoulder charge', meaning that was what the referee had decreed.

This is no criticism of Wolstenholme, you understand. Those were deferential times, when government ministers were routinely called 'Sir', warmly thanked for deigning to speak to the media, and asked to explain in detail what great benefit their latest initiative might bestow upon the nation. In 1957, the questioning of an authority figure on TV was as unlikely in Britain as a decent cup of coffee.

Imagine if a similar scenario were to unfold now. Quite apart from the technological advances enabling the incident to be viewed from a multiplicity of angles, there would be a hue and cry involving sports broadcasters, podcasters, bloggers and tweeters from every corner of the globe. Short of a major natural disaster, or a celebrity chef caught in a crack house, it would be lead item on the six o'clock news. Round-the-clock police protection would be the least that the referee would require.

Our small gathering, the boys more than the grown-ups, thought Villa's 2–1 victory unfair on United and Wood, but were prepared to blame it on the dreaded 'Wembley Hoodoo', a phrase favoured by Wolstenholme and the press at the time to explain a series of injuries suffered in the pre-substitute finals of the 1950s and '60s. Almost every year, the famous hoodoo reduced one team in the final to ten men, often with an injured player hobbling along the wing to keep the numbers up. Players had to be more or less immobilised before they actually left the field of play. Some viewers followed the Wolstenholme line that it was the 'lush Wembley turf' that made players mysteriously prone to injury, but whatever it was, the Wembley Hoodoo was a quaint belief the nation clung to in those years, just as we believed dairy butter would do us good and that Arthur Askey was funny.

The crowd at Lichfield Drive that Saturday was miffed about McParland's assault, but mostly we felt if Wolstenholme said it was the hoodoo, then hoodoo it was. Even the Association Football correspondent of *The*

Times (still the great Geoffrey Green, though *Times* correspondents were then anonymous) felt moved to refer to it:

> The best team in Britain lost Wood, their goalkeeper, with a depressed fracture of the cheekbone and with it lost the Cup final … So now there is little left to do but ponder the same sort of cruel fate that year after year seems to strike down one team or another at Wembley. The Cup final is the apotheosis of the English game; it crowns the season and is attended by royalty. Yet five times in the last six years the imp that lives in that velvet turf has shown its spite to create unequal odds and spoil the occasion.

These included the most famous injury of all: Bert Trautmann's broken neck the year before. My view is that these injuries all contributed to the mythology of the FA Cup – substitutes were not allowed in English Football until the 1965–66 season – and helped it grow into the behemoth of an all-day television event it later became.

Already, by 1957 the Cup final coverage had been granted an extra ten minutes, and continued until five o'clock, to allow for the presentation of cup and medals by the Queen and the Duke of Edinburgh, but it was off-air in time for the *Lone Ranger*, the synopsis of which in that day's *Radio Times* runs as follows: 'For many years an old settler has been saving to buy a harp for his wife on her birthday.' (I am not making this up – *a harp*.) 'On his way into town he is attacked and robbed by the ne'er do well son of a powerful ranch owner. Helpless against his rich enemies he is tricked into the clutches of the sheriff on a charge of attempted murder. One witness alone can save the day, but can the Lone Ranger and Tonto find him?'

I feel fairly safe in saying we may have abstained from *The Lone Ranger* that evening in favour of further discussion of the Ray Wood incident. On the specifics of that, by the way, *The Times* agreed with the verdict of the Lichfield Drive jury. 'Some of the physical challenges in those opening stages went beyond the bounds of respectability,' Green wrote.

'Indeed the way McParland accelerated over the last few strides to thunder into Wood after the Manchester goalkeeper had saved his header seemed quite unnecessary.'

Wolstenholme, however, was not a man to make a fuss about an injury to a football player, or a free kick not given. Nor, quite frankly, however unjust it seemed, was a stiff upper-lipped nation, proud of its recent defiance of the Nazi jackboot, and only recently delivered from the privations of food rationing. My sister, six years older than me, used to tell me about sweet rationing – which finished in February 1953 – to indicate how easy we young 'uns had it. But stoicism for Ken Wolstenholme meant more than doing without aniseed balls and bubble gum. A man who had flown missions over Germany in a period of exceptionally heavy night fighter activity, and seen countless of his young comrades fall from the skies, was unlikely to be caught making a hoo-ha about a fractured cheekbone. You sometimes now see footballers presenting a team shirt to a sick or disabled child, or appearing in a testimonial for a fellow player struck down with cancer, where they will pay lip service to 'putting the game in perspective'. Fresh from the horrors of the war, Wolstenholme truly did have it in perspective.

Arguably, he had the whole business of commentating on football matches in perspective. As the *Daily Telegraph* noted in its obituary, 'he did little research for games, arming himself with not much more than a pencil and a copy of the match programme'. Not that this was too much of a problem back then. Nobody was blogging, or taking part in asinine football phone-ins, or indeed writing semi-humorous columns about broadcast sport. Also, there were no replays, no highlights programmes, so if Kenneth got something wrong or missed a salient point, there was little in the way of evidence for the court of public opinion to pore over.

In a way, Wolstenholme was Oliver Hardy to Peter Dimmock's Stan Laurel. Not that they were Laurel and Hardy in an incompetently trying-to-move-a-piano-up-a-huge-flight-of-steps way, but in the sense that the real Oliver Hardy reportedly used to swan blithely around the golf course while Stan Laurel, the brains behind the unit, came up with the stuff.

Mind you, Ollie's more subtle talent did make a major contribution to the finished product, and similarly Wolstenholme's role in embedding the FA Cup final as a TV institution should not be discounted.

Seymour Joly de Lotbinière, from whom all wisdom on commentating flowed until the mid-1950s, considered Wolstenholme a kind of bridgehead between the officer class in the BBC commentary box, and the more plebeian types who were about to take over (although there was a definite touch of the NCO about Barry Davies). He called Wolstenholme 'a fair compromise … since he sounds neither posh nor common.'

For Wolstenholme, who was then as indispensable to the BBC as Ollie was to Stan, the time was right. *Look Back in Anger* had dragged theatre audiences out of the country house drawing room, and pop singers like Tommy Steele and Terry Dene emerged from East End coffee bars. The kind of commentator who had helped establish BBC television sport at the 1948 Olympics no longer spoke for the nation.

As evidence, I give you Lieutenant-Colonel Dudley Lister, a First *and* Second World War hero who won the Military Cross near Ypres, and was mentioned in despatches after the first raid on the Lofoten Islands in 1941. He was also a services boxing champion whose work at the 1948 games is preserved in the Alexandra Palace Television Society archive. Lister can be seen interviewing South African boxer Douglas Dupree in a very funny clip, in which he consoles the bandaged boxer for receiving 'a creck on the head'. He wishes all the 'South Efricans' well, on behalf of Great Britain, in a closing address which makes Celia Johnson sound like Arthur Mullard.

Quite apart from Tommy Steele and John Osborne, though, there was an even more compelling reason for the BBC to unbend a little in the 1950s: a new kind of television that threatened to speak to the nation beyond the metropolitan elite.

SIX

WAITING FOR
J. FRED MUGGS

Remember I said that office politics was the primary function of the BBC? Well, I may have been overstating for comic effect, but there's no denying it can be a nest of vipers in there. I am struggling to think of another organisation where as much back-stabbing and jockeying for position goes on; the Mafia, I suppose, and obviously Yorkshire County Cricket Club, where members can't wait to get the tedious business of the cricket season out of the way so that the backbiting and mudslinging can start.

The problem with the BBC is that it is such a damned fascinating, all-consuming, place. I have worked for the Corporation as a freelance on and off for nearly thirty years, which puts me in a privileged position as an observer – being *in* the BBC, but not *of* the BBC – and I can easily see why it takes over people's lives.

The first job I ever did there was present a show for Radio Two in the middle of the night in Broadcasting House. All the studio entrances round the back of the building were closed in those days, so the only way to get in was via the prow of the ship, through the magnificent front entrance in Portland Place, under the motto, 'Nation Shall Speak Peace Unto Nation' (although in my case it was more 'Nation Shall Play Neil Diamond Records Unto Nation'), into the grand art deco entrance hall, and then to the first-floor studios on the starboard side of the building (or it may be port, forgive a poor landlubber) through some of the miles of corridors.

I had had a walk-through the previous day with a producer, and been tempted to do the Hansel and Gretel trick of marking my route with breadcrumbs or small pebbles, but instead arrived early and wandered the corridors, past the portraits of broadcasting giants, treating myself to a peek in some of the offices, and the magnificent boardrooms with the heavy oak tables. George Orwell, who worked in the building from 1941 to 1943 and named the infamous Room 101 in his novel *1984* after a BBC conference room, called Broadcasting House, 'a cross between a girls' school and a lunatic asylum', but it struck me as more than that.

I felt it was like its own independent statelet, not subject – its critics would argue – to any of the normal laws of economics, and far more interested in what was going on within its own borders than anything happening in the nation outside. As I write this, I have just listened to an hour-long discussion on BBC Radio Five Live about whether the channel is living up to its remit or not. The BBC loves talking about itself, and you will never run short of people with an opinion. Is it any wonder that, in that atmosphere, intrigue, internecine struggles and just plain gossip and blather all flourish? The danger is that while concentrating your gaze inwardly, you lose sight of the bigger picture.

In 1947, Norman Collins was a popular appointment, Peter Dimmock told me, to replace the disillusioned Maurice Gorham as Controller of the BBC's underfunded Television Service. Collins was something of a renaissance man, turning out a series of popular novels, and two plays in the 1930s. His best-known work was *London Belongs To Me*, a real page-turner set in a seedy Kennington lodging house in 1938 where, with the world on the brink of war, people, according to Amazon, 'continue to work, drink, fall in love, fight and struggle to get on in life' (something for everyone there, as the saying goes).

All the while he was writing his novels and plays, Collins was working as a radio producer, rising in 1946 to Controller of the Light Programme, the BBC's more populist, entertainment-based network, which had grown out of the Forces Programme, set up to entertain troops with some light dance-band music. At the time, the Light Programme, the forerunner of Radio Two, was very much the poor relation of the Home Service within the BBC, but Collins greatly strengthened its hand, introducing the hugely popular *Dick Barton – Special Agent*, which ran for 711 episodes between 1946 and 1951, and *Woman's Hour*, which is still running (on Radio Four) today. His success led to his appointment as Controller of Television, where he gave Dimmock and Orr-Ewing enthusiastic support – and such resources he could lay his hands on – for the televising of the 1948 Olympics, television's first big triumph. But Collins made the fatal mistake of rocking the boat.

Like Gerald Cock before him, he went to America and saw the future, and wrote in the *BBC Quarterly Review* in 1949: 'Once TV is truly national it will become the most important medium that exists. Everything that it does or does not do will be important ... its only rival will be the wireless, and the rivalry will not be strong. Indeed, the first casualty of television, possibly the only casualty, is not the local cinema or the country theatre, it is sound radio.'

It is easy to see what excited Collins. In the bracing commercial atmosphere of the US, television was making great strides in the late 1940s, and according to the archive of the Chicago-based Museum of Broadcasting Communications, sport was driving the expansion. As Harry Coyle, one of NBC's pioneering directors of live sport reminisced: 'Television got off the ground because of sports, Today, maybe, sports need television to survive, but it was just the opposite when it first started. When we put on the World Series in 1947, heavyweight fights, the Army–Navy football game, the sales of television sets just spurted.'

There were 190,000 sets in use in the States in 1948, and the networks – NBC, CBS and the now-forgotten DuMont – saw sports not so much as a means of selling advertising, but as a driver for selling the equipment (interestingly, a not dissimilar strategy adopted by Sky in its early days). 'Sports did indeed draw viewers,' says an article on the museum website, adding, 'Although the stunning acceptance and diffusion of television cannot be attributed solely to sports, the number of sets in use in the US reached ten and a half million by 1950.'

Back at Broadcasting House, though, radio was still king, so Collins's cheerleading for TV was not about to have him chaired shoulder-high round the building. As it turns out, the invention of the transistor radio in 1954, and its ubiquity in the 1960s, enabling me to listen to *Pick of the Pops* and my dad to growl at Raymond Glendenning, scuppered Collins's prediction about the wireless, but on the rest he was spot on. 'Everything that it does or does not do will be important', words to ponder as you read the latest front-page splash about a soap star or talent show winner.

The television sceptics in Broadcasting House, including John Reith and his successor William Haley, had their revenge, though. In 1950, Haley created a new post – how BBC is that? – Chief Executive of Television, and appointed not Collins, but a radio man, George Barnes, straight from the BBC's hoity-toity Third Programme, over Collins's head. 'In doing so,' according to Andrew Crissell's *Introductory History of British Broadcasting*, 'Haley handed a piece of heavy artillery to the Corporation's enemies. Collins promptly resigned and devoted himself to masterminding the campaign for commercial television, something he did with great skill.'

What was it President Lyndon Johnson said about the crazed head of the FBI, J. Edgar Hoover? 'I'd rather have him inside the tent pissing out, than outside the tent pissing in', a little presidential wisdom the BBC has never grasped. Johnson, the undisputed master of the urine-related quote, also said, 'Making a speech on economics is a lot like pissing down your leg. It seems hot to you, but it never does to anyone else', which could easily apply to some of the BBC's navel gazing.

Collins's departure came at a crucial time. In 1949 the Labour government had appointed a committee under Lord Beveridge to look at the state of broadcasting and in 1951, despite some reservations, Beveridge recommended the continuation of the BBC's broadcasting monopoly. However, the Tories' victory in the election that year rendered that largely irrelevant. The new government wanted to have a look at broadcasting for itself, although at least two of Beveridge's strictures about commercial TV became enshrined in future legislation, and some would say have shackled the sector until very recently, 'Its alertness to the danger that advertising would influence programme content ensured that ITV would carry "spot" commercials and not sponsorship,' wrote Crissell, 'Second, its disapproval of what it termed the excessive "Londonisation" of the BBC provided the inspiration for ITV's regional structure.'

The campaign for commercial television of some sort was unstoppable, though. The antis, according to another writer, Simon Cherry, were an alliance of 'dyed-in-the-wool Tories who thought the BBC was a hotbed of left-wing propaganda and wanted to see its power checked, manufacturers of television sets who wanted to expand the market, and advertisers who wanted a new platform at a time when newsprint was still rationed.' Collins was prominent among the orchestrators of the campaign through a company he had set up with the aim of capturing one of the franchises (in the event, he joined forces with Lew Grade's ATV).

It was a debate that crystallised at times into an argument between British and American values. Opponents of commercial broadcasting cited the supposed vulgarity of TV in the US. Lord Reith could hardly conceal his distaste in a speech in the House of Lords in May 1952, in which he compared the introduction of commercial television to Britain with the introduction of 'dog racing, smallpox, bubonic plague, and the Black Death.' (An interesting selection, especially as he lived just long enough to enjoy Harry Carpenter's commentaries on the Greyhound Derby on the BBC's *Sportsnight* in the early 1970s.)

If Reith was unable to stem the tide, those of a like mind, including a large chunk of the press, fearful they might lose advertising income to TV, were handed a powerful weapon in the shape of celebrity chimpanzee J. Fred Muggs. The chimp, dressed like a baby in a nappy, was the mascot for NBC's *Today* show, and featured in advertising when America showed a recording of the Coronation. Britain, or at any rate the BBC, was outraged.

A headline on the front page of the *Daily Express* of 9 June 1953 read: 'BBC Protest Over J. Fred Muggs: The row boiled up again today over J. Fred Muggs, chimpanzee star of American commercial TV, and his appearance between scenes of the Coronation,' reads the story, 'The BBC protested to the three big American TV networks on the way they allowed advertising for goods from cars to deodorants to be sandwiched between scenes of the Coronation.' In December 1953, the Muggs issue was raised by a speaker in an Oxford Union debate in favour of commercial television, and helped defeat the motion.

Muggs or no Muggs,* the Television Act was given the Royal Assent in July 1954 – with a clause banning advertising breaks during broadcasts featuring the Royal Family, still apparently adhered to, as you will have noticed if you watched the wedding of Prince William and Catherine Middleton on ITV.

It would be wrong to say the BBC panicked at the prospect of competition, although there was some concern, in the months before the launch of ITV, at the salaries being offered to trained BBC staff to switch sides. The director general at the time, Sir Ian Jacob, was normally reluctant to match these offers because of the effect on the BBC's pay structure. But, according to Leonard Miall in his book *Inside the BBC*, when Sir George Barnes (he was knighted in Coronation year) reported an approach had been made to Dimmock, Jacob told his Director of Television, 'You've got to keep him. Make any sort of personal arrangements for him that are necessary.'

'Dimmock was a special case because of his skill in negotiating sports contracts,' wrote Miall, 'He had established excellent relations with all the sporting authorities. His unique knowledge of the BBC's sports contracts could have been invaluable to ITV had it wanted to offer a first-class sports service.'

In the event, commercial TV was not initially very interested in sport. There is a story told about Lew Grade at ATV, taking one of his

---

* Fred was last heard of in 2004, in retirement, aged sixty, at Citrus Park, Florida. The *New York Observer* reported that he had gone 'a little grey, mostly in his beard'.

underlings to task for negotiating over rights with the Amateur Athletics Association. Grade is reported to have said, 'I don't want amateurs, get me the professionals.' As with many Lew Grade stories, it is probably apocryphal, but like the quote about his film *Raise The Titanic* ('It would have been cheaper to lower the Atlantic' – occasionally suffixed with 'My life') it's not far from the truth.

What all this meant for Dimmock was that he became one of the best-paid people at the BBC. A later director general, Charles Curran, pointed out to him, 'We're paying you too much in BBC terms, you're getting near my salary.' Dimmock replied, 'Dear boy, I'm not paid too much, you're paid too little.'

This had not been what Roy Thomson meant at all when he said the launch of commercial TV constituted a licence to print money. But Dimmock got the BBC's money back many times over when he was appointed general manager of the Corporation's selling arm, BBC Enterprises, in 1972. He reorganised the ailing outfit, and brought in millions from the sale of BBC programmes overseas. To people of my generation, though, Dimmock will chiefly be remembered as the smooth, moustachioed, George Cole-style (young George Cole, of *The Green Man* vintage, not *Minder* George Cole) presenter of *Sportsview*, the BBC's first sports magazine show, launched in April 1954.

It was devised and produced by Paul Fox, later to become Controller of BBC1 and managing director of Yorkshire Television, and Sir Paul. 'It was a time when anything was possible in TV,' said Fox. 'I went to Peter and said, "How about making a sports programme?" and a month later we were on air with *Sportsview*. You could do that, because the chain of command was so short.' Having joined the BBC from Pathé News, Fox was ideally placed to produce a fast-moving magazine show, and Thursday night – later Wednesday – with Dimmock became a regular date for sports fans.

It was also the first programme on BBC TV to have its own permanent team, which was quite a big deal at the time. A dedicated head of sport was still two decades in the future, so the *Sportsview* unit was the first indication of how important sport was to become. 'We got very lucky,' says Dimmock, 'The second week in we got a tip-off about Roger Bannister trying to break the four-minute mile at a meeting in Oxford. He rang Fox and said, "Look Paul, I think Roger may break the four-minute mile. I think it's worth your having a camera there." We raced back with Roger – and the film – from Iffley Road, Oxford, and got him into the studio live for the programme. Bannister said afterwards he'd never ride again in a BBC car.' Fox recalls the car journey being interrupted so that the record-breaker could go into his house in Harrow and change into a suit and tie, because he refused to appear in the studio in a tracksuit.

Another first for *Sportsview* was the introduction of the teleprompter, which Dimmock had first seen in January 1953 when he went to Washington to observe their coverage of the Eisenhower inauguration. It was beyond Dimmock's budget but he happened to mention it to a variety director back in London, who said he had used one in a stage magic show, and it was just two sheets of glass.

So with the two sheets of glass, a mangle, some white paper and a black pen, Dimmock had the first autocue device in British TV. 'I did the first lot of *Sportsview* like that,' he told me, 'and, of course, everybody was very jealous, and said to me, "Peter, how do you manage to speak so quickly?" It was because I was reading it. People would write to me as Head of Outside Broadcasts and say, "We've seen you on *Sportsview*, would you come and do an after dinner speech?"

'I'd write back and say, I'm terribly sorry, and they used to think it was because I was stuck-up, but it wasn't. It was because I bloody well knew I'd make a balls-up of it without a prompter. Cliff Michelmore, who did *Tonight* in the studio next door, wanted to use it as well, but I said no, no, no, it's exclusive to us. We kept it very much to ourselves.'

Sportsview also created its own event, the *Sports Personality of the Year*, inaugurated in December 1954 at the suggestion of Paul Fox. It was a minimalist affair compared to today's much-hyped Christmas road show but even then it had a certain style, coming from the Savoy Hotel in London. Carl Doran, the current producer of the show, says it was groundbreaking, 'For the first time you were seeing people you knew from the world of sport away from a sporting environment, in what was roughly an entertainment setting. It is all about giving the public just a little glimpse of the personality behind the sports person, and *Sportsview* undoubtedly started all that.'

Maybe it was Fox's background in newsreel that propelled him towards the human interest behind the sport, although he is adamant that without his smooth front man *Sportsview* would not have flourished. Dimmock himself reckoned the main reason he was chosen as front man was because he was staff and so cost nothing. 'Paul Fox would send me the script around 4.30pm and I would do my best to rewrite it in my own words. I really didn't know what the hell I was doing at the time.'

It worked for us viewers, though and, in sport at least, it meant the BBC was ready for the challenge that lay ahead.

SEVEN

EARLY EXCHANGES

There were no monkeys in nappies when the first ITV channel launched at 7.15pm on Thursday 22 September 1955. It was all rather sedate and very British. Associated-Rediffusion, who had won the weekday franchise for London, started with a five-minute news-reel-style portrait of the capital. 'Tonight we add another sentence to the long history of London,' intoned Cecil Lewis, Deputy Controller of the channel.

Over pictures of 'one of the most mighty and venerable cities in the world,' Lewis gave a short history of broadcasting from Marconi's invention of wireless, through 1936 and the 'strange and new antenna rising from a crumbling amusement hall called Alexandra Palace' to 1955 when, after less than twenty years, Lewis's sonorous tones announced, 'one home in three throughout the British Isles sits spellbound several hours a day before a magic tube'.

Unfortunately, there were not as many people sitting spellbound as Lewis, and the manufacturers of Gibbs SR toothpaste, ITV's first advertisers, might have hoped. The BBC's response was to air the most dramatic episode yet of its already long-running radio soap opera, *The Archers*. Normal territory for *The Archers* in those days was minor marital discord and amusing storylines about rivalries at the county show, alongside clumsily concealed messages from the Ministry of Agriculture about crop yields and potato blight.

Out of this clear blue bucolic sky, on the night ITV launched, there was a fire at Brookfield stables during the course of which one of the younger, more attractive characters in the show, Grace (Ysanne Churchman), newly married to Phil Archer, was hit by a falling beam as she ran into the stables to rescue her horse, Midnight. Grace lost her fight for life 'to the shock of millions', according to the front page of the following day's *Daily Express*.

'Who killed Grace Archer?' asked the newspaper, and more pertinently, 'Was it just coincidence it happened on ITV night?' It reported BBC offices swamped by complaints by telephone, with parents saying their children were upset, and their evening had been spoiled. As is standard practice in these cases, 'one farmer's wife asked when the funeral would be, and where she could send flowers'. While this was on the front page, the launch of ITV made it no further than page five. As if to justify all the high-minded talk in Lewis's short opening film, ITV's first programme was an outside broadcast from a black-tie dinner at the Guildhall in the City of London, featuring speeches from the Lord Mayor and the Postmaster General, and a performance by the Halle Orchestra of Elgar's Cockaigne Suite.

The real business started just after eight o'clock with a variety show showcasing some of the stars of the new network, introduced by the dance bandleader and disc jockey Jack Jackson. After this, the channel signalled its intent to make sport part of its schedule by showing a Southern Area middleweight championship fight between Terence Murphy and Lew Lazar, from Shoreditch Town Hall, a Jack Solomons promotion.

Solomons featured in a trailer for Associated-Rediffusion, alongside footballer Danny Blanchflower and snooker player Joe Davis, promising all sorts of sporting riches ITV ultimately found it impossible to provide. The opening night boxing match, however, was a 'really good fight', according to the *Express*. And Bernard Levin, reviewing the evening for the *Guardian*, went even further, 'How often we have been infuriated by a description of something we could perfectly well see for ourselves. There is no need to mention names here, except that of Mr Richard Dimbleby, but anybody who has ever watched, say, a sporting programme on BBC television will be able to add half a dozen. But Mr Len Harvey and Mr Tony Van den Bergh confined themselves almost entirely to inter-round summaries ... and let the cameramen tell the story for us.'

Between rounds there were adverts for beer, radio sets, and electric lamps. Only brief clips of the opening night still exist, but I am told the first beer commercial ever shown in Britain, featuring a glass being drained with a satisfying slurp, was followed immediately by a shot of one of the combatants at Shoreditch spitting a mouthful of saliva into a bucket, a foretaste of the unfortunate clashes between adverts and programmes ITV would face. After the boxing came a newsreel, presented by Christopher Chataway, who only nine months earlier had beaten Roger Bannister to become the BBC's first Sports Personality of the Year.

Of the 188,000 homes in the South-East available to view, an estimated 100,000 were sufficiently immune to Grace-grief to tune in. It was years before the BBC admitted categorically that the Grace Archer conflagration was more than a coincidence, but a memo in the BBC's archives confirms it. H. Rooney Pelletier, then Controller of the Light Programme, writes in the note, 'The more I think about it, the more I believe that a death of a violent kind in *The Archers*, timed, if possible to diminish interest in the opening of commercial television in London, is a good idea.'*

A genuine coincidence was that the very day ITV launched, and scored its critical triumph with the boxing coverage, was also the first day at work at BBC Sport's Lime Grove HQ for a young, ambitious,

---

* In his 1996 book *The Archers: The True Story*, William Smethurst suggested that Grace may have been chosen for sacrifice because Ysanne Churchman, who played the part, was trying to get her colleagues, many of them amateurs chosen for their convincing country voices, to join a trade union. When he put this to Ms Churchman, she 'replied darkly: "Dead girls tell no tales."' The good news is that Ysanne herself lived on, appearing in many BBC dramas, most recently as 'woman in street' in a 1999 production of *Oliver Twist*. At the age of eighty-five, last heard of, she was alive and well and retired. And the idea of troublesome soap opera stars being summarily despatched made for a classic *Hancock* episode in 1961, entitled 'The Bowmans'.

plain-speaking Lancastrian, who was to be a hugely important ally of Fox and Dimmock in meeting the challenge of ITV. Bryan 'Ginger' Cowgill (the soubriquet going far beyond his hair colour) was another ex-military man, the youngest commissioned officer in the Royal Marines in 1944 at the age of eighteen, and fresh from editing the family-owned newspaper, the *Clitheroe Advertiser and Times*. As Cowgill said in his autobiography *Mr Action Replay*, 'The joke at the time was that you couldn't get through the door at Lime Grove without being knocked down in the rush of people dashing through it in the opposite direction to join Independent Television to grab the fat pay packets that were on offer.'

As we know, Peter Dimmock was one of those approached, 'They made me a very big offer, which I considered. But I said, look, you are all individual companies, what pre-emptive rights would I have over your OB equipment, because, say an event comes up and I want to cover it and I need two units, can I be guaranteed automatically that I will have two units out of all the companies?

'They said, "We'll have to think about that," so I went away, and then I went back to see them a second time, when they said, "Well, for a very special occasion we might be able to do it." That worried me because if I was going to go to ITV, I wanted the best outside broadcasts.'

As it happened, Dimmock had identified one of the key factors that prevented ITV competing with the BBC on sport for at least its first fifteen years: the difficulty in achieving any kind of consensus in an organisation comprising fifteen disparate regional companies. Not only would regional interests come into play – a live rugby league match might be a big draw in Widnes but prove less popular in Weybridge – but in the macho alpha-male world of television management in those days, it would take a politician of genius to get Dimmock his OB units. There may only have been fifteen regional controllers bickering and jockeying for position, but it brings to mind General De Gaulle's famous line about his difficulties as French president, 'How can you govern a country that has 246 varieties of cheese?'

However, while the BBC managed to keep both Dimmock and Paul Fox it found it more difficult to hold on to its viewers. Under the veneer of respectability, ITV's formula comprised cheerful variety shows like *Sunday Night at the London Palladium*, introduced by music-hall comedian Tommy Trinder, simple-minded quizzes hosted by mid-Atlantic hucksters with painted-on sincerity and messy personal lives and American imports such as the Lucille Ball comedy vehicle *I Love Lucy* and the police drama, *Dragnet*, with its distinctive dum-de-dum-dum signature tune and satisfyingly imitable catchphrase, 'Just the facts, ma'am.' Millions were lured over from a BBC that, according to even Asa Briggs's official history, had become 'dull and complacent'. In just two years, ITV won over 72 per cent of the available audience share.

Trebles all round. But, as the trailer featuring Blanchflower et al demonstrated, sport was definitely seen as part of ITV's plans. Yet having failed to sign Dimmock or Fox, it found itself notably short on the talent to take on the BBC. It was easy to make a success of one night's boxing, a sport, that as the boxing writer Kevin Mitchell puts it, was the easiest possible TV option. 'You can have a fixed camera, positioned above the level of the ring, looking down on this theatre, because that's what it is. You can't miss. The camera doesn't have to go anywhere, it doesn't have to follow a ball up and down a field or anything like that.'

But ITV could not rely on boxing to deliver a mass audience. Following a ball up and down a field was exactly what the network needed to do. As Sky – and ITV itself – demonstrated years later, football, Cardus's game of the people, was the only sport whose appeal vaulted age and sex barriers, and would attract the buyers of toothpaste and Cadbury's milk chocolate in their multi-millions. Had the network had the will and the unity it could have courted football, splashed out on it, and changed the course of the history of televised sport.

It did make piecemeal attempts to get into football in the 1950s, with Kent Walton, who later became the voice of professional wrestling, commentating live on the second half of some less than riveting midweek matches: like Bedford Town v. Arsenal in an FA Cup third round replay in 1956, or a friendly between Chelsea and Sparta Prague in 1957. In audience terms, though, and for entertainment value, it would have probably served the channel better to screen another half-hour of Broderick Crawford screaming 'ten-four' into his radio on its top-rated US police import *Highway Patrol*.

(I ought to declare an interest here. My father set up a small raincoat factory in the 1950s and, though producing raincoats in Manchester sounds like a foolproof business plan, he was only ever one dry summer away from going bust – until he switched to making *Highway Patrol* jackets, some kind of zip-up imitation leather thing with a nylon fur collar, allegedly just like Broderick's. Thanks to the power of ITV, we moved from our terrace in Salford to a nice semi-detached in Prestwich. So I didn't personally lament the lack of decent football on ITV, just as long as there was a jowly cop on a motorbike in pursuit of miscreants.)

ITV's first foray into league football – Britain's first-ever Football League game to be televised – was also no Broderick Crawford or Lucille Ball when it came to audience appeal. On 10 September 1960, ITV screened the second half of Blackpool v. Bolton Wanderers billed as *The Big Game*. The game, however, turned out to be slightly less Big than the Wembley contest between the same teams seven years earlier, partly because of the absence of Stanley Matthews, who was injured. Bolton scraped home 1–0 after a drab game played in a half-empty stadium.

It was supposed to be part of a £150,000 deal to screen twenty-six league matches, but ITV withdrew from the deal when Arsenal and Tottenham Hotspur refused permission to televise their matches against Newcastle and Aston Villa. They showed the *Nat King Cole Show* instead. All in all, a not exactly unforgettable attempt to become the home of football.

The BBC, meanwhile, was busy courting the League secretary, Alan Hardaker, with whom they agreed in 1964 a deal for a Saturday teatime highlights programme. From documents in the BBC archive, it seems to have taken the League a dinner or two (on the licence-payer, of course) and a few months of negotiation to get the facility fee for highlights of thirty-six matches up from £18,000 to £20,000. They also agreed on a forty-five-minute programme rather than the fifty-five minutes the

BBC had wanted, and the League turned down the BBC's request to announce in advance the match being covered, thus saving for the nation the sport of guessing which game the BBC would show.

The word 'derisory' had not yet become common currency at this time – that came during the labour disputes of the 1970s – but it might have been used to describe the BBC's £20,000 payment. As F.W. Deards pointed out in his column in the *Sunday Citizen*, 'The season's take comes out at about £600 each club, which will hardly pay for bootlaces. It looks like a proper clanger to me.'

Match of the Day was certainly not universally welcomed in the football world. Kenneth Wolstenholme introduced the programme on the newly launched BBC2 channel on 22 August 1964, but it was only available in London, so an audience of just 20,000 viewers, less than half the size of the crowd in the ground, saw Liverpool beat Arsenal 3–2, and heard Wolstenholme's introduction delivered from Anfield, 'Welcome to *Match of the Day*, the first of a weekly series on BBC2. This afternoon we are in Beatleville.'

Alec Weeks, doyen of BBC football directors, worked on the first programme, which offered one of the early uses of videotape. In his memoir, *Under Auntie's Skirts*, he underlines how vital a project *MOTD* was, since one of the factors that helped England win the bid to hold the 1966 World Cup was a guarantee that every match would be covered with electronic cameras.

'So at 2.45pm a videotape machine recorded the introduction and first half of Liverpool v. Arsenal until 3.45pm, when another machine took over for the second half whilst editing began on the first,' said Weeks, 'We were on air at 6.30pm, which left us very little time to edit 90 minutes down to 45, and as we had only edited six matches on videotape prior to this one, experience was another commodity we were short of.'

Weeks described one edit where Liverpool's central defender Ron Yeats took a throw-in from one side of the pitch, and the ball landed on the other, at the feet of ... Ron Yeats, 'The match, or the television version of it, was full of interesting touches like that.'

Despite the gaffes, though, the show was a hit, and not just in Britain. In a modest foretaste of later Premier League success, BBC Enterprises sold *Match of the Day* around the world. A letter in the archives from Findon, South Australia, dated 21 December 1964, said the programme was enjoyed by thousands of expats, as well as a growing number of Australian converts to soccer, but added, 'the only flaw concerns the title shots which leave us aghast. Wherever did you find the group of Skid Row characters who assault our vision each week?' The pasty-faced Scousers swaying on the terraces at Anfield must have looked deprived indeed to the tanned outdoor types Down Under.

Often the commentator on the main match – just two matches were shown in the 1960s and 70s, later three – would appear from the ground on the football preview slot on *Grandstand* on Saturday lunchtime, shot in close-up with just a glimpse of the location in the background, which prompted fierce debate amongst school chums as to where exactly he was.

In the days before live football, people would also go to extraordinary lengths to avoid hearing the scores, to make the *MOTD* experience as 'live' as possible. I would use the cinema as a safe haven. I remember living in Oxford, going to the Moulin Rouge cinema in Headington, where they often had double bills of classic MGM musicals and where I knew that, unless they broke into Gene Kelly and Jerry Mouse's dance routine in *Anchors Aweigh* with the scores, I was safe.

For its first run, *MOTD* had a 6.30 start time, but the following season it moved to a post-10pm slot, and by the 1966–67 season, thanks to the increased popularity of football following England's World Cup triumph, it had moved to BBC1 and become a cornerstone of Saturday night. When people talk about a golden age of British television, they invariably refer to what you might call the BBC's consensus schedule on 1970s and '80s Saturday evenings: a middle-of-the-road comedy show like *The Two Ronnies*, Michael Parkinson chatting to a Hollywood Film Star, and *Match of the Day*. It was a line-up for the whole family to unite around, although *Sunday Times* TV writer Stephen Armstrong attributes its success to the fact that this was an era before central heating became widespread in Britain, and the room with the television was often the only warm and welcoming spot in the house. Whatever the reason, *Match of the Day* became one of those BBC programmes, like *Blue Peter*, that has somehow managed to defy what the late broadcaster Eamonn Andrews called the 'shifting, whispering sands of time'.

By the mid-1970s, *Match of the Day*'s audiences peaked at 12 million as part of a highly competitive schedule, put together by someone who had no public service qualms when it came to shafting the opposition with a cleverly concocted killer line-up. Bryan Cowgill had become Controller of BBC1 in 1974.

F.W. Deards' wrong-headed prediction that *Match of the Day* would fail because of the paltry fees was balanced by an extraordinarily prescient forecast that pay-TV would be the 'Eldorado of all the big sports promoters'. He explained, 'Selling the FA Cup final or the Derby to half a million people at ten shillings a time all over the country would make everyone lick their lips.'

He was nearly forty years ahead of his time and a little shaky on how it might work, although a short-lived and largely forgotten experiment in pay TV did launch in London in 1965 and in Sheffield the following year. It was run by British Home Entertainment, a consortium led by the film producer Lord Brabourne, amongst whose triumphs were the gritty *Up The Junction* (1968), and Franco Zeffirelli's decidedly non-gritty *Romeo and Juliet* (also 1968).

Viewers paid via a meter clamped to the side of the television set into which you dropped shillings as into a gas meter in a student flat. Early offerings were racing from Kempton Park and the National Theatre's production of *Othello* starring Laurence Olivier (not in a double bill, I suspect). The big coup was to grab the Henry Cooper–Muhammad Ali heavyweight championship fight in July 1966, in partnership with Jarvis Astaire, who showed it in Odeon cinemas. An estimated 40,000 watched in cinemas and another 30,000 at home. Lord Brabourne reckoned a quarter of a million subscribers were needed for the service to make money.

Just as with pirate radio, the government showed little enthusiasm for media innovation, imposing a limit of 150,000 customers on the company, and by October 1968, the three-year trial period was over and the idea of pay TV lay dormant for nearly a quarter of a century. For the time being, then, the battle remained between BBC and ITV, which was joined in 1963 by the future star *Guardian* columnist Frank Keating, plucked from inky fingerdom to set up and head an outside broadcast unit for Rediffusion, the company providing Monday to Friday programmes for the London region.

'I was spectacularly unqualified,' admitted Frank, who had only ever worked in newspapers. 'I did not so much apply as send them an essay on what they should do, and amazingly that got me the job. I went from £22 a week to £76, and found myself producing ITV's coverage of the Opening of Parliament.'

There were, it will probably not startle you to learn, cock-ups, the most famous being in 1965 when ITV screened highlights of an England v. Austria friendly at Wembley, but neglected to show Austria's winning goal in a 3–2 victory. Steve Minchin, a recruit to ITV from the film industry, was the director that night, and told me he takes responsibility, citing extenuating circumstances, which is what circumstances often were at ITV in those days. 'I was still editing the second half as the first half was going out,' Minchin told me, 'And we had two bits of the game on the floor – one was Austria's third goal, the other was the national anthem. When we put it together, unfortunately, we got the anthem. They were not actually my hands on the offending piece of film, but the buck has to stop with me.'

This was the kind of incident that served to undermine ITV's attempts to be credible rivals. All those fans who had placed themselves in a media black hole to avoid finding out the result in advance (even if they had not actually gone to see *Anchors Aweigh*) went to bed that night convinced the match had ended in a draw. You can only imagine the sense of shock felt by those of us settling down in blissful ignorance for England v. Austria, watching four goals go in, then picking up the morning paper and finding a fifth had been scored.

Twenty-year-old Toni Fritsch's winning goal in the eighty-first minute was a historic one too, sealing only the third-ever defeat at Wembley for England by foreign opposition, after Hungary in 1953 and Sweden in 1959. It was Fritsch's second of the match, and earned him the nickname 'Wembley Toni', still used even when he went to America as a placekicker in the NFL with the Dallas Cowboys and the Houston Oilers.

To get an idea of the cultural importance of 'Not Finding Out', you only need pop in to the British Film Institute's Mediatheque on the South Bank, search through famous British situation comedies, and find that one of the most celebrated is the episode of Dick Clement and Ian La Frenais's *Whatever Happened to the Likely Lads?* from 1973, the entire plot of which hinges on the main characters, Bob (Rodney Bewes) and Terry (James Bolam), trying to avoid the score of an England match in Bulgaria.

Despite the seat-of-the-pants nature of the Rediffusion operation, though, Keating and his Head of Sport Grahame Turner did get some decent, even groundbreaking, stuff onto the air. Unconsciously maybe, they were developing a strategy that would enable ITV, if not exactly to fire a shot across the BBC's bows, to at least to give their rivals a backside full of buckshot. Because the BBC had the tradition, the expertise, the long-standing relationships with the sports bodies, and the faces and voices the public knew, Keating and Turner had to – forgive me, but for these purposes, the management cliché works perfectly – think outside the box. 'We covered Wimbledon in 1965 and 1966, trying to take on the Beeb,' Keating told me, 'Well, we had one tent, like the English before Agincourt, and there was the BBC in their splendour with their many marquees. Frankly we were looked on as absolute scum by the All-England club.

'I remember we had a floor manager who wandered round that awful concourse at Wimbledon, standing in front of the big scoreboard relaying the scores to us, saying "six–nil, six–nil" rather loudly. Anyway, eventually there was an announcement over the PA asking if ITV's editor Mr Keating will kindly report to the chairman's office, where I was told, unless you stop "this camp little man" shouting "six–nil, six–nil" you are going to be banned from Wimbledon for the fortnight.'

It became apparent to Keating that his raggle-taggle army was unlikely to go far towards rivalling the BBC in providing a comprehensive service for tennis fans – 'ITV being ITV, we had to fit everything in before five o'clock when children's programmes began' – so he set about producing something a little racier. 'We went on from half-one till about four as I recall, and to make it different, we had a theme of the day which I brought people like Peter Cook and Clement Freud to talk about. I remember Mary Holland doing a very funny memoir about being a convent girl, and Lord Arran did a sort of snooty critique. I also hired Willy Rushton to draw a cartoon summing up some aspect of the day's play.' Rather good cartoons, too. Keating still has one in his study.

He also enlisted some of his old journo chums to provide informed, independent comment, often to interesting effect. In 1966, Roy Emerson, hot favourite to repeat his men's singles triumph of the previous year, skidded into the umpire's stand during his fourth round match, injuring his shoulder, and ending his tournament. The sainted Geoffrey Green of *The Times*, who appeared to have lunched rather well, was asked who might be the new favourite. Green, turned to the camera, looked straight down the barrel, and said, 'I can tell you that Wimbledon 1964 is now as wide open as Gina Lollobrigida's legs.'

One can only imagine such audience as there was at home sitting there open-mouthed like the front row at Mel Brooks' 'Springtime For Hitler'. In the event, it all turned out for the best. The popular Manuel Santana won the title, and Rediffusion somehow escaped a lawsuit.

I wish I had seen some of that coverage – Peter Cook, Willie Rushton, well-refreshed sportswriters, what's not to like? It earns its place in sport's broadcasting history, not only as a forerunner of some of those sports panel shows, like Sky's *A League of their Own*, or BBC radio's *Fighting Talk*, on which comedians sit alongside sports people, and treat their trade irreverently, but also as an example of how sport could be covered differently from the way the BBC had always done it. 'There was a sense in which we would have a go at anything,' said Keating, as proven by the 1964 Olympics when ITV, with just a Eurovision feed and perhaps fewer viewers than the BBC had staff in Tokyo, somehow tried to compete.

Kent Walton was ITV's front man, co-presenting with the Yorkshire runner Derek Ibbotson from a tiny studio near the Middlesex Hospital, covering the games off-tube, as TV professionals call it. 'We would take the feeds from the stadium and swimming pool, and commentate on them from our sound booth,' said Frank, 'Meanwhile, I would run out and get the first editions of the *Evening Standard* and *Evening News*, and as I was running back with them I would be ripping out the stop press for Kent to read out, straight from the newspaper. The Press Association would have done us proud with British winners, and if we needed to fill a hole, Kent could always read out the modern pentathlon results. I don't think anyone much was watching, but we were running all day, and it was glorious fun.'

Keating's memories are virtually all that remains of Rediffusion's coverage of the Tokyo Olympics – and indeed of Wimbledon. The reason for that, he says, is that 'history is written by the winners', and my research suggests that so is YouTube. Frank assures me, though, that it was not an utter disaster, 'We were Heath Robinson certainly, but it turned out to be a successful Olympics for the Brits which made for a good programme.' Britain won four athletics golds, the star of the show being the long jumper and mum Mary Rand.

Keating recalled, 'When she was competing in the long jump, we thought it would be a good gimmick to get her three-year-old daughter and bring her to the studio, to celebrate with us if Mary won the gold. A fellow athlete Diane Leather was babysitting, as it happens, and she brought Mary's child down to us. Unfortunately, I was left holding the baby for the rest of the day. There I was trying to produce the show while looking after the little girl. Anyway, when her mother broke the world record, I said to Kent, for the close of the show, stand up, and pace out the twenty-two-and-a-half feet that Mary had jumped to give the audience an impression of just how far it was.

'So, delivering his script, looking to camera, Kent very carefully started pacing out the length of the jump, but on about nineteen paces, he suddenly hit the wall with a huge clang, half knocking himself out. Everything was live then, nothing recorded, and that was the end of our show, Kent on the floor, alongside this bloody baby. It was a very small studio.'

By 1968 and the Mexico Olympics, ITV had become considerably more professional, having been joined by the legendary John Bromley, who tried valiantly – not without a degree of success – to knit the ITV network together, and eventually provide the BBC with truly viable opposition.

For ITV, though, the brutal truth was that the BBC had not only won the early exchanges by shrewdly bagging the lion's share of sports rights, but had also spent the late 1950s and early '60s developing a weapon which would ensure their dominance of sport on TV – bar the occasional hiccup – for thirty years.

EIGHT

SATURDAY AFTERNOON IN

I wonder if *Grandstand* would have lasted forty-eight years and 3,000 editions if it had been called *Saturday Afternoon Out* and included Scottish country dancing?

I only ask because I found a note from Peter Dimmock in the BBC archives, written in July 1958, three months before *Grandstand* went on air, when a title for the show had not yet been agreed, 'I think that *Saturday Afternoon Out* is about the best generic title that we can find,' wrote Dimmock, 'And it would have the advantage of allowing us to include other events, e.g. *The Kilt Is My Delight* and country dancing when there is not sufficient sport available.'

The Kilt Is My Delight. I am not making it up, I promise you. And to think as a youngster I used to complain when the BBC's flagship sports show included volleyball.

A month later, Dimmock was still scratching his head over a title for the proposed Saturday afternoon sports show. He and his two lieutenants, Paul Fox, editor of his *Sportsview* unit, and producer Bryan Cowgill, must have been like one of those bands we all had a bash at in our youth, spending more time arguing about a name than rehearsing.

'Having thought a great deal about the various titles that have been suggested, I am afraid that none of them really appeals to me,' Dimmock wrote to Paul Fox, '*Lookout* is too much like *Outlook* and *Look*. *Sports Parade* is too definitive and will make it awkward to include events other than sport (still keeping a light burning in the window for that Scottish country dancing, then?), *Spectator* will be too easily confused with the intellectual magazine of the same name.'

I must say I rather like the thought of some tweed-jacketed type switching on his TV on a Saturday afternoon for a little right-wing polemic or a wryly ironic take on popular culture, and instead finding himself confronted with a swimming contest from Blackpool baths.

According to Cowgill, the notion of the programme had arisen during the 1958 Commonwealth Games in Cardiff. 'We felt out on a limb in Cardiff with many other sporting events going on around Britain. Somehow all these disparate events needed pulling together into one overall programme,' he wrote in his autobiography. 'At that time all Saturday afternoon sport was co-ordinated through the Presentation Department from a studio in London. The announcers often didn't know anything about the sport being covered and it sounded like it.'

A simple idea, really, to have the sport presented not by a plummy-voiced continuity man, but by somebody engaged with it, but back then it was tantamount to revolution. The announcer was a ubiquitous figure in the BBC in those days. Everything had to be announced: the news, drama, gramophone records. It was the way things had always been done. Even comedy shows, like *Round The Horne* and *The Goons*, used announcers – announcers sending themselves up, but announcers nonetheless. The pirate radio stations of the 1960s forced the BBC to unbend a little in the pop music area, replacing announcers with chaps who sounded like they actually wanted to play the records, but it was years before journalists were allowed to read the news.

Until I checked dates I did not realise just how groundbreaking the idea of the Saturday afternoon show was. I had assumed that like a lot of TV ideas in the 1950s it had been borrowed from America, but ABC's *Wide World of Sports* did not start until three years after *Grandstand*. With no template to follow, the birth pangs were difficult, and the title was not the only issue. The BBC scheduling people wanted the programme to end at 4.45pm (no need to explain to football fans the absurdity of that plan) to leave room for children's programmes, and also so as not to diminish *Today's Sport*, a 5.40 round-up where the classified results were traditionally given, along with a regional opt-out covering local sport. Eddie Waring used to read the Manchester one, as I recall.

Because the regions were involved, there were a lot of BBC vested interests – I refer you to previous comments about internal politics – wanting *Grandstand* to end at the most unfeasible time possible, about which Paul Fox was not happy. 'Quite frankly,' he thundered in a memo, 'unless we can give the results <u>as they come in</u> and stay on the air until five o'clock to present them in tabulated form, the programme is not worth doing at all. I see this as a sports news programme and I do not see how we can go off the air at the very moment <u>the</u> news of the day is happening.' (Fox's underlinings.)

Fox copied the note to numerous people with important-sounding initials: H.P.P.Tel, S.P.A.I., S.P.A.II, H.O.B.Tel (Dimmock, I assume, Head of Outside Broadcasts), and several others too inscrutable to mention, but initially (pun intended) lost his battle. Then there was the issue of the compère. Fox and Dimmock had identified a young journalist, David Coleman, working in Birmingham for the BBC Midland Region, who they thought ideal for the Saturday Afternoon Project – as the ex-military men often referred to it in memos, as if it were a new top-secret submarine – but they did not have the budget to employ him, so more memos had to be sent to people with initials to try and get him seconded to the programme. 'I am absolutely certain in my own mind that we need someone of Coleman's calibre and experience – particularly in the football sense!' Dimmock wrote to Fox, urging him to 'convince the establishment that there really is not anyone outside capable of doing this job and that therefore there is a dire need to second Coleman'.

Ironically, when one considers the BBC's later policy of delivering great pantechnicons full of money to presenters like Jonathan Ross and Graham Norton, Fox had to jump through all sorts of BBC hoops to get

Coleman. 'Would it be possible for Coleman to be seconded to *Sportsview*, preferably for the whole week, but alternatively for Saturday only?' he wrote. 'Were he with us just for Saturday, he could still do his news reporting duties and office routine, leaving his Saturday programme duties to be performed by a freelance, who would be paid by us. I think there is someone available in Birmingham who could do this Saturday work, so long as Coleman is available during the week in the office.'

By September, a month before the programme was due to begin – as a three-month experiment at first – Fox appeared disheartened by the problems. 'I am sorry to be so lukewarm about the new Saturday programme,' he wrote to Dimmock, 'I don't want to go back over old ground, but such setbacks as the 4.45 ending and the lack of a developing tank [a container allowing photographic film to be developed in daylight] are burdens that appear both unreasonable and unimaginative.' He listed seven points he felt needed to be solved before the programme's dummy run, which was just two weeks away, among them 'Reconsideration of the title.' 'I re-submit *Grandstand*, Fox wrote, 'and submit *Now See This, Saturday Parade, Good Afternoon …*

'I think we are wrong to go off at half cock,' he added. 'We are wrong to go off without a full-time compère; we are wrong to use a title none of us really like. Unless some consideration can be given to these points, I would strongly urge a postponement of the series until January.'

Maybe the ultimatum was just Fox's way of seeing some action (even today, people in the BBC sometimes refer to the various strata of management they must consult as the Programme Prevention Committee). As we know his re-submitted title was accepted, and served the programme reasonably well for nearly half a century, most of his technical needs were met, and *Grandstand* launched on 11 October 1958, although without Coleman and still with the 4.45 end time (which led, in an early programme billing, to the less-than-irresistible offer to football fans of '*some* full-time results'.)

Fox continued to angle for Coleman, and also complain in a series of memos about the ridiculous end time. He also had to fight to get an article plugging the show in the *Radio Times*, where television in those days struggled for space, not only against radio, but also against the copious pages devoted to advertisements for garden sheds, greenhouses and quaint 1950s food products. '*A delicious surprise for tea? It's easy if you always keep a few jars of Brand's*', boasted a well-known manufacturer of bloater paste.

You would not guess from the feature in the issue of 5–11 October that Fox had any misgivings, 'Nearly three hours of non-stop television – with the accent on sport: that is the aim of the new BBC Television Outside Broadcasts programme *Grandstand*, which makes its first appearance on Saturday,' he wrote. '*Grandstand* is a one-word title for an all-action programme – though it is really many programmes. All the items that used to appear here and there on Saturday afternoons will now come under the *Grandstand* umbrella.

'*Grandstand* plans to provide a new type of sports survey. Throughout the afternoon there will be football newsflashes, together with half-time scores. There will be a complete up-to-the-minute racing service with, of course, the starting prices. So the quickest way of knowing what has happened in sport on Saturday will be to watch *Grandstand* throughout the afternoon. Sports news of the day will be given as it happens – and whenever possible, where it happens.'

(Provided it doesn't happen after 4.45.)

'We shall be bringing you swimming – long a TV favourite – motor-racing, motor-cycling, skating, table tennis, and, if our hopes are realised, boxing. Yes, boxing on Saturday afternoon is one of *Grandstand*'s planned events. Another is the return of a famous sports personality, Joe Davis. The greatest snooker player of all time has signed up for a series of special challenge matches. Joe Davis will travel around the country challenging his fellow stars – his brother Fred Davis, Walter Donaldson, and John Pulman. The first match – Joe against brother Fred – is due on 18 October.'

There was rather too much swimming, and Joe Davis playing snooker in black and white, for my taste in the early days, serving only to dampen down the excitement created by an exciting title sequence one would be tempted to call iconic had the word not been overused to the point where it is now meaningless, like 'legend.'

The tune was 'News Scoop' by Len Stevens, clearly grabbed off an album of library music ('urgent, insistent, news and current affairs theme, full orchestra') over which there was a shot of a four-turret lens camera – which again I am tempted to call iconic as it was the model for the Sports Personality trophy – with a different sport going on in each lens: boxing, horse racing, swimming and rugby league. '*BBC Television Outside Broadcasts bring you Grandstand. Today's Sport As It Happens…*' read the captions, ' … And all the football and racing results.' Behind that caption was a shot of busy men sliding team names and scores into wooden slats, basically an old-fashioned scoreboard.

Perhaps my favourite of all the *Grandstand* memos in the BBC archives is one from late in 1962 from one of the producers, Alec Weeks, to a young assistant in the design department, taking him to task for the state of the scoreboards. 'The football boards used for *Grandstand* have been considerably damaged during the past three weeks, presumably during their assembly and disassembly,' Weeks wrote. 'These boards are now in a desperate need of refurbishing, i.e. repainting, repairing of broken slats and lining. Could this work please be put in hand immediately?' The young set designer to whom the message was sent was Ridley Scott. I like to think that the first thing Scott did when he won his Best Picture Oscar for *Gladiator* was send a message back to *Grandstand* telling them to mend their own bloody scoreboards.

Dimmock presented the first three *Grandstands* while Coleman was awaited, and his tenure, while as smooth as always, emphasised the need for a football specialist. Scottish football especially remained a murky area to the presenter, according to Cowgill, who says Dimmock floundered when confronted with Cltc 3 Ptk Th 1 on the teleprinter. Finding no help forthcoming via his earpiece, the Head of Outside Broadcasts announced somewhat hopefully, 'Celtic 3 Purr Thaaa 1.' As Dimmock was the first to say, 'David Coleman took over and was brilliant, absolutely brilliant.'

The first show included the World Amateur Golf from St Andrews, three races from Ascot, and the Junior Show Jumper of the Year from Harringay. There was also a filmed interview between Kenneth Wolstenholme and England centre forward Nat Lofthouse. The budget for the show was £497, mostly spent on items like film and teleprinter lines, with a few guineas here and there for contributors. Wolstenholme got ten guineas for his interview, while Lofthouse is charmingly listed in the budget as costing 0 guineas. Almost the most expensive item was 'Suit for Peter Dimmock – £61'. A pencil note alongside it reads 'Huntsman, Savile Row'.

Viewer reaction to the first show makes interesting reading. The BBC duty office received three complaints about Peter Dimmock talking too much, ten saying the programme was too bitty, eleven calls saying too little time was given to showjumping, and six complaining that a plug for *Six-Five Special*, the rock 'n' roll show, was included in the programme. Balanced against that, there were twenty-seven calls after a boy at the Harringay show had misused his whip on his horse.

Who, you might wonder, was calling the BBC duty office in 1958? Someone with a home phone, obviously, the preserve of the more prosperous in those days. (Even in the mid-1970s when I was a newspaper reporter, if we wanted a quote from someone on a council estate, we often resorted to ringing the only house on the street with a phone, and asking if he or she could go and bring our interviewee to the instrument.) It was also, most likely somebody watching alone. If others were present, views might be shared rather than phoned in.

As a veteran of late night Radio Two, I am something of an expert on the duty officer's log, which we disc jockeys used to peruse to see what the audience thought of us – or to check that our mates had remembered to call up to praise our show. We quickly formed the view that the duty office was an early example of what would now be called 'care in the community'. I remember particularly one call where a colleague, a sweet and inoffensive female presenter, was criticised for 'advocating oral sex' on her show. Turned out she had described a party she hosted, and mentioned how difficult it was to talk 'with a mouthful of peanuts'.

The point is people who call the BBC are not always the most reliable witnesses, so professional research was commissioned during *Grandstand*'s experimental period. Paul Fox's 'half-cock' worries, despite seeming fully justified to the professionals, did not seem to worry the audience. An Audience Research Report into 'the new-style, non-stop parade of sports and events' reported overwhelmingly favourable reaction. 'It is just what all keen sportsmen must have dreamed of for a very long time,' ran one comment. 'Well done, BBC – you have done a grand job for all us outdoor sports lovers. Long overdue, but very welcome.' A housewife (they still existed then, and the BBC was allowed to describe them as such) reported 'a very pleasant afternoon by the fireside' (they still existed in 1958 as well) 'on a dull October day'.

Audience ratings during the first few weeks were no higher than they had been prior to *Grandstand*'s launch when a ragbag of sports – swimming, cricket, horse racing – appeared in Saturday afternoon's schedules on an ad hoc basis, but they grew exponentially during the Coleman era (1958–68) and by the time ITV achieved sufficient network unity to launch its rival, *World of Sport* at the start of 1965, *Grandstand* was embedded as part of the nation's sporting furniture. In the words of Professor Steven Barnett, '*World of Sport* faced the perennial ITV problem: it could never match the consistently higher ratings being achieved by *Grandstand* with its longer tradition and more prestigious events.'

Under Coleman, *Grandstand* became what we now know as a brand, although at the time *Olympic Grandstand*, *World Cup Grandstand*, and *Sunday Grandstand* were just seen as convenient programme titles. One of the most popular programmes on the roster was *Grand National Grandstand*, which recorded a Reaction Index (known as RIs among initial fans at the BBC) of 86 for the 26 March 1960 show, well above the average (76) for thirty-one editions of *Grandstand* that year, according to an Audience Research document. 'Great credit was due to all those responsible,' said one respondent, 'for the way the coverage had been organised by the BBC.' David Coleman, says the report, was 'well liked by most viewers. As always, many of them said, he controlled the programme admirably, without ever getting flustered. They find him a likeable personality and admire his confident, assured manner.' Peter O'Sullevan was also singled out, 'When it comes to describing a horse race he is in a class of his own.' My favourite sentence in a detailed report reads, 'A Bakery Manageress (their capitals) thought, "the commentaries could be improved if a man with a deep voice finished the commentary at the last few laps of the race."'

Mind you, the nation's Cornish pasty specialists would not have had a Grand National to watch at all were it not for Dimmock's canny negotiations – and possibly his snappy Savile Row suit – and prolonged courting of everyone connected with the race.

Mirabel Topham, who owned Aintree, would have nothing to do with television, believing it would discourage crowds from attending the National. In fact, the Topham family was so opposed to the BBC that in 1952 the family barred radio coverage and did their own commentary. However, as even the official history of the National concedes, 'If anybody is in any doubt that race commentary is a difficult job then a brief listen to this commentary will tell you different. It can only be described as dreadful and it was soon handed back to the professionals.'

It took years for Dimmock to talk Mrs Topham round – 'Most of my grey hairs are a result of that woman,' he says – but the National was televised from 1960 onwards, the last of the major sporting events to succumb to TV. The first contract was a three-year agreement at a cost of £35,000 a year, and Mrs Topham was rewarded with a mention in the *Radio Times*. 'It may surprise listeners to know that the general manager of the course (Aintree) is a woman, Mrs A.R. Topham, who yields place to none in efficiency and enterprise.'

'Yes, you could say that,' comments Dimmock.

There was a time when you could mark the passing of the seasons with *Grandstand*: the bleak cheerless Saturdays of January and February meant Five Nations rugby, with its invitation to toast a crumpet and luxuriate in the warm Celtic glow of Bill McLaren and Cliff Morgan, then early spring and the Grand National and Boat Race, followed by the two cup finals, rugby league and football, often bathed in May sunshine, before summer proper and a couple of weeks at Wimbledon.

Sure, there were weeks when the line-up was limp. I give you 7 January 1978, which featured the second half of a half-decent rugby league match, but otherwise nondescript racing from Haydock, surfing, and squash (a sport that has never worked on TV, and never will). On that sort of week, the teleprinter took over – by early 1959 Paul Fox had won his battle for a five o'clock finish – and Coleman (Frank Bough in the 1970s) and the printer could chatter away happily together, until the Lone Ranger, or Billy Bunter, arrived to entertain the kiddies.

There was always something to fill the unforgiving hours between the football preview and the teleprinter, even if it was squash, or tug of war (also on that show of 7 January 1978), or obscure boxing bought in from America. Always, that is, except in the harsh winter of 1962–63 when everything out of doors was frozen off for months, and producer Alec Weeks asked the Controller of Television, Stuart Hood, for permission to run a feature film in the slot where horse racing would normally be. The feature film pulled off the shelf for the 29 December programme was *D.O.A.*, a 1949 film noir starring Edmond O'Brien.

Unfortunately, the film turned out to be a little more noir than either Weeks, Coleman, or the audience was expecting. I have the script for the show, and Coleman announced the movie as follows, 'And now for our feature film which stars Edmond O'Brien and Pamela Britton. It's a thriller and a story of mystery and murder, a story of a man in fact who was "dead on arrival".' What followed was hardly a suitable curtain raiser for the other main attraction, an ice skating gala from the Silver Blades rink at Streatham. Weeks says he did not know the film, but he thought it 'a whodunit that would keep our viewers happy for a couple of hours'. The film is known to me, and I remember Neville Brand going well over the top as one of those smiling psychopaths he specialised in, Edmond O'Brien being poisoned, a number of corpses, and dialogue such as, 'If you so much as look cross-eyed at anybody, I'll blow the back of your skull off.'

Hundreds of mothers, says Weeks, were calling Television Centre demanding the film be taken off immediately. 'Is this what you call family viewing?' was a typical comment. 'How dare you put this film on?' another outraged viewer asked, 'I'm the mother of five children who have been glued to the screen ever since this film started. You can have no idea what five children are capable of.' As the big freeze continued into the New Year, *Grandstand* showed another noir classic, *Farewell My Lovely*, on 5 January 1963, leading to the suspicion the programme was being put together by the earnest young cineastes of *Cahiers du Cinéma*.

After Coleman left the programme in 1968, *Grandstand* was fortunate in finding another everyman figure to replace him. If the nicely modulated Stockport tones of Coleman shook the BBC out of the cut-glass era of actor/announcers, Frank Bough, from a few miles down the road in the Potteries, continued in similar vein. Bough was *Grandstand*'s longest serving presenter, fifteen years covering the golden, self-confident era of BBC dominance up until 1983. In the 1970s they even gave him a new theme tune, this time specially written for the programme by Keith Mansfield and – impossibly – even better than the original one. Sometimes I would tune in just for the titles, and switch off once Frank started going on about the horse racing and golf.

Like Coleman, Bough came from regional TV. In the early 1960s he joined the BBC as presenter of *North at Six* in Newcastle, one of the early regional magazine programmes, 'reflecting on the issues of the day in that area, to highlight the aspirations of the people, their character and sense of humour', as Frank explains it in his amusingly Pooteresque 1980 autobiography *Cue Frank!*: 'Each of the regions was given twenty minutes early in the evening to make their own programmes for their own people.' Local news for local people, as the business was later characterized in the comedy show *League of Gentlemen*.

Much more on Bough presently – the sex, the drugs, the one-day cricket.

NINE

THE LORD'S DAY

'What is it about this unobtrusive game? What is its magic? For magic it must surely be that makes men sit and watch, and dream of past occasions, and of wistful yearnings never quite fulfilled. Magic it is that makes the hush when captains meet.'

The words are Sir Ralph Richardson's in a short British Council film called *Cricket*, produced by the Pathé Documentary Unit in 1951. 'Only sunny days and history are long,' intones Sir Ralph (in that marvellous voice, and probably with the mournful eyes too, although impossible to say as he is out of vision). 'All thought and spirit concentrated on a square of green, a subtle battle between a slice of willow and a round of leather.'

Richardson was entitled to be misty-eyed, as he was talking over footage of the peerless Donald Bradman's last Test at Lord's, the second of the 1948 series, which Australia's 'invincibles' won 4–0. A crowd of 30,000 was packed into the headquarters of English cricket that day, and the film has footage of the be-suited throng outside the ground, stretching further than the camera could see, queuing patiently to get within viewing distance of the battle.

The scene is redolent of those years after the Second World War when sporting events of all sorts drew record crowds. The 158,000 who attended the Second Test at Headingley that series remains a record for a Test in England, while the Football League also broke its record in

1948, when 83,260 watched Manchester United play Arsenal at Maine Road.* Those huge crowds for live sport may account for the reluctance of some of the sports' bodies, as the 1940s slipped into the 1950s and television became more popular, to let the new medium get too close. Not quite as reluctant as Mrs Topham at Aintree racecourse, who took ten years to be ushered into the television age, but wary nonetheless. Back in 1948, though, BBC television was still a relative novelty, not perceived as too much of a threat to the live event, and was welcome inside Lord's, and also at The Oval for Bradman's final Test appearance when he was given a standing ovation by the crowd, and three cheers from the England players, on his way to the wicket.

Famously, he was bowled out for a second-ball duck by Eric Hollies, yet cheered to the rafters once again as he returned to the pavilion, a moment that Brian Johnston in the TV commentary box, called the most poignant he could remember. John Arlott, meanwhile, was painting a word picture for radio listeners. 'What do you say under these circumstances?' he asked, 'I wonder if you see the ball very clearly in your last Test in England on a ground where you've played some of the biggest cricket of your life and where the opposing side has just stood around you and given you three cheers, and the crowd has clapped you all the way to the wicket. I wonder if you see the ball at all.'

On radio, Arlott, the poet, was allowed the words, whereas Johnston had to be more economical in the TV commentary box, as he himself accepted in a piece he wrote in 1956 for a BBC publication called *Armchair Cricket*, in which he drew up a number of golden rules for TV commentators.

Firstly, he warned, 'Never speak unless you can add to the picture showing on the screen at the moment. So you must always watch your monitor.' Secondly, 'Never refer to the players by their Christian names only. Personally, although I know some people do not, I like Len Hutton, Denis Compton, Peter May etc. But to use just Denis or Peter without

---

* Old Trafford was being rebuilt after wartime damage.

the surname is inexcusable.' (It is a lesson some of today's football pundits could well learn.*)

Finally, in a classic Johnnersism, he counsels, 'Do not describe the obvious. If you want to draw the viewers' attention to an aeroplane in the picture do not say, "Ah, an aeroplane!" – but something like "I wonder if the chap in that aeroplane can pick out Wardle's chinaman."'

After the euphoria of England's Ashes success in 1953 – by now the BBC had transmitters in the North and Midlands, so for the first time all five Tests could be covered – the BBC began to negotiate for the following summer's cricket with the MCC, who now severely restricted the hours the BBC was allowed to broadcast the matches. On Mondays, Wednesdays, and Thursdays for example, TV coverage was limited to half an hour between 1pm and 1.30, and then two hours after tea, from 4.30 to 6.30. On a Saturday, TV was permitted only between 4.30 and 6.30.

This was not a tactic to get more money – the money the BBC paid was now up into the (very low) thousands – but the old, old worry of the effect televised cricket might have on the paying punters. The MCC knew it could get people through the gates at Test matches, even if televised, but the counties understandably felt their attendance figures would suffer if a Test was on the TV, and demanded the restricted hours. I mean, who would want to be present to witness what Cardus called the 'creeping paralysis' of a 'decaying contemporary industry' – this was not exactly how the counties put it – when the real action was clearly going on elsewhere, and could be seen without leaving home?

According to Chris Broad and Daniel Waddell's history of cricket on the BBC, even the restricted coverage caused internal problems, particularly with the producers of Children's Hour. They wrote, 'Plans to halve Children's Hour on Test match days were resisted, even when the sports

---

* For some unfathomable reason, Owen and Rooney are constantly referred to as 'Michael' and 'Wayne', yet mysteriously none of the other players are (almost as if Michael and Wayne are special chums).

department offered to adapt the commentary to cater for children.' (I am not making this up. They were quite serious.)

In an internal memo in June 1957, Joanna Spicer, the Head of Programme Planning (or H.P.P., as she will have been known within the BBC) explained her opposition to the child-friendliness notion, 'While Brian Johnston is more than capable of adjusting his commentary to children, other announcers would not be so good at it.' (I am still not making this up).

Later that year, Freda Lingstrom, the head of Children's Programmes (H.C.P.) rebuffed attempts to move the children's programmes from 6.30pm back to 3.30pm. 'Children should be, and generally are, out playing themselves at this time on fine Saturday afternoons … We will be encouraging them indoors when they should be out in the fresh air …' she thundered (in the voice of Joyce Grenfell, I like to imagine), '… 6.30 to 7pm is a much better time for children to be viewing, as they will then be indoors after tea and ready to go to bed afterwards.'

Wow. If it's social history you want, look no further. I think I know what the matter is – with apologies to Lionel Bart – with kids today. There are not enough Freda Lingstroms around to ensure children get plenty of fresh air and are in bed at a reasonable hour.

Despite the strictures you may have read in this book about the BBC's dedication to children's programmes – the problems it caused for *Grandstand*'s results service for instance – as a father of four I bless the public service broadcaster for looking after our children. In order to write my newspaper column I have to have a complete Sky package, and all sorts of mind-numbing rubbish comes into my house via Disney and suchlike, but as long as my little ones are in the safe hands of the BBC I am happy. Of course, I would rather they were out in the park, Freda Lingstrom-style, but that's not always possible.

By 1959, the Corporation had negotiated a new contract with the MCC, was paying more money, and was allowed to broadcast Test matches without restriction. That did not solve internal scheduling problems, though, which had to wait until BBC2 came on the air in 1964.

As for the terminally ill county game, its life support system came courtesy of a young county secretary trying to save his club from financial ruin. Unlike the rest of the nation, in the spring of 1962, Mike Turner was not worrying about the Cuban missile crisis, or queuing up to see John Wayne and James Stewart in *The Man Who Shot Liberty Vallance*, but burning the midnight oil in his office at Grace Road, Leicester, scratching his head over the balance sheet of his county, Leicestershire, trying to calculate how long the club could survive. He reckoned that if all went exceptionally well, the county he had just taken over might just about have five years of life left.

The creeping paralysis Cardus had spotted in the county game had spread to all areas. It was dying on its feet. The format of the County Championship had been little changed since 1890 and excited almost nobody. Seventeen teams played between twenty-eight and thirty-two fixtures, all three-day games, producing the county champions in late August or early September.

Turner's eureka moment came when he examined that season's fixtures and noticed there were three days in May when neither Leicester-shire nor neighbouring counties Nottinghamshire, Northamptonshire, or Derbyshire were playing. 'I had a word with the chairman of the club, and we agreed it would be a really good idea to play a regional knockout tournament that weekend. So I phoned round all the secretaries, we agreed a format, and the Midland Counties Knockout Cup was born.'

The tournament, involving one-day games with a novel limited-overs format was an instant success – 'Champagne Cricket' was the headline over the *Leicester Mercury*'s report of Northamptonshire's triumph in the inaugural competition. It was an idea whose time had come – frankly, it had probably come several years before – and by November 1962, contracts were being signed for a national 65-over knockout tournament the following summer, which mutated into the Gillette Cup. The BBC got involved, and it delivered healthy audiences. In fact, so popular was it that Peter Dimmock suggested – not with a huge degree of confidence – that it might be worth trying to sell it to the United States.

The number of overs per side was soon cut down to sixty in the interests of everyone getting home before midnight, and two memorable matches established the competition as a firm favourite: Yorkshire's victory over Surrey in the 1965 final, featuring an innings in which Geoffrey Boycott shed all his inhibitions to score 146, and the remarkable semi-final between Lancashire and Gloucestershire at Old Trafford on 28 July 1971 which, long before floodlights on cricket grounds, went on until almost 9pm.

'It's my view that it was that match that put one-day cricket on the map,' says David Lloyd, Lancashire's opening batsman of that evening. 'I vividly remember the ground being packed, with kids right up to the boundary rope. I think there were 24,000 in there, and in the gathering gloom David Hughes scored 24 in one over to put the teams level. There were kids running all over the place, and we had to wait while they were all ushered back behind the rope to score the winning run.'

Lloyd says that when he raised the problem of the fading light with the umpire Arthur Jepson, the official pointed to the sky, and asked, 'What's that up there?' The baffled batsman replied, 'The moon', to which Jepson responded, 'Well, how far do you want to see, then?'

Nick Hunter, one of the BBC's producers that evening, remembers *Points of View*, the programme scheduled for 8.50pm being dropped after telephone calls from the scanner van, while another producer Jonathan Martin, later the BBC's Head of Sport, had a more fevered conversation about the possibility of the nine o'clock news being delayed. 'We've got to go to the news now,' he was told. 'This *is* the fucking news,' he replied. As it turned out the winning run was scored, as darkness descended, in the nick of time.

Hunter recalls that when it was all over, both he and the commentator, Jim Laker, were bursting for a pee. 'The pair of us made a desperate dash for the loo when it finished and if anybody got in our way, then God help them. It was pitch black, and I thought, "ten minutes ago people were still playing cricket". It was unbelievable.' 'We got letters at Lancashire from irate wives,' said David Lloyd, 'They said their husbands had rolled in last thing at night claiming to have been at a cricket match, asking us to confirm this was true.'

My brother, who would have been twelve at the time, went to the match, and I remember him coming home singing 'Lancashire la la la, Lancashire la la la la', to the tune of the theme from the TV show *The Banana Splits*, which must have been the first time exultant football-style chants had taken hold at cricket grounds. Another favourite was 'Ooh Lanky Lanky; Lanky, Lanky, Lanky, Lanky, Lankysheer', adapted from Chicory Tip's hit song, 'Son of My Father'. Cricket had truly joined the modern age.

Thanks to one-day cricket, then, the patient seemed now to be sitting up in bed, taking a little light refreshment, and, to stretch the metaphor almost to breaking point, television was there under the covers too, no longer in a twin bed, or with one foot on the floor, as in a 1950s sit-com.

The crucial figure in helping consummate this relationship was a half-forgotten figure rejoicing in the unlikely name of Bagenal Harvey. Actually, probably more than half forgotten: the only Bagenal Harveys who turn up on an internet search are a Commander of the United Irishmen in the 1798 rebellion, and a restaurant in County Wexford presumably named after him.

This Bagenal Harvey was a sports agent, probably the world's first. Harvey's agency stemmed from the England cricket tour of South Africa in 1948–49, when journalist Reg Hayter was handed a suitcase full of unopened letters by his travelling companion, Middlesex and England batsman Denis Compton. 'Christ, Compo, you're sitting on a fortune,' said Hayter, as he began reading the mail, some of it six months old. There were offers to take fees for after-dinner speaking, to make public appearances at the opening of stores and new theatre productions, offers to write books and newspaper columns, as well as the £1,000 a year to be the face of Brylcreem. Hayter thought his shrewd friend Bagenal might be able to help.

The first deal Harvey struck was for Compton to be photographed putting on the hair cream, with Harvey taking 10 per cent (of the fee, not the Brylcreem). There were lots more 10 per cents, but more importantly, Harvey also sorted out the minutiae of Compton's life off the field: tax demands, insurance, bank accounts, all those brown envelopes, the niggling matters sporting heroes (Compton was the David Beckham of his day) and quite frankly even those of us not busy being the golden boy of English cricket, find too irritating and time-consuming to deal with.

It is why so many sports agents are former accountants or financial advisors. In one of those periodic rows that break out at the top of the Labour Party, Nye Bevan once called Hugh Gaitskell 'a desiccated calculating machine'. Well, that is exactly what you want in an agent. Someone who understands money.

Bagenal Harvey was more than that, though. Despite never getting the 'executive producer' credit which agents are so keen on these days, that was effectively his role in cricket's next big step forward. In 1965, recognising the clamour for the one-day game, Harvey, whose charges now included a variety of sportsmen and broadcasters, put together the Rothmans Cavaliers, with suitable sponsorship from the cigarette company.

The team was comprised of international cricketing greats like Compton, Laker, Graeme Pollock, and Gary Sobers, alongside the occasional exciting youngster like the West Indies' Clive Lloyd, and played 40-over matches against a county eleven each Sunday afternoon, often from some colourful venue, like Tichborne Park in Hampshire, the private ground at the home of Sir Anthony Doughty Doughty of Tichborne (really, not stolen from a Wodehouse novel). The matches were shown on BBC2, but not before some correspondence between Bryan Cowgill and the BBC governors, asking for permission to run the cricket into the so-called God slot, the religious broadcasting hour which began at 6pm, and was then more inviolable even than the Children's Hour. As presenter Frank Bough wrote in his autobiography: 'Cricket, the game of manor house, village church, pub, and village green, was clearly vital. The governors persuaded themselves that the sight of a world-class batsman in full flow was as much an uplifting experience as *Songs of Praise*, and without doubt, to the greater glory of God!'

The football commentator Brian Moore actually preceded Bough as presenter of the Cavaliers cricket matches – now there's a recondite snippet of broadcasting history – but only for one match. A passionate cricket fan, Moore was chosen despite being football correspondent at the time for BBC radio. After his first stint on Sunday cricket, his radio boss decided that was where he should stay. So Bough took over and made it his own! (Tribute exclamation mark.)

All those interviews you now see at the end of Test matches and knockout cup finals, well, this was where they started. It was Bough who spoke to players as they went to the wicket, after the matches, and during the tea interval as well, often also seeking out 'interesting people' not necessarily connected with the game, rather as Garry Richardson now does for the BBC during Wimbledon fortnight. In his book Bough describes a memorable teatime encounter with the international playboy Nubar Gulbenkian, a famously tough cookie who once sued his father's company for ten million dollars for refusing to allow him to claim a $4.50 lunch of chicken in tarragon jelly on expenses, and was said by a friend at Cambridge to 'tire out three stockbrokers, three horses and three women before lunch'.

Bough asked him cheerily if he was fond of cricket. 'Not particularly,' replied the bearded and monocled bon viveur, as he walked off, 'I came here to see Evelyn Rothschild for a meeting about the local hunt.'

Bough also stage-managed the post-match presentation – in a style that has since become familiar – of the winners' cheque, which was pretty fiercely contested by the teams. The matches were anything but exhibition games, thanks to Cowgill's insistence the sport be as competitive as he himself was. (As Bough explained, 'Above all, it must be a series that would bring the crowds back to the game, but even more important, because Cowgill competed over every inch of life, it must get television viewers watching his programmes!')

John Arlott and Sir Learie, later Lord, Constantine were the commentators, joined in 1968 by Jim Laker, the former England off-spinner known not just for his canny punditry but also for never being knowingly guilty of pronouncing a 'g' at the end of a word. Laker was a popular member of the BBC's Sunday cricket team right up to his death in 1986. Nick Hunter, who produced the broadcasts, sees them as a television revolution, 'Beforehand you went along to cover a Test match and you were expected to live by all the rules and regulations that were set by the authorities, so not a toenail over the boundary line, that sort of thing. The Sunday cricket changed that completely,' he told me.

'We sort of felt it was our tournament, and we could break ground by doing different things at tea, with the interviews and so on. And by having John Arlott and Learie Constantine commentating, it gave it a different feel to our Test match coverage.' Having an in-vision presenter welcome viewers, and set up the game's key figures was also an innovation. 'Frank knew his cricket,' says Hunter, 'But he was also able to ask journalistic questions to people as well, and was friendly, so the whole broadcast had a relaxed air about it, particularly compared to Test cricket.'

Hunter is spot-on in identifying a shift in sports broadcasting, one that was not lost on Bagenal Harvey. Jimmy Hill, a Harvey protégé, described in his autobiography a meeting set up by Harvey in 1967, at the Berkeley Hotel (at which he ate grouse – Hill is not as profligate as Bough with the exclamation marks, but matches him on irrelevant detail). His dining companion was Michael Peacock, managing director of the soon-to-be-launched London Weekend Television, who asked Hill, 'If you owned a television channel and your rivals held exclusive contracts for the major sporting events, how would you compete?'

'I suppose,' Hill reports himself as replying, 'you'd be forced to devise your own competitions, which you would own. You'd need money to tempt the leading professionals to take part and presumably a sponsor might provide that if he could be guaranteed sufficient exposure. It's a three-legged stool.' It's a three-legged stool still standing today. The PartyPoker.com Premier League snooker, Whyte & Mackay Premier League darts, and even the Stobart Super League are all direct descendants of Harvey's Cavaliers.

Of course, this triumvirate of agent, broadcaster and the performers does leave the sport's administrators out in the cold rather, a situation the newly formed Test and County Cricket Board decided to remedy in 1969. Huge crowds, they noted, were paying good money to watch a product the BBC would televise, and sponsors were happy to finance, and yet they were not seeing a penny of it.

And so their own competition, the 40-over John Player League, took over on Sunday afternoons, and was immediately popular with fans and with the BBC. I recall being at rugby matches on Sundays in the 1970s and '80s, going into the clubhouse afterwards, and joining the cluster around the TV for the last few overs.

All such sports fixtures were testing the boundaries of the Sunday Observance Act, originally passed in 1780 and subsequently amended, creating a labyrinthine collection of rules and regulations – you could buy a pornographic magazine on a Sunday, for example, but not a copy of the Bible. But one of the clearest taboos was selling tickets for a sporting fixture on a Sunday.

, I remember living near Holloway Road in London in the 1970s, where there was a rather good bakery standing next door to a specialist store selling a range of black leather items clearly intended for use in what you might term boudoir activities. While the bakery was shut on the Lord's Day, the leather shop was open, which meant you could buy a gimp mask on His day, but not a Cornish pasty.

Attempts to reform the act nearly always failed because of the fierce opposition of the Lord's Day Observance Society. As early as 1953, the Labour MP John Parker was pointing out some of the absurdities of the act in a parliamentary debate: 'One is not allowed to play billiards in public or to dance in public on a Sunday, but one can organise a billiards club or a dancing club with a subscription of one shilling a year, and the public can attend, provided they are not charged for admission, and then one can have all the billiards and all the dancing that one wants.'

Mike Turner, who acted as consultant to the John Player League, remembers that spectators gained entry by buying a programme, which coincidentally was sold for the exact price of admission. 'The John Player League, with 40 overs a side on a Sunday afternoon, and a two o'clock start was a superb package,' said Turner.

'They could have their Sunday lunch before they came and the game was over by 6.30. It also brought a boom in catering at the ground. We used to have two sittings for lunch. Every Sunday afternoon, one match was televised in its entirety by BBC2, and that generated boundary-board advertising, which we had not had before in cricket.' Turner also recalled, in a Sky Sports documentary, that not everyone approved of the Lord's Day being used for flogging adverts, and two servings at the carvery, 'I got a letter about it from the Bishop of Leicester beginning "Dear Sinner … "'

By 1972, a third one-day competition, the Benson and Hedges Cup, had begun, set up with the help of the BBC front man Peter West, who by that stage was the West of West Nally, a company just getting into the relatively new field of sports sponsorship (the BBC seems to have been more relaxed about possible conflicts of interest back then). That year also saw the first international one-day matches in Britain, sponsored by the Prudential insurance people.

The only people not sharing in the new found wealth of cricket were the players, who were paid little more than the average wage, and found themselves having to drive hundreds of miles at the weekend to fulfil fixtures. Lancashire, for instance, could be playing in a County Championship match at Blackpool, in the middle of which a Sunday League fixture in Somerset might be scheduled. The players would therefore have to drive down to Taunton on a Saturday night or very early on a Sunday morning – at a time when Britain's motorway network was anything but complete – and then drive back after the match to finish the county fixture. While cricket might have been skipping around the convalescent ward, its players still felt very sick indeed. Within a decade that would change thanks to events over the other side of the world.

World Series Cricket, a breakaway professional cricket competition staged between 1977 and 1979, was a prime example of the Jimmy Hill method in action. Organised by Australian media tycoon Kerry Packer for his television company, Nine Network, the matches ran in opposition to established international cricket, and grew out of Packer's frustration in trying to secure the rights to televise the sport. He is quoted as saying, at a meeting with the Australian Cricket Board, 'There is a little bit of the whore in all of us, gentlemen. What is your price?'

The timing was propitious, as Packer's impasse over rights coincided with a growing feeling among the top cricketers that they were being underpaid. The Australian fast bowler Dennis Lillee complained that the Australian Cricket Board treated players as amateurs yet made securing outside employment prohibitive, and other recruits also rallied to Packer's cause, including the Chappell brothers, Viv Richards, Imran Khan and England captain Tony Greig.

Greig was an early and enthusiastic Packer disciple, and embraced the new world with great fervour. He was a man with an eye for a deal, as attested by his numerous endorsements in Australia, notably for Nutri-Grain – catchphrase, 'It's just like a cricket bat with holes'. He is on the Channel Nine payroll to this day as a commentator.

When Packer died in 2005, the obituary in the *Sydney Morning Herald* ran, 'Boardroom tyrant or sporting visionary? It usually depended on which side of the bargaining table you sat. As Australia woke to the news of Kerry Packer's death, the sporting community was left to ponder the legacy of a man whose media empire forever changed the face of cricket and rugby league in this country.'

There was little enthusiasm for Packer's 'rebel' Tests at the start, though. He was estimated to have lost around £2 million in his first season. But eventually the Aussie public grew to love it, embracing the concept of night matches, colourful kit, and modern television coverage, even propelling the WSC theme song 'C'mon, Aussie, C'mon' performed by the Mojo Singers to the top of the Australian charts in 1978.

'Packer was the catalyst for change,' the England and Wales Cricket Board commercial director John Perera told me. 'Cricket was very conservative before Packer. We had only just moved out of the Gentlemen and Players era. Players were getting paid, but not enough for a full-time career, not even the top ones. Overnight, Packer changed all that, and obviously with full-time professionalism, standards improved accordingly. It spawned new trophies, and for the first time we had players wearing non-white clothing.'

Packer revolutionised TV coverage as well. 'I grew up watching BBC covering matches from just one end,' said Perera. 'You either saw the bowler, or the batsman, often obscured by the wicketkeeper's backside. As well as all the gimmicks, Packer brought in more cameras, forcing TV directors here to rethink the way they did things.'

Meanwhile, back at the end of the 1960s, there was another sport, even more eager than cricket to shake off the dowdy garb of its low-budget monochrome past, a sport that had been a handy, inexpensive filler for TV ever since the early days, but could now benefit from the scheduling possibilities of BBC2 – and even more from the arrival of colour.

TEN

SPOT THE REDHEAD ...
AND THE PINK

I don't recall any great clamour for colour television in Britain, certainly not in Lichfield Drive. My mum gave the device the gimlet eye – not literally, she wouldn't have one in the house – harrumphed a little, and carried on watching in black and white. Admittedly, she may not be the best example, having taken a similarly sceptical attitude to other 1960s phenomena, like space travel and recreational sex, but in this case she was not alone.

Sir George Barnes, the BBC's Director of Television, who went to New York in 1954 to monitor developments, set the tone, 'Extraordinary to think of how much skill and money are being expended on a marvel that the public, so far as one can tell, is perfectly content to be without,' was his assessment, according to *The New Yorker*. He was probably right as well. After all, in 1954 Britain had only just got bananas.*

There had been colour programmes in the US since the 1950s. Not many Americans had sets capable of taking advantage, but popular series like *The Cisco Kid* and *The Lone Ranger* were filmed in colour. The first regular weekly colour programme, on NBC in 1959, was *Bonanza*, a Western series about four brothers setting fire to a map (they did other

---

* The import of bananas was effectively forbidden during the war and they were considered a luxury, an attitude to fruit still prevalent in parts of the UK.

stuff as well), and from the mid-1960s the sets became more affordable and ownership began to grow rapidly.

But in Europe, and certainly at the BBC, there was less in the way of commercial pressure to rush colour onto our screens. Experts were unhappy with the American NTSC system, which suffered hue, or tint, problems, and decided to go with a 'phase alternating line' system (don't ask me, I'm just a humble newspaper columnist), or PAL, developed in Germany. Even so, we were not too far behind viewers on the other side of the Atlantic. Most of America had found the tantalising prospect of watching full colour gunslinging in the comfort of their own homes – while lounging round eating bananas, no doubt – surprisingly resistible.

By 1964, only 3.1 per cent of television households in the US had a colour set, according to the Museum of Broadcast Communications, and it was only when NBC announced that its prime time schedule for autumn 1965 would comprise mostly colour programmes that the blue (and red and yellow) touch paper was lit.

A year later, David Attenborough was the man charged with bringing the future to Britain. He was already on his way to becoming a national treasure, having produced and presented a three-part series, *The Pattern of Animals*, featuring full and frank disclosure on the courtship rituals of some of the denizens of London Zoo (keeping the nation entertained at a time when such detail on the horizontal pleasures of pop stars and professional footballers was some distance in the future). He also presented *Zoo Quest*, and produced several highly praised natural history documentaries. Attenborough was appointed Controller of BBC2 in March 1965, and the following year announced what these days we would call a soft launch of colour television, showing four hours of colour programmes a week on BBC2, rising after a year to ten hours a week.

There was no ballyhoo about the experimental programmes, which were often either the Western series *The Virginian*, or *Late Night Line Up*, the late night arts and discussion programme where Joan Bakewell and Tony Bilbow impressed grammar school boys like me with talk about poetry, and films with subtitles. True to his word, Attenborough stepped up colour output in July 1967 with a four-hour outside broadcast of Roger Taylor against Cliff Drysdale at the Wimbledon Tennis Championships, followed a few days later by the first recorded programme in colour, a highlights show featuring that year's men's final in which John Newcombe beat Wilhelm Bungert.

Tennis was made for colour: the bronzed limbs of the players, the crisp white kit, the lawns, the muted yellows of the Robinsons' Barley Water (stop me before I turn into John Betjeman). This was certainly the kind of thing that entranced the *Daily Telegraph*'s broadcasting correspondent L. Marsland Gander, who wrote, 'Mr David Attenborough, the head of the channel, introduced the service on the screen, looking suntanned from his recent trip to Serengeti, and other surprises concerned the yellowish tinge on the grass and that one of the ball boys, often prominent, was a perky redhead.' There is a case to be made for the red-haired ball boy who turned up with suspicious regularity at the big matches as the first star of colour television in Britain.

The following month saw the first colour football coverage in Britain, highlights of the FA Charity Shield, a 3–3 draw between Manchester United and Spurs, notable for Tottenham's second goal, scored by goalkeeper Pat Jennings whose long punt downfield bounced in front of United's goalie Alex Stepney, went over his head and into the goal. I am sure I am not alone in remembering that goal in black and white. It was not until the run-up to Christmas that people really started talking about colour television, prompted by the news that the Queen's 1967 Christmas Day broadcast, which in those days had almost liturgical status, was to be part of the new service.

In recording the item, according to a piece in the William Hickey diary column in the *Daily Express*, Her Majesty faced similar problems to John Logie Baird's dummy Stooky Bill. 'For two hours she sat under hot arc lights in the Bow Room of Buckingham Palace. On Thursday afternoon she had spent a further two hours doing rehearsals,' the paper reported. The Producer Anthony Craxton explained: 'Because of colour we had to wait a little longer between each take. You cannot hurry these things.' He says the Queen could not have been more patient, but I like to picture a scene of extreme forelock tugging, and Prince Philip somewhere in the background, cursing.

But the painstaking and generously staffed operation – a hallmark of the BBC over the years, attracting admiration and opprobrium in roughly equal measure – reflected well on the boss. As James Thomas wrote in the *Daily Express*, 'Britain has shown the world a quality colour service unrivalled anywhere – and Attenborough, the man from the jungle trails, has at forty-one placed his feet securely on the ladder to the top hierarchy.' (Except that after his triumph at BBC2, which saw programmes like *Monty Python's Flying Circus* and *The Old Grey Whistle Test* enhance the lives of teenage viewers, followed by a short spell running both channels, he decided to go back to making programmes in the jungle, which he possibly found less treacherous than the top floor at TV Centre.)

Thomas predicted that ITV would bring forward its planned launch date – they were certainly under pressure from retailers and manufacturers to do so – but much as they may have wished to speed things up, colour did not come to BBC1 and ITV until its scheduled date, November 1969. These were difficult economic times, and the sets remained out of the reach of average earners for a while.

In the run-up to that first Christmas, Currys, advertising a 25-inch Decca set about the size and weight of a small family car, were keen to plug their hire purchase deal which came with 'full maintenance, parts, and labour', and boy did you need it back then. Many people chose to rent sets because they were famously unreliable and, in the case of colour, still horrendously expensive: 328 guineas (about £344) for the Decca, the equivalent of nearly £5,000 today. And that was a rock-bottom price.*

Not having the requisite guineas, I looked around for friends who did: the hunt became frantic in January 1968 when the Beatles' new

---

* A guinea in pre-decimal currency was equivalent to 21 shillings, £1.05 after decimalisation. If you wonder why prices continued to be quoted in terms of a coin that went out of circulation in 1813, I believe it was to confuse cocksure Americans who thought they had got the hang of our quaint money.

film *Magical Mystery Tour* was scheduled to be shown in colour. It had already appeared – disastrously – on monochrome old BBC1 on Boxing Day night 1967, traditionally a time for cosy family entertainment, which meant it was sandwiched incongruously between mildly satirical middle-of-the-road comedy *Frost Over Britain* and *The Square Peg*, a Norman Wisdom film in which Norman plays a council workman mending the road outside an army camp with what would have probably been considered hilarious consequences, I expect.

The black and white meant the psychedelic sequence around the song 'Flying' appeared in a kind of muddy grey. The film was universally and comprehensively mauled – I remember Chris Welch writing in *Melody Maker*, 'On Christmas Day, we showed our home movies to the family, and then on Boxing Day, the Beatles showed theirs'. But this made some of us even more determined to see it in colour, as the Fab Four intended, when it was re-shown on BBC2 ten days later.

There were fewer than 200,000 colour sets in Britain at the time, but I was fortunate enough to have a friend whose father was a market trader with surplus cash that was better placed in a big fat Sony Trinitron TV than in the bank where the taxman could see it. The set was so heavy that once it had been lifted onto the table you did not take lightly the decision to lift it off again.

As far as the picture went, there were individual controls for each colour, which people kept fiddling with so that instead of full living colour the programmes kept hiding behind a pink or an aquamarine filter – and the Beatles film was still a disappointment, even in colour, after the triumphs of *A Hard Day's Night* and *Help!*

By now, American colour television was well established and getting cheaper. In 1966, all three US networks launched a full service in prime time, selling it quite aggressively. Elizabeth Montgomery, for instance, might pop up between programmes to say, 'Hi, I'm Elizabeth Montgomery. Stay tuned for *Bewitched*. Next. IN COLOR!'

Two events in particular made 1969 a key year for colour television in Britain: the Apollo 11 moon landings, shown in colour on BBC2 on the night of 20–21 July and – if you will forgive the bathos – the first edition of the snooker show *Pot Black* just three days later. (By the way, if you think I am guilty of jumping from the sublime to the ridiculous, BBC1, who simultaneously showed the moon landing in black and white for the majority audience, built up to it with *Dr Finlay's Casebook* and *The Black and White Minstrel Show*, where colour was something that came out of a tin of boot polish.)

Just as David Attenborough had used sport to widen the appeal of BBC2 in its early days by working with the Rugby League to create the Floodlit Trophy, so sport became an important element in BBC2's new colour service, and what sport could be a better fit than snooker, with its array of differently coloured balls (even though they all still looked blue on my friend's set).

The *Pot Black* tournament – a single-frame snooker competition with a round robin format – was devised by TV (a Birmingham producer called Philip Lewis gets the credit) for TV, which time and again has proved the route to ratings success. Older readers may remember a fair amount of snooker on TV before *Pot Black*, but that was obviously in black and white, which gave it an unwanted air of mystery, and in retrospect seems a little like juggling on the radio (I was seriously once offered a juggler as a guest on my late night radio show. I protested that there would be no sound, only to be told by his manager, 'Don't worry, from time to time, he drops something').

Snooker was a useful makeweight on *Grandstand* on frozen Saturday afternoons: producers would get the incomparable Joe Davis in to play A.N. Other at short notice. 'Joe more or less owned the game in the late 1950s and early '60s,' recalled the snooker commentator Clive Everton. 'He would decide who turned pro, and the players would get something like a tenner or twenty quid to appear on those early *Grandstand* shows.'

Pot Black was the right idea at the right time. 'The Controller of BBC2 wanted low budget programmes to which colour was intrinsic,' said Everton, 'and you could not get anything much lower budget than snooker in those days. There were no rights to pay for, the players got about £100 each, and the whole thing was recorded in three days at Pebble Mill in Birmingham. It was as basic as could be.'

In the early days, however, even on BBC2, large numbers of viewers were still watching on their old sets, which gives me a chance to lay to rest a threadbare old joke. I don't think *Pot Black* commentator 'Whispering' Ted Lowe ever did say, 'For those of you watching in black and white, the pink is behind the green.' It just seems too well honed, not to mention well worn. I cannot find a recording of it anywhere, nor can I find record of any football commentator saying anything like, 'For those of you watching in black and white, Spurs are in yellow,' which has been variously attributed to David Coleman, John Motson, and Barry Davies. Until I receive tangible evidence, my scepticism stands.

Despite the ad hoc, bargain basement nature of *Pot Black* the show found an audience and rose to number two in the BBC2 ratings, just behind the *Morecambe and Wise Show*. 'People liked the formality of it,' said Everton, 'the players wearing dress suits and being polite to each other and so on.' Philip Purser in the *Sunday Telegraph* wrote, '... such a change from the hysterical pooves of the football field'. (Those were the days when the *Telegraph* knew its audience.)

For the players, the result of the *Pot Black* tournament was less important than the exposure. 'Nobody could take seriously a game consisting of just one frame,' says Everton. But TV appearances meant players like Ray Reardon, John Spencer and the Australian Eddie Charlton got more bookings to play exhibition matches, and possibly a tenner or so extra on the fee. That was the only way professional snooker players could make anything approaching a living in those days. There were very few tournaments. In fact, for several years not even the World Championship could find a promoter. 'The 1957 tournament was held in Jersey, with just four entrants,' says Everton, 'The players were on a share of the gate, and I don't think there was much gate to share. Joe Davis killed it off really, because he retired from the World Championships after winning in 1946. He had this thing about retiring undefeated, but what promoter would be interested in the competition if the best player isn't in it?'

On the exhibition circuit you had to have some trick shots and some patter, and some players were clearly better at that than others. In 1971 the best of them all arrived from the snooker halls of Belfast, with both the shots and the charisma, Alex 'Hurricane' Higgins.

If sport on TV sells on personalities – from the Matthews Final to Botham's Ashes to Jonny Wilkinson's World Cup – Higgins was the key player in the transformation of snooker in less than a decade from working-class subculture to a sport that BBC executive Jonathan Martin felt able to describe as 'bigger than football'.

Higgins thought so too. As he said in a BBC interview in 1999, 'I was the one that made it a spectator sport, an entertainment. If I hadn't started the ball rolling like that, I doubt you'd have the young boys in the game that there are now, because most of them were inspired by Alex Higgins. I have created an audience of millions who have never even played the game.' It may sound like bombast and blether, but you will struggle to find anyone in the snooker world who disagrees. The great Canadian novelist and screenplay writer Mordecai Richler (*The Apprenticeship of Duddy Kravitz*), who was a poolroom hustler as a youngster in Montreal, wrote a book called *On Snooker* shortly before he died in 2002. In it, he quotes the former world champion Fred Davis's view that Higgins was 'the only true genius snooker ever had', describing it as 'an accolade which I fear Higgins would dismiss as an understatement'.

But Higgins alone was not enough to take snooker forward. In the early 1970s, Clive Everton was not only writing about this sport, but also managing British squash champion Jonah Barrington. He went to see Peter West's sponsorship company West Nally about Barrington and, later in the conversation, mentioned that snooker was looking for a sponsor for its championship. West Nally sold that idea to the Gallagher tobacco company who earmarked it for Park Drive (an appropriate sponsor at the time, being a fairly downmarket smoke favoured by tramps, and school kids who thought of them as starter fags, as they were available in affordable packets of five).

At first it only produced a few glimpses on *Grandstand*, but by 1976 sponsorship had edged a notch upwards to Embassy, and Glenda Jackson was making the draw out of an ashtray in the green room for the old early evening news programme *Nationwide*.

And the final, held at the Forum Theatre in the unprepossessing Manchester suburb of Wythenshawe, caught the attention of the sports producer Nick Hunter. 'I thought it was great,' Hunter told me. 'I was working out of BBC Manchester at the time, and always looking for sport we could get on the network, and the snooker championships seemed to fit the bill to me.' In 1977 a former amateur player (snooker being a strange, enclosed world), Mike Watterson took over as promoter.

It was, however, Mrs Watterson who was responsible for snooker's next great leap forward into the TV sports pantheon. Having been to a play at Sheffield's Crucible Theatre, she told husband Mike she had found the perfect venue for his newly acquired property. And so it proved. Watterson hired the theatre for £6,600 for two weeks, and to this day the theatregoers of Sheffield have to endure a fortnight of Chekhov and Ayckbourn-deprivation.

The BBC got good figures in 1977, but in 1978 (Ray Reardon's sixth win), they took the plunge to cover the event from first break to last pot and were richly rewarded. The numbers kept on rising, peaking late one April night in 1985 when bespectacled Dennis Taylor beat the hot favourite Steve Davis in the final before 18.5 million viewers, still a record for BBC2 and for any channel post-midnight. No sports enthusiast old enough to remember that era has to think where they were the night Taylor won: they were in front of the telly.

Women liked snooker because the players came over as the type of chaps who would open the car door for you, pull back your seat at a nice but not-too-flashy restaurant, and generally handle you with the same care and attention they might give a recondite blue that needs to be nicked into the centre pocket. Such a change from the wham-bam-thank-you-mam badly behaved footballers. And for those with a taste for a touch of danger, there was the rakishly good-looking firebrand 'Hurricane' Higgins, the undisputed star of snooker's golden era.

At one time Higgins considered billing himself as 'Alexander the Great' but 'Hurricane' seemed to fit so much better, on and off the table. As Mordecai Richler wrote: 'Higgins confirmed his hell-raiser's bona fides by wrecking hotel rooms, pissing in the nearest available plant pot, punching officials, tussling with opponents, heaving his cue at fans, head-butting a referee, scribbling apologies on toilet paper, indulging in reckless gambling, being bounced out of too many bars to count, and for good measure, getting stabbed in the chest while living with a bimbo in a caravan.' The plotline needed one man like that to balance the nice guys.

Quite apart from the personalities, though, snooker is a sport made for television. With four cameras per table, the position of the balls is never lost on the viewer, but the so-called money shot is arguably when a player misses a pot, leaves an opening for his opponent, and slumps back in his chair, condemned to watch the other player build his break. As the balls roll in, the close-ups of the player watching, as well as those of the man concentrating on his shots, build up a compelling story. 'You can lose a match sitting down, not playing a shot,' says Nick Hunter. 'I remember Jimmy White playing Steven Hendry. He was 14–8 up and coasting, and then Hendry won a frame to make it 14–9. We got a great shot of Jimmy, and to look at his face, you would think he was losing 14–9. He sort of lost it upstairs. I'm absolutely convinced that if you have got yourself into a winning position, and then you have to sit there and watch your opponent benefit from all the hard work you did getting the balls into a potable position, you start thinking about what you did wrong. If you can't control that, the match will slip away. That is the story we are telling.'

Thanks to the exhaustive TV coverage, Embassy got tremendous value. Though the BBC was restricted in the amount of mentions they could offer, the branding was everywhere. A number of players smoked, which helped as well, and given snooker's roots in smoky halls and working men's clubs, Embassy's message was less subliminal than it might have been. In fact, I distinctly remember an incident during the 1980 championships, when the snooker coincided with a running news story about Iran's diplomats in London being held hostage in their offices by Arab separatists, which eventually ended with the SAS storming the building. I swear that during the coverage, a continuity announcer interrupted, saying, 'We are leaving the snooker now to bring you the latest from the embassy siege,' and I felt compelled to comment, 'Bloody hell, are they sponsoring that as well?' Had Twitter been around then, I would have tweeted.

Clive Everton commentated on the World Championships from 1978, the first year that the tournament got too big for Whispering Ted Lowe, the BBC's hushed voice of snooker, to manage alone. 'Ted used to whisper because he was actually commentating from a seat in the audience, sometimes just a few feet away from the player, but he carried on for the sake of atmosphere, even when there was a soundproofed booth.'

The comedian Mark Watson, who was only five the night Taylor beat Davis, turns out to be an unexpected fan. And when Lowe died in 2011, Watson wrote in the *New Statesman* of his childhood ambition to be a sports commentator, how Ted was a role model for him, and how he regretted the 'rather self-conscious art form' commentary has become:

'Commentators are armed with dozens of facts about each player and team, which they throw in with apparent nonchalance, often on the most spurious pretext ("the free-kick is going to be taken by Gomez ... Gomez, of course, is the great-grandson of the man who invented the typewriter and he'll be trying to type the word 'goal' here"). There is a tendency to waffle, to sentimentalise and to deliver obviously prepared spiels. A stadium becomes "this great Viking fortress of the north-east"; players are "gladiators"; a last-minute goal is a "knife in the heart" of the losing team. Even in sports more sedate than football, there is a pressure on commentators to augment the drama.'

What Watson admired most was Lowe's restraint. As he told me, 'Even at moments of high intensity, his patter was so minimal that if you joined the game midway through, you might think he had forgotten to turn up.'

Snooker is certainly no longer in the market for an audience of 18.5 million, but then nothing much is. Audiences have fragmented, not just in sport, and snooker has to work harder to keep its appeal. Barry Hearn, the chief of World Snooker Ltd, has been trying to tempt TV back with something called Power Snooker, a short form of the game he sees as snooker's equivalent of Twenty20 cricket. He needed to do something: snooker lost out when tobacco sponsorship was outlawed in 2003, although the sport was given special dispensation to continue its association with Embassy until 2005, when the era of free and easy partnerships between sport and fags finally came to a close. (I remember being horrified when I took my ten-year-old son to a rugby league cup final sponsored by Silk Cut and he came home with dozens of free fags courtesy of the sponsor's 'cigarette girls.' I was at least twelve before I took up smoking.)

But it was colour TV, not cigarettes, that made snooker. Not that a whole lot of new sets were sold on the back of it. Nor were they when *Coronation Street* finally entered the new era in 1969 (although it caused a mild shock to southern viewers who thought life up north was only ever in black and white anyway). What the nation really wanted to see in colour was football.

Think back to your very first football match, and the visceral thrill of climbing the steps, emerging into the light and seeing the greensward in front you? Didn't it look greener than any green you had ever seen, even when careworn in midwinter? This was to be football's next step as it emerged from the flat-cap era: green grass, blue shirts, blood scarlet on Terry Butcher's brow. The first World Cup we had a chance to watch in colour was Mexico 1970, which brought a spike in set sales: up from 235,000 by the end of 1969 to half a million in time for the tournament.

But oddly, even though most of us watched it in black and white, it somehow seems to be remembered in colour. In part, this is because we have had forty years of seeing the clips – Pele's brilliance, Banks's save, Bobby Moore's arrest. But I think it might also have something to do with the TV coverage, which was undoubtedly more colourful, in the widest sense, than any other tournament before or since.

ELEVEN

A WHOLE NEW PANEL GAME

It is 1970, the World Cup is underway in Mexico, and the BBC is about to get rid of Kenneth Wolstenholme, war hero and honorary member of the Boys of '66. He said in his autobiography: 'It wasn't all that long after the 1966 final that someone on the BBC staff said to me, "You know those words you said at the end of the World Cup final? Well, box clever, because they may just come true."'

Wolstenholme must have spent the best part of four years between suspecting it was all over and 'It is now', waiting for the stab in the back, which may account for the extraordinary outpouring of bitterness and regret between pages 151 and 171 of his memoir, *50 Sporting Years ... and It's Still Not All Over*, written in 1999, in which he examined in minute detail the circumstances of his departure. Nicholas Sellens summed it up more tersely in his book *Commentating Greats*: '... Every time he looked over his shoulder, there was the young pretender David Coleman, performing ominous stretching exercises on the touchline.'

In his own book Wolstenholme devoted almost as much space to his sacking as he did to his war exploits, which were pretty dramatic. Having anticipated the call-up by joining the RAF reserve as an eighteen-year-old in 1938, he flew more than a hundred sorties over occupied Europe. He was awarded the Distinguished Flying Cross in May 1944, and the following year a Bar was added. When Wolstenholme flew his last mission in 1944, he was still just twenty-three, the kind of figure who would be played on-screen by one of those square-jawed English leading men like Kenneth More or John Gregson. When he was fifty-one, however, and sacked by the BBC, the stiff upper lip failed him.

Wolstenholme had a contract that guaranteed his position as the BBC's No.1 football commentator, but in the atmosphere of uncertainty bordering on paranoia that is possibly piped through the air conditioning at TV Centre, Ken did not sleep easily at night; not with the Head of Sport being Bryan Cowgill, best man at Coleman's wedding, and the two going out to lunch together, sometimes with a senior producer joining the party.

'Then, early in 1970, the mafia struck,' he wrote. He was called to a meeting with Cowgill, who told him he wanted to give Coleman more experience of covering England matches, so the plan was for the young pretender to follow England in Mexico, while Wolstenholme commentated on West Germany's group. 'As the tournament went on I still had my deep suspicions that I would be told I was not going to do the commentary on the final,' Wolstenholme added. He found out for sure by getting someone to send a copy of the *Radio Times* out to Mexico. The billing read: 'World Cup Final 1970. Join David Coleman in the great bowl of the Azteca Stadium for football's greatest drama.'

One thing delayed the break-up: England's 3–2 quarter-final defeat against West Germany, after they had squandered a 2–0 lead. Funny thing is, I watched that match and I could have sworn it was Wolstenholme, not Coleman, who commentated, although I may not be the most reliable witness, as there were four of us watching it on an old black-and-white TV in a student flat, sharing big party cans of beer, and illegal roll-ups. Until I picked up the papers next day I was also convinced England had won.

But back to Wolstenholme's account, 'England's defeat was a bitter blow to the BBC [to me too, once I found out], and I can imagine the discussions in Television Centre between Paul Fox and Bryan Cowgill. David wouldn't be too keen on doing a commentary on two foreign sides.' (For younger readers; yes, there really was a time when expecting England to reach the World Cup final was not considered dangerously delusional.) So Wolstenholme got to call one of the great World Cup performances – Brazil's 4–1 defeat of Italy – and returned to England for what he sensed would be his last season with the BBC. 'The whole plan was a David Coleman takeover,' he concluded. 'I felt angry, I felt humiliated. I felt insulted. And I think the BBC behaved in a despicable fashion.'

Peter Dimmock's take, it will hardly startle you to learn, is slightly different. He told me Coleman's agent had threatened a move to ITV unless his man was given the 1971 FA Cup final (which was then considered more important than any foreign nonsense). 'I thought about it, and discussed it with some senior colleagues, and we decided we had to bite the bullet. I didn't particularly want Coleman to do the FA Cup final because Kenneth did it very well. But we couldn't afford to lose him, because he was doing *Grandstand* and was very good on athletics.

'When Kenneth came to see me, I said, "I've got some good news for you, and some bad news. I'm prepared to increase your salary by a very substantial amount, but the bad news is, it means letting Coleman do the FA Cup final." Well, he sprang out of his chair and left the room, slamming the door behind him. Later I rang him at home and said, "Kenneth, I hope you have had time to think about it." I told him he would still do some of the top matches, and that Coleman probably would not want to do the Cup final for long, but he said, "No, no, no, I'll go to ITV."'

So, farewell then, Kenneth Wolstenholme. He did do the 1971 FA Cup final, and the European Cup final three weeks later, between Ajax and Panathinaikos at Wembley. But that was it. After leaving the BBC, he did some match reports for the *Sun*, commentated for a while on ITV's Tyne-Tees regional programme, *Shoot*, and later added voiceovers to Channel 4's Italian football coverage. I am happy to report that he bought shares in TWI, the company that produced the *Football Italia* show, and that they performed rather well for him. He could therefore,

I am even happier to report, slip into blameless retirement in Torquay, surrounded by friends and family, playing a lot of golf – if that's your idea of a good time.

Meanwhile, as Wolstenholme dealt with his personal nightmare, tossing and turning in his Guadalajara hotel bedroom, wondering if that feeling at the pit of his stomach was the Mexican food or the thought of Coleman, ITV's commentary team of Hugh Johns, Gerald Sinstadt, Roger Malone, and Gerry Harrison could take quiet satisfaction in an unprecedented triumph. For the first time in broadcasting history, ITV was beating the BBC in the ratings for a simultaneously broadcast event. Not that it was the commentary that had us all migrating to the commercial channel – although I was quite a fan of Gerald Sinstadt, who did Granada's local footy in Manchester. It was the twenty minutes before the match, the five minutes at half-time and the half-hour after the final whistle. We had never seen or heard anything like it.

Manchester City's flamboyant, fedora-wearing, bunny-girl-chasing coach Malcolm Allison, the garrulous Northern Irish international Derek Dougan, Manchester United's Scottish midfielder with a twinkle in his eye Pat Crerand, and the Arsenal defender with the unfeasibly bushy sideburns Bob McNab, were 'The Panel', ostensibly engaged to provide informed punditry, but mostly selected because they mirrored the famous 'Englishman, Irishman, Scotsman' joke, and because of their potential for entertaining disagreement.

These four – with the exception of Bob McNab (a touch of genius, hiring a quiet one) – would have been pretty lively sober, but John Bromley, ITV's executive producer, ensured their tongues were loosened still further by locking them up for the duration of the tournament in the Hendon Hall Hotel, giving them the keys to the mini-bar, and insisting they were woken each morning with a bottle of vintage champagne.

I was pretty sure this was myth, part of the John Bromley legend. Brommers, as he was affectionately referred to by almost everyone I interviewed for this book, was one of those characters, like Sam Goldwyn or W.C. Fields, around whom a whole mythology has grown; one of those people to whom raconteurs like to attach their stories to make them that bit funnier. All sorts of tales about outrageous expenses claims, or seat-of-the-pants TV production, have been wantonly stamped with the Bromley brand, but this one, it seems, is definitely true.

As a viewer – and I am working from imperfect memory here – I should have said part of Brommers' genius as a producer was to keep the alcohol consumption at just about the right level. Nobody on the panel appeared roaring drunk, or even embarrassingly tipsy. I don't remember a George Best or Oliver Reed moment (both of whom guested on TV chat shows at various times, having apparently drunk the green room dry). Bromley, mind you, had a certain amount of specialist knowledge in this area. Being something of a party animal himself, he will have been familiar with that point at the party where you have had a loosener or two, just enough to impress the gathering with your charm and wit, but where another glass might tip you over into crashing-bore territory. The results – and the viewing figures – suggest it was all perfectly calibrated.

'For the first time during the coverage of sport on television we had passionate, controversial, confrontational discussion,' recalled Brian Moore, who was the party's on-screen host. 'It was sometimes outrageous, even bigoted,' he told the *Daily Telegraph*, 'as when Allison suggested the Russians and Romanians were all peasants and the protests practically jammed the switchboard.'

So, maybe not absolutely perfectly calibrated then, although I think Allison, universally recognised as something of a coaching sophisticate, may have been referring to the primitive nature of their football. Allison was also often seen chugging on a cigar during the show, those being the days before both political correctness and smoke alarms. Among the panel's more outrageous strokes was the ceremonial ripping off and flinging to the floor of their Union Jack kipper ties when Germany knocked England out, with Allison adding for good measure his view that the England midfielder Alan Mullery was unfit for international football. When Mullery returned from Mexico, Brommers got him in the studio, where he flung his England cap at his critic.

It was unrealistic, I suppose, to expect the free spirits of the 1970 panel to remain unfettered – even a movement like the punk rock revolution, forged in an anarchic rush, ended with Johnny Rotten advertising Country Life butter. However, the ITV panel did successfully reconvene for the 1974 World Cup, with Brian Clough and Jack Charlton replacing Crerand and McNab. When those two panels are discussed, as they frequently are in football nostalgia shows, the role of Moore as mild-mannered arbiter is often undervalued. Although far from being a force of nature to match the extraordinary Coleman, Moore played as important a part in ITV's successes as his counterpart did for the other side.

Moore had been poached from BBC radio, for whom he commentated on the 1966 World Cup final, and was one of Jimmy Hill's early signings for LWT, together with director Bob Gardam, brought in from Anglia. Gardam and Moore were key figures in the launch in 1968 of *The Big Match*, ITV's Sunday football highlights show in the southeast, which, with more cameras, Hill's punditry, a great theme tune ('The Young Scene' by Keith Mansfield, TV theme genius), and a funny montage at Christmas featuring Terry Venables mugging to the camera, was way ahead of what we were watching in the provinces. In his book, Kenneth Wolstenholme noted his surprise at the primitive nature of the equipment at Tyne-Tees – lack of replay facilities and so on – when he landed there after the BBC.

John Nicholson, who runs the football365.com website, wrote in his book *We Ate All The Pies*, 'In an era where football presenters are all too often smug, vacuous heads that talk a lot but say nothing, Brian Moore stands as a shining example of how the gig should be done. Loved and respected by all who knew him and a giant of the genre he all but created, he left a peerless legacy. I can't imagine that we'll feel the same way about Richard Keys or Ray Stubbs, somehow.' Moore died in 2001, on the day England beat Germany 5–1 in Munich.

Nicholson rightly draws attention to Moore's relationship with the quirky, combative, and frankly occasionally intoxicated Brian Clough. Stop me if this sounds too flighty, but I see Moore as McCartney to Clough's

Lennon, providing the evenness to balance the fabled manager's spikiness. As Nicholson said, 'On the legendary occasion in 1973 when England drew with Poland 1–1 at Wembley and Brian Clough was thoroughly disparaging of Tomaszewski, the Polish keeper, calling him a clown, Brian rebuked him, saying the Pole had played magnificently for his side. That took bottle because Cloughie was a fierce, sneering firebrand who could and did shred weaker men with one well-honed sentence.'

Perhaps Clough's second most famous television performance was on local TV the following year, on the evening Leeds United sacked him after just forty-four days as manager. Yorkshire TV invited him onto the local news programme *Calendar*, and ambushed him by confronting him with his predecessor Don Revie, with whom he had previous, for a live discussion about what went wrong. The station cleared its schedule for what it billed as *A Calendar Special: Goodbye Mr Clough*. It comprised nearly half an hour of the most riveting television you will ever see – it is on YouTube – an example of one of ITV's regional fiefdoms working as it should and examining a local issue in depth. The chances of seeing anything similar in today's manicured, PR-driven world of sports broadcasting are more than remote. Getting two well-known figures from any field who dislike each other the way Clough and Revie did, to sit down for a live discussion is pretty unlikely in itself. The meeting is dramatised in the film of *The Damned United*, but fails to crackle like the original. Nothing could.

The presenter Austin Mitchell, who went on to become a Labour MP, was brilliant on the show, just gently prompting, not goading, in complete command of the material, and unfazed by the sulphurous atmosphere. The result is a fascinating argument about the craft of managing a football club. For a man who has just been sacked, Clough is hardly cowed. He is one of the reasons football on TV in the 1970s is remembered fondly.

Brian Moore is undoubtedly another. As a commentator, he was no smartarse phrasemaker, although his description of a goalkeeper, during a 1970s goalmouth scramble, 'flailing around like a man in a nightmare' makes it into the odd anthology. But when he was commentating on those FA Cup finals ITV shared with the BBC in the 1970s and '80s, there were many viewers – including this one – who opted for Moore's fan-friendly commentary over the more mannered offering on the other side.

The football fanzine *When Saturday Comes*, for instance, felt David Coleman's greeting of a goal – almost his signature phrase – with a momentous '*ONE–NIL*' was delivered 'in the style of a man meeting his dead brother on the stairs'. This may be a little unfair on the doyen of BBC sport, acknowledged by almost every executive we spoke to for this book as the finest commentator Britain has produced and a key figure in raising and maintaining standards at BBC Sport, but what can I say? I derived more fun from the operatic swoop of Moore's voice. All the stuff that Coleman brought to the game – the preparation, the quick-wittedness, the capacity for coping with cock-ups – was important, but half the battle is just sounding like someone you might want to spend time with, and Moore had that. Avuncular is a word often used in association with Moore – or Mooro, as I feel tempted to call him – and that is exactly what he was when he was hosting the panel: a much-loved uncle, smiling indulgently at the antics going on around him.

A pale imitation of the panel is now a staple of major tournaments, but the true children of the revolution are today's hugely successful reality shows, like *The X-Factor* and *Strictly Come Dancing*, where the kind of stinging criticism aimed at international footballers is now applied to glorified karaoke singers, or bit-part players from soap operas having a go at ballroom dancing.

The journalist Will Buckley, who covered sport on television for the *Observer*, reckons the line-up of judges on *The X-Factor* almost perfectly replicated the 1970 World Cup panel: 'Simon Cowell is the outspoken Malcolm Allison character, Dougan would be Louis Walsh, constructively critical, Paddy Crerand, at a pinch, is Cheryl Cole, the nice one [you are losing me now, Will], and Bob McNab is Dannii Minogue, inoffensive, a bit of eye candy.' Maybe that is stretching it a little, but it was undoubtedly groundbreaking television, and if there are too many inter-ested parties – lawyers, agents, and so on – and too much compliance for sports broadcasting to be so outspoken these days, every panel show that tries to get a laugh or a little controversy out of sport shares some DNA with Bromley's original team. The 1970s panels were the apotheosis of ITV Sport, where the values of Lew Grade, and all the old showbiz types who got commercial TV off the ground, merged with those of the BBC, and the sport was never more than a moment away from tripping into light entertainment. Memory is imperfect but when I think of FA Cup finals on ITV, I see Jimmy Tarbuck wearing a Liverpool scarf or Freddie Starr marching round in full Nazi regalia.

Saint and Greavsie was a rousing example of the ITV way of doing sport. In the four years before the advent of Sky and the Premier League (1988–92) ITV had the rights to league football, and used the former internationals Ian St John and Jimmy Greaves to present their Saturday lunchtime preview. What made it superb TV was the fact that Greaves had a back-story well known to us, which promised at the very least some unpredictability.

The best striker in Britain with Chelsea, and later Spurs, Greaves missed out on the 1966 World Cup triumph for tactical reasons. He also played for Milan for a few months but got homesick and returned home. In the twilight of his career he signed for West Ham, where he made headlines for a spectacular goal at Manchester City, and also for sneaking out of the team hotel in Blackpool to go drinking on the eve of a 1971 cup-tie that West Ham subsequently lost 4–0. A recovering alcoholic, Greaves had not had a drink since 1978.

His past flakiness, though, gave the programme an edge you would not get from a Bob Wilson or a Frank Bough – certainly not in the pre-cocaine years. And with St John as the straight man, *Saint and Greavsie* was a hit. St John's shtick was to laugh helplessly at most of what Greaves said, and chip in with the odd pertinent football question from time to time. In an old show I watched recently, Saint kicked it off by saying, 'We'll be at the FA for news of a big shake-up in football.'

'Yeah,' chipped in a languid Greavsie, 'a big shake-up, Graham Taylor's buyin' a drink.'

The football world soon caught on, realising they could avoid awkward questions by playing a Greavsie interview for laughs. Jimmy interviewed the Manchester City chairman Peter Swales, who had just sacked City manager Mel Machin (for not having any 'repartee' with the fans, as I recall), and put to him a number of names being suggested as successors. 'We're hanging on for you, Jimmy. You don't seem to be doing anything much there,' replied Swales, with a self-satisfied smile (his habitual mien, as City fans of the era will recall).

After ITV lost league football, and *Saint and Greavsie* died, Jimmy went as a TV reviewer to TV-AM, where he would sum up an expensive new drama production on one of the main channels by saying something like, 'Well, it's a bit of a friller, really.' There is footage of Greaves on YouTube in a cerise jumpsuit wrestling Kendo Nagasaki on *World of Sport*, which tells you more or less everything you need to know about Jimmy.

Whenever sport became more serious, ITV tended to cede the ground to the BBC. At the Olympics, for instance, they were always soundly beaten. They did not bother with it in 1984, and in 1988, the very last time they were at the Games, they shared coverage with Channel 4, and had the film critic Barry Norman among the presenters.

At the BBC, meanwhile, vast resources were put into Olympics coverage, often to the chagrin or ridicule of licence-fee payers and the press. As for getting a laugh out of sport, the BBC contented itself with its own long-running light-hearted sports quiz, which has consistently delivered a big family audience. The success of both was largely down to one man.

TWELVE

COLEMANTATING

There is a fine dividing line between being a perfectionist and a complete pain in the arse, and opinions varied on which side of the divide David Coleman stood. Years ago, in the days before YouTube and mp3s, reel-to-reel tapes used to float around the BBC with bloopers – off-air moments that should not have been recorded – and one of the most popular was labelled *David Coleman Loses It*. It is Coleman fluffing a pre-recorded opening for a *World Cup Grandstand* programme from Mexico in 1970, apparently because of some confusion as to which camera he was on. His producer tells him, 'We'll have to go again on that,' sparking the following rant:

> 'Jonathan, keep it simple. You've got a bloody zoom there, and a camera that's racing all over the bloody studio. I mean, Christ almighty, you'd do better on one camera for God's sake. Get in your original position, and let me do the opening link again, then. I mean, don't try and be bloody clever. Shoot it on one camera if necessary, and keep the link camera covering me.
>
> *[Now almost spitting out the words]* 'A bloody din, and racing all over the place. He must be in the shot there, isn't he? You can't move that, he's against the desk. Keep your camera still now. Bloody chattering all the way through it. Get your bloody finger out, and leave the cameras in the same position.'

It was quite unusual in the pre-digital, pre-Auntie's bloomers era, for this kind of recording to exist. Nowadays, every hair-lacquered local news presenter and bit-part actor in *Casualty* is saying cute things or swearing on the end of foul-ups just to get in the Christmas tape. But for Coleman's 1970 rant to be lovingly preserved on magnetic tape, and still being gleefully exchanged around the BBC in the mid-1980s when I first joined, it must mean he had enemies at the Corporation.

Jonathan Martin, however, the recipient of the sharp end of Coleman's tongue on the tape, was not one of them. He believes that it was the influence of Coleman, together with the demanding standards of the former *Grandstand* chiefs Bryan Cowgill and Paul Fox, that enabled the BBC to survive ITV's small victories and maintain its dominance in televised sport until the birth of satellite TV. 'He was difficult to work with,' says Martin, 'but that was because he had high standards and he expected the same from everyone else.'

Coleman retired from the BBC in 2000 after the Athens Olympics, and was last a regular *Grandstand* presenter in 1978, so I had to remind myself what a preternaturally confident presenter and commentator he was. The BBC archives kindly gave me a recording of the 1972 FA Cup final between Leeds and Arsenal, and the contrast between Wolstenholme a year earlier, his notes scribbled on the team sheet, and Coleman, head bursting with information, could not be more stark.

Not that Coleman felt constrained to share interesting facts with you, in the tiresome way some of his successors do. But you know he could if he wanted, and that was what was important. Just once or twice, and only when appropriate, he passed on a nugget, 'There's the oldest man on the pitch tackling the youngest: Jack Charlton, thirty-seven, and Charlie George, just twenty-one.'

But then, if we had seen him presenting *Grandstand* we would already know he was the fount of all knowledge. This was no accident. According to the football producer Alec Weeks, 'Of all the presenters, David was the one most able to proceed without notes. He would walk near his home in Chalfont St Giles for eight to ten hours on Thursdays learning all the details he needed from football and rugby. He went through every bloody match on the fixture list. And then he would just pick up the lip microphone we had lying next to the teleprinter and start talking.'

The teleprinter was a feed of sports news from the Press Association, and it was the idea of *Grandstand*'s first producer Paul Fox to put it in vision. For a young viewer, it was the highlight of the show. It started chattering away at about 4.37, spewing out the Scottish results. Despite starting at the same time as matches south of the border, for some reason Scottish matches always finished earlier. I don't know whether this was because Scots players were made of sterner stuff, and did not need the full ten minutes' interval, as it then was, simply trotting into the dressing room for a quick bowl of porridge and for broken limbs to be mended, before rejoining the fray. But it was Coleman's chance to get into his stride, and you could immediately feel the benefit of those Chalfont St Giles perambulations: 'That's a rare away win for Kilmarnock, this the best start the Ayrshire club have had for four years, McCormack, who's on the fringe of the Scottish under-21 squad, the scorer there.' (All facts and names made up by me – but say it quite quickly, and you get an idea of how it went.) Coleman incidentally was recorded at 200 words per minute when commentating on David Hemery's win in the 400 metres hurdles in the 1968 Mexico Olympics.

Fortunately, Swinton, the rugby league team I supported, was only about five minutes away from home, and as our match was usually over by 4.25, I could be in front of the TV in time for Coleman's *chef d'oeuvre*. What bliss it was to watch the master keep time with the chattering of the printer. The Scottish results, and one or two rugby scores, were the aperitif, before a waiting nation was brought news from Darlington and Torquay, and then First Division scores began to filter through, and the urgency in Coleman's voice was ramped up accordingly, in deference to the premier competition in British football.

I liked it when the printer paused, chattering away so you knew it was still working, but keeping the scores to itself. Teleprinter consti-pation. 'What news from Burnley? What happened in the Merseyside derby? What's the latest from East London?' you would ask yourself, as Coleman filled expertly, 'The last we heard from Spurs, Manchester United were two up,' he would say, as you took another bite of crumpet, wondering if they had held on, or if Tottenham had staged a late comeback. These, remember, were the days before there was a reporter on the blower or on an ISDN line at every ground, or those scoreboards at the side of the screen, which some nostalgists reckon spoil the 4.40 fun.

Apart from when President Kennedy was assassinated, this was the nearest we got to breaking news. The teleprinter was Coleman's party piece, but his commentary on that Leeds–Arsenal final – not classic TV, just another day's work for Coleman – was phenomenal in terms of how completely on the ball he was. As far as I could see, he barely got a call wrong in ninety minutes. Just before half-time Alan Ball fires a fierce shot into a crowd of players defending the Leeds goal, and the ball somehow ricochets back out. Paul Reaney, it appears, has cleared the ball off the line, but I couldn't see what had happened, even very close to the screen, with my reading glasses on. Coleman, though, is spot on: no confusion, no equivocation and no pointless flowery detail. No replay either, giving the commentator time to recollect the incident. The action replay system was running in 1972, but used very sparingly, probably fewer than a dozen times in the whole match.

Also used sparingly were co-commentators. Coleman had the Derby manager Brian Clough and Manchester United's Bobby Charlton in the box with him, but, as was the convention at the time, both only spoke during intervals in play, either a long injury break or at half-time. So it was more or less a one-man show, performed as only an artiste utterly untroubled by self-doubt can perform.

There is a telling moment in the match when Leeds's combative midfielder Billy Bremner is booked for talking back to the referee, and Coleman comments, 'Bremner, booked for something he said. Bremner, unreasonable to himself, perhaps, in the way he drives himself, but really he demands so much from his players, and is also so competitive in every sense as a player and captain.' I wonder if Coleman was thinking there was somebody else on duty at Wembley that day to whom those words could equally apply.

In the preface to the compilation of his classic TV columns in the *Observer*, Clive James wrote: ' ... letters started arriving to prove that David Coleman aroused the same kind of perturbed reverence in other people as he did in me'. *Perturbed reverence* is exactly right. You marvelled at Coleman's capacity to deliver information when apparently in a state of fevered excitement, but never felt entirely comfortable with him, in the way that you did with, say, Brian Moore, or Des Lynam. And Coleman took more than his fair share of flak from the rest of the press as well. The magazine *Private Eye* named its column of sports broadcasters' gaffes, 'Colemanballs', after him, and he made plenty. But who wouldn't, in hours of live broadcasting? Rarely did that criticism come from his fellow professionals, either in sport or broadcasting.

Brian Moore, who was ITV's commentator on the Leeds–Arsenal match, got a taste of Coleman in Billy Bremner mode round the back of the stadium by the scanners before the match, when the dark genius of the teleprinter gave him the traditional greeting. 'He always had a well-rehearsed barb aimed in my direction,' recalled Moore in a 1992 interview with the *Independent*. 'He'd say to me, "Oh, here he is, seeking an inferior audience again." You'd curse yourself for not having a rejoinder ready, but it was just his way of hyping himself up and trying to get one up on you. He was the last word in competitiveness.' If you are looking for the TV equivalent of the uncompromising Leeds United of David Peace's *The Damned Utd*, you have him in Coleman. But Moore remained a committed fan, 'His player identification was absolutely 100 per cent. Whereas some of us mumble and stumble when goals are scored that are difficult to call, I can't ever recall David getting a thing wrong.' Not only did Coleman rarely get much wrong in his football commentaries – despite the 'Colemanballs' column – his tone, as he delivered his catchphrase, 'One–nil', suggested he had known the goal was coming all along.

Coleman also earned the respect of the athletes he worked with. As the Olympic gold medallist David Hemery put it, 'What was so special was just his identification with the delight of it.' Hemery said that Ron Pickering, a professional coach with whom Coleman formed a double act at most big athletics meetings over three decades, had the breadth of knowledge, 'but he didn't have what Coleman brought, a level of enthusiasm as the race heated up, to be able to verbalise what many people were feeling.'

This enthusiasm and empathy may have stemmed from Coleman's own blighted athletic career. He was a promising middle-distance runner, and in 1949, at the age of twenty-three, he became the first non-international to win the Manchester Mile. Were it not for a persistent hamstring injury forcing him to hang up his spikes, he may have fulfilled his own ambition to compete at the Olympics. Instead, he covered fourteen Games, winter and summer, for the BBC. And as Nicholas Sellens put it, 'Coleman's contribution to the movement was far greater than would have been achieved by a solitary appearance in a heat of the 1,500 metres. Since the war, Britain's successes at the Games have been little more than spasmodic, but whenever an athlete did strike a track and field gold, it was inevitable that Coleman's emotional accompaniment would be there, capturing the moment for the nation's sporting scrapbook.'

Coleman cared. I suppose that was the key. During the 1978 World Cup in Argentina (one of those the England team swerved to avoid, leaving Scotland to enjoy the disappointment and recriminations), Clive James commented, 'ITV, despite frequent appearances by Brian Clough, outperformed the BBC in every department throughout the World Cup. None of this stopped me watching the Beeb, however. It isn't just that there are no commercials and no Dickie Davies. It's something deeper, something occult, something to do with the personality of David Coleman. Just by being so madly keen, he helps you get things in proportion. Anything that matters so much to David Coleman, you realise, doesn't really matter much at all.'

Something occult? Could it be that Coleman exerted some sort of weird spell over people like Clive James and me? Unlike him, I liked Coleman's enthusiasm, his lack of doubt. 'And who cares who came third?' he said after Hemery's victory in 1968, giving short shrift to the British bronze-medal winner John Sherwood. But if the Dark Lord says, 'Who cares?' dare anybody?

As Harry Pearson wrote in his *Guardian* column in December 2010: 'As the runners entered the crucial phase of an Olympic middle-distance race … Coleman was given to gurgling "Oh my word – and has he gone too early?" Viewers often feared that Coleman himself had gone too early, reaching a pitch of excitement in the final curve of major finals that seemed unsustainable without access to helium. Yet somehow, just when you thought he was going to yodel his lungs out through his nostrils and let the final fifty metres pass in blissful silence, the great man found something extra. Coleman was a commentator whose hysteria knob went up to 11, and probably way beyond that.'

It is also worth considering Coleman's no-nonsense, virtually classless vowel sounds, forged in Stockport, not-quite-Manchester-not-quite-Cheshire, as a factor in his rise and rise. In the 1960s and 1970s when Coleman bestrode the world of broadcast sport like a colossus, the broadcasting landscape had not assumed its later shape, when Scouse, Geordie, and Northern Ireland accents would be widely heard; especially on children's TV, and the only presenters using what we used to call Received Pronunciation were the Asian ones. Back then it was a breath of fresh air to hear a presenter who sounded like your geography teacher rather than Lady Isobel Barnett.

If you want to see the master at his best, there is a clip of him looking straight down the barrel of the camera, introducing highlights of Chile v. Italy in the 1962 World Cup, which is distilled Coleman: 'The game you are about to see,' he says, 'is the most stupid, appalling, disgusting and disgraceful exhibition, possibly in the history of the game.' Who could resist a come-on like that? 'The national motto of Chile,' he continued, 'reads "By reason or by force". Today, the Chileans were prepared to be reasonable, the Italians only used force, and the result was a disaster for the World Cup. Now, if the World Cup is going to survive in its present form, something has got to be done about teams that play like this.

Indeed, after seeing the film tonight, you at home may well think that teams that play in this manner ought to be expelled immediately from the competition. Just see what you think.' During his commentary, not a kick or sly punch is missed, and he names the guilty men. Boy, does he name them, in a match he says 'will surely become known as the Battle of Santiago', on which point he was spot on.

'He was a critical observer,' said his BBC contemporary Michael Parkinson. 'He loved the sport and the people who played it, but reserved the right to say "no, that's not right". That is what we are missing in sport today.' This view was echoed by the Olympic gold medallist turned supremo Sebastian Coe: 'He moved on from the bland soft-soap interview, which actually we have gone back to. If you were a top sports administrator and Coleman was interviewing you, you were very naïve to go on unbriefed.'

Some idea of Coleman's status in the BBC can be gathered from the fact that when the Beatles flew back into Heathrow Airport in February 1964, after their triumphant tour of the United States, it was the *Grandstand* presenter who met them, opening the show from the observation platform. 'This is perhaps the most sought-after grandstand in Britain today,' he announced.

Ever the journalist, Coleman asked the group what plans they had to reclaim a spot in the Top Ten, having dropped out for the first time in their career. Paul McCartney, just as sharp and professional himself, replied, 'What do you suggest? John's going to go into the Old Vic, I'm trying tap dancing and Ringo is doing comedy on the highway.' Lennon said later he knew the band had made it when he saw David Coleman waiting for them.

Coleman's journalistic training became even more relevant at the 1972 Olympics when he broadcast live and unscripted for several hours after the Israeli athletes were held hostage in the Olympic village, rarely tipping over into bathos. But still he got sent up: the satirical puppet show *Spitting Image* represented Coleman with a mannequin that occasionally spontaneously combusted, and Clive James invented the term

'Colemantating' and he wasn't being flattering. What saved Coleman from turning into an Alan Partridge was that it was never a performance. You got the feeling that for him, fame was no spur. He was not an opening-supermarkets kind of guy.

I did, however, find a rather embarrassing newspaper ad from May 1965, forgivably early days for Coleman: 'David Coleman, top sports commentator, is one of television's best-dressed men,' it reads. 'Like so many of today's successful men, he makes sure his shirts are by Peter England. For style. For comfort. For the quality fabrics, the pace-making designs. And especially for the exclusive Formalic collar that stays smart always. Bri-nylon 49/6. Nkalon Royal De Luxe 42/-. Royal Ho-Iron 33/11.'

I hope this was not true. I don't like to think of Coleman in the heat of Mexico getting all excited in man-made fabrics. Those shirts would be sopping wet before we got anywhere near the 100 metres final. The Formalic collar brings back memories, though. There was a craze at the time for stiffening collars and giving the process some sort of technical-sounding name so it sounded like something to do with the space programme. My dad was doing it all the time with the jackets he made, always inventing stupid claims, like 'now includes new, exclusive, Extremitron for that shiny mod look'. You could get away with that sort of thing in those days.

But Coleman did not seem to get involved in much nonsense. Carl Doran, who produced him for more than ten years in *A Question of Sport* and became a close friend, says Coleman was the model of a dedicated family man, who might commentate on a match in the North of England for *Match of the Day*, then fly back down south, rush off to have supper with his family, before driving very quickly into London (one of the few newspaper cuttings I could find about Coleman's private life was about a speeding offence) to present the highlights.

In May 2011, Doran produced a tribute show called *The Quite Remarkable David Coleman*, which looked like an obituary but was actually a tribute to the commentator on his eighty-fifth birthday. 'I tried to persuade him to do one for his seventieth, seventy-fifth, and eightieth, and finally he agreed, although he would not be interviewed.'

For Coleman it was all about the sport. The former runner understood athletic endeavour, and wanted the television viewer to understand it too. If he could be a tartar at times, it was on behalf of us, the viewers. It was not some rock star demanding a bowl of M&Ms with all the blue ones taken out, just because he could. Jim Reside, a former executive producer at BBC Sport, said, 'He used to broadcast with the adrenalin sloshing around, and it somehow had everybody else on the edge of their seats too. It made them very sharp, very focused. Everybody was on their game all the time when David was broadcasting.'

Nobody pretends Coleman was an easy man to work with. He was secure in his abilities and knew, almost certainly better than management, where his talents could best be utilised. So, in 1977, when contenders like John Motson and Frank Bough were taking some of the plum jobs, he felt he was being under-utilised, and refused to sign a new contract. He was off our screens for a year during which, according to Alec Weeks, he was approached by ITV. That encouraged the BBC to settle.

It was a difficult year but, as was typical of the man, Coleman did not issue what the sports pages used to call a come-and-get-me plea. The BBC displayed its pique by failing to include Coleman in a programme called *Commentators' Choice* in July 1977, featuring the BBC's most famous voices of sport. The William Hickey column in the *Daily Express* called it an 'extraordinary omission'. Dorian Williams, Harry Carpenter, Henry Longhurst, Alan Weeks, Bill McLaren and Peter O'Sullevan were the choices. 'But not, amazingly, the mustard-hot Coleman,' wrote Hickey. The BBC said the selection was based on 'the producer's editorial judgement'.

Ironic then that since Coleman retired, the BBC has been trying to persuade him to participate in a tribute programme. When Coleman left the BBC in 2000, after his eleventh Olympic Games, Doran tells me he requested no ballyhoo, no leaving parties, no on-air fuss, although he was honoured by the Olympic movement for his contribution to the Games. 'He would have been completely out of step with today's celebrity culture,' says Doran.

It was Coleman's good fortune to reach his peak as a commentator just as British middle-distance running was reaching its peak, and so his voice will always be linked with the towering achievements of Coe and Steve Ovett. But while his gifts were being exercised to salute the single-minded dedication of Britain's stars of the running track, elsewhere the celebrations were for the endeavours of those for whom sport meant diving off cliffs in Acapulco, propelling motorcycles over double-decker buses, or putting on a shiny leotard and sitting on other chaps' heads.

THIRTEEN

COME ON EVERYBODY, BIG SMILE!

ITV's *World of Sport* marked out its territory from the start, somewhat to the left of *Grandstand*. Before going on air in January 1965, its first major signing, hired to sprinkle some fairy dust on the horse-racing coverage, was actress Eunice Grayson, rather better known for playing 'seductive' Sylvia Trench in the film of *From Russia With Love* than for any knowledge of the turf, and often referred to in those unenlightened times as a 'glamour girl'.

According to the *Daily Express* the day before the programme launched: 'Television's big battle for Saturday sports viewers broke into a row last night over actress Eunice Grayson, helping to pick winners at Catterick races.' David Coleman is quoted in the piece: 'Having a glamour girl pick winners with a hatpin is an insult to women viewers,' he said. 'Women are interested in serious sport. Women are quite happy to watch me – I don't find them running away from me on or off screen.'

'I don't use a pin,' Eunice responded. 'It depends more on the sound of the horse's name.' She only lasted a few weeks, but was symptomatic of ITV's problems in sport. Showbiz was at the core of commercial TV's appeal in Britain, and a mere ten years after its launch, the men who controlled the ITV channels eyed sport suspiciously.

There was certainly no great enthusiasm for *World of Sport* around the network, and in 1966, with the programme just eighteen months old, ATV, who were in charge of London broadcasts at the weekend, allied themselves with most of the regional stations to try to get the programme curtailed at 3pm and replaced with *Danger Man*. It was only the intervention of Lord Hill, chairman of the Independent Television Authority, that ensured the continuation of *World of Sport* through Saturday afternoon, although ATV did get permission to opt out of the wrestling at 4pm for *The Rifleman*, and an Italian puppet mouse called *Topo Gigio*.

A lesser man might have wilted under the indignity of being usurped by an Italian mouse, but not John Bromley, the executive producer of *World of Sport*. 'Bromley was magnificent. He never lost his enthusiasm for the show whatever was thrown at him,' says Dickie Davies, full-time host of the show from 1968 and a summer stand-in from the very early days, 'We knew we were up against it with the BBC having all the rights, but Brommers never lost faith in our capacity to rattle the opposition.'

'Ten seconds to go now, come on everybody, big smile,' Dickie told me, was the habitual last-minute instruction Bromley gave him as he went out to battle David Coleman on a Saturday afternoon. Not that *World of Sport*, which launched on ITV on 2 January 1965 and ran until September 1985 was ever really much of a rival to *Grandstand*. 'It was a completely different audience,' says Davies, 'It became particularly noticeable on FA Cup Final day when we went head-to-head against the BBC, and we would come on at about 11.30 in the morning, with all kinds of stars, comedians and the like, our Cup final panel, and we'd put the wrestling on early, and beat them hollow in the ratings – until about quarter to three, and then everyone would switch over to the BBC in time for kick-off.'

The apotheosis of this kind of Cup final coverage was probably the comedian Freddie Starr, whose strut in full Nazi get-up came on the lawn at the Everton footballers' hotel in 1984, and the song-and-dance man Michael Barrymore before the same final, blacked up for an impersonation of Watford's John Barnes. Normally, ITV tended to do showbiz shtick better than the BBC, and *World of Sport* became a much more potent competitor – and not only on Cup final day – than the BBC ever thought possible. Before launch David Coleman, while taking a swipe at Eunice, had famously crowed, 'We'll have them off the air in six months,' a comment Dickie Davies, who hosted the show from 1968 until the end, wears like a campaign medal.

The BBC's triumphalism was not unjustified, though. Peter Dimmock's efforts had ensured the Corporation held long-term rights for most significant sport. 'I always tried to leapfrog,' Dimmock explained. 'If there was two years left on a contract, I went for another three. In that way I was able to ensure that the fees did not become outrageous, and also protect the contracts. Before I left, for instance, I left them with quite a few years of Wimbledon.'

But perhaps the BBC underestimated the efforts of Bromley, although competing for sports rights did not appear to be at the top of his list of priorities when he turned up for an interview in 1964. His *Daily Telegraph* obituary in 2002 quotes Brian Tesler, the executive who hired him: 'Brommers was irresistible. Absolutely. The first thing he asked me was, "Is there an expense account?"'

Satisfied on that score, Bromley left his job at the *Daily Mirror* where he had been writing a sports gossip column, and launched *World of Sport*. 'We had no idea what we were doing, blind leading the blind, darling,' Bromley later admitted. His first move was to hire Eamonn Andrews as host, a shrewd move given Andrews's reputation both as a boxing commentator and as long-time presenter of radio's *Sports Report*. 'The trouble was that while Eamonn was red-hot on boxing, his knowledge of other sports was not as sound,' according to Frank Keating. 'He was not really interested in football at all, and I remember him once reading out a Formula Two motor racing result, calling it Formula Eleven because it came up in Roman numerals.'

I barely remember Andrews on *World of Sport*. Like everybody else I associate the programme with Dickie Davies. Andrews, for me, and I suspect others of my generation, will forever be the rather awkward uncle on the BBC children's programme *Crackerjack*, which he presented from 1955 to 1964. He had been a boxer (All-Ireland Juvenile Champion) and still moved like a prizefighter. Forgive me if I am trampling on the memory of a much-loved presenter, but Andrews seemed a little too tall, barrel-chested, and pug-nosed to be working with children – Gulliver amongst the Lilliputians. He did invent the best feature on the show, though, 'Double or Drop', a general knowledge game in which three contestants plucked from the audience – invariably in school blazers – were awarded toys or boxed games for each correct answer, but if they dropped an item, they were given a cabbage. It operated on a three-cabbages-and-out basis, a formula that could be usefully applied to *Question Time*.

However, it is plain to see why Bromley picked him. The big, slightly ungainly Irishman was a television animal, and there were not all that many of them about in those days – not clever in a conventional sense, but clever with television, at home in a studio. He brings to mind a quote from Artie, the producer played by Rip Torn in the TV satire, *The Larry Sanders Show*. When Larry is thinking of abandoning his chat show, Artie is horror-struck, 'You can't. You belong here. You're like some goddamn creature from Greek mythology: half man, half desk.'

That was Eamonn Andrews. As well as *Crackerjack*, he presented a couple of shows on the BBC that my parents used to watch: *This Is Your Life*, the famous biographical format which Andrews later took to ITV, and *What's My Line*, a middlebrow twenty-questions-style parlour game where panellists in full evening dress had to guess what working-class people did for a living, based on a mime. This was in the days when the country was awash with lamplighters, saggar-maker's, bottom knockers, wheeltappers and shunters, and the like. My mum enjoyed it because it had well-spoken people in it, while we young ones sat around bored, waiting for the Beatles to be invented.

Andrews smiled affably through the show, and always seemed a little less smart – because he was – than the panellists, very much the Alan Partridge figure. But there is always room for a Partridge in sports broadcasting, and given the content of *World of Sport* some weeks, it must have been a positive advantage to have someone front of house without an ironic bone in his body.

As evidence I produce a bundle of letters the young Eamonn sent to the BBC in the late 1940s. In January 1948 he wrote to Seymour de Lotbinière, 'While Stewart McPherson is away I wonder if you would allow me to do a boxing commentary for you. I know that to go to London (or wherever the venue might be) for a single commentary would not be a financial proposition. But I would be glad of the opportunity to display my wares. You may have heard some of my boxing work at some time or other, but I do assure you (with as much modesty as I can command!) that I can give a better commentary on this particular sport than any I have heard from the excellent men you have at present.'

To this, Lobby replied, 'I am afraid there is very little likelihood of our being able to ask you to take the place of any of our present commentators. However, it is comforting to know that you would be available at any time if the occasion did arise.'

Rather than simply sending a short note reading 'Sarcastic bastard' to Lobby, Andrews kept writing in similar vein, so regularly that by August 1949, he felt obliged to start his letter, 'I suppose you'd feel the seasons weren't changing in the normal way if a letter didn't arrive from me very soon!' By 1950, he had engaged a showbiz agent, Edward Sommerfield, to lobby Lobby on his behalf: 'I should be extremely grateful if you would bear him in mind for any OBs for which you consider him suitable,' Sommerfield wrote, 'especially a fight commentary, at which we are all confident he will excel.'

In fairness, according to my dad, Sommerfield's confidence was not misplaced. Andrews was a heck of a boxing commentator. I have heard his commentary (Eamonn's, not my dad's) on Cassius Clay, as he then was, boxing in the Rome Olympics in 1960, where Eamonn says, 'I think we are going to be hearing a lot more of this young boxer,' which you cannot fault as a prediction.

The doggedness Andrews displayed in his letters followed him into his broadcasting career. Sommerfield angled to get him on *Housewives'*

Choice, describing him as 'an attractive personality with a warm rich voice, and a devil of a lot of Irish charm', all of which was true. And in time he pioneered the chat show format in Britain, with the *Eamonn Andrews Show* on ITV, on which he often seemed to be interviewing Zsa Zsa Gabor. He was sent up mercilessly by the BBC's *Round The Horne* radio show, which based a character on him, Seamus Android, making fun of his occasional awkward non-sequiturs: 'Talking of cheese sandwiches, have you come far tonight?'

World of Sport was modelled on ABC's *Wide World Of Sports*, which launched in America in 1961. Like its now-forgotten British namesake,* ABC in America was hampered by not having the rights to the plethora of major events that NBC had, and so filled its screens with sports like hurling, rodeo, and jai-alai, a version of the Spanish sport pelota. Bromley originally planned to call his British version *Wide World of Sports* as well, until he looked down the line up for the first show, and saw table tennis from Wembley, racing from Sandown Park, and wrestling from Lewisham, and decided it might be prudent to drop the 'Wide'.

'Brommers did a deal with ABC in America,' Davies told me, 'picking up all kinds of sports not usually shown over here. Our rivals at the BBC used to laugh about some of the stuff we showed, like the New York Fire Brigade sporting events, log rolling, cliff diving from Acapulco, but these were things people talked about in the pub.'

In the early days, horse racing was usually the programme's main event. The ITV Seven was still more than four years away, so the unique selling point of the horse racing, post-Eunice, was the fact that its main presenter, a trilby-wearing chap called John Rickman, used to raise his hat as he wished us 'Good afternoon.' Rickman was a charming old-fashioned gent, who was once presenting from the commentary box/ studio at Sandown Park, when the telephone rang on the desk in front of him – this used to happen on TV – so he picked it up, and said, quite

---

* The British ABC grew out of the cinema chain and had the contract for weekend ITV in the North and Midlands until 1968, when it mutated into Thames TV. It produced *World of Sport* for the programme's first three years.

calmly, and perfectly enunciated, 'I'm terribly sorry. I can't talk to you at the moment. I'm a little busy, I'm on air.'

He was a respected racing journalist who had won the *Sporting Life* naps table, one of several old newspaper mates who Brommers called on to fill his show in the early days. An early running order featured, as well as Rickman, Peter Lorenzo of the *Sun* analysing the latest football news, and summing up the day's games, and Ian Wooldridge of the *Daily Mail* reporting from South Africa on the MCC tour. Its other mainstay was British professional wrestling, which had been on ITV since the very early days of commercial TV, commentated on by the faux-Canadian Kent Walton.

Walton, who died in 2003 at the age of eighty-six, was actually about as Canadian as the Duke of Windsor. His real name was Kenneth Walton Beckett, and his father was financial minister in the British colonial administration in Cairo, where Walton was born. The future voice of grapple and grunt was educated at Charterhouse followed by drama school, and flew with RAF bomber command during the Second World War. Afterwards, Walton found work at Radio Luxembourg and affected the transatlantic accent to present some shows as a disc jockey. He was also in a few British films, including a football movie, *Small Town Story* (1953), too obscure even for *Halliwell's Film Guide*. In it, Walton played – guess what? – a Canadian, a talented footballer who signs for Arsenal but then moves to plucky little Oldchester to save them from extinction. Some scenes are shot at Arsenal's ground, and the film includes cameos by Denis Compton and my dad's favourite, Raymond Glendenning.

With this unimpeachable background in sport, and his radio experience, Walton was a natural for Associated-Rediffusion, the pioneer commercial TV company which launched in 1955. The first head of programmes Roland Gillett, who was (genuinely) transatlantic, having been recruited from American TV, recognised a kindred spirit in Walton, and gave him the sports presenting gig, as well as a music show a year later called *Cool For Cats*, bridging the gap between wimpy British pre-Beatles pop and the nascent rock 'n' roll scene. Frankly, in those days there was so little pop music around we were grateful for anything we could get. As long as the DJ was fast-talking and sounded vaguely American we were happy and, with his Luxembourg pedigree, Walton fitted the bill.

The wrestling, as Walton admitted, was not an obvious job for him. A *TV Times* pull-out supplement from the early 1970s called *Kent Walton's Top 50 Guide to Wrestling* begins, 'When Kent Walton was asked in 1955 "What do you know about wrestling?" he replied "Nothing." Yet five days later he was giving a stylish commentary on his first wrestling match. Today, thousands of bouts later, Walton is acknowledged as an expert on the sport.' That first bout, from West Ham baths on 9 November 1955, featured Francis St Clair Gregory and Mike Marino. Marino, I can tell you, thanks to Kent Walton's guide, was a Libran, and his 'ring speciality' was the grapevine (a kind of headlock). Gregory, sadly, does not make the Top 50.

Initially, the wrestling was on a Wednesday night, effectively marking out ITV's dominion, downmarket of the BBC. If the BBC was Lady Isobel Barnett, its commercial rival was the Catford Crusher. By 1958, ITV's brand of wrestling had become sufficiently entrenched in popular culture to be the subject of an episode of the popular radio comedy *Hancock's Half Hour*. In 'The Grappling Game', Hancock's secretary Miss Pugh (Hattie Jacques) accompanies him reluctantly to a wrestling bill at Cheam Baths – 'There'll be some heads caved in tonight', Hancock says joyously – but becomes so involved she ends up in the ring. 'A punch up the bracket never did anyone any harm', is another favourite Hancock quote from the episode.

That sort of encapsulated the spirit of the sport which, when it migrated to *World of Sport*, was a big hit with the female audience. My mum did not watch it, of course, but I expect some of the chaps standing beside my dad and me at the rugby or football on a Saturday afternoon had little ladies at home with the TV on in the background, while they prepared the evening meal. Walton's Top 50 clearly plays to this audience, with details of the grapplers' star signs, children, interests, and so on, alongside their signature moves.

The Rev. Michael Brooks, for instance, was a Methodist Church Minister in Newcastle-upon-Tyne, whose hobbies were nature study and gardening. 'His specialities,' reported Walton, 'are the flying cross-buttock, and the Irish whip.' And I expect there are only a select few Methodist ministers of whom you can say that.

Mick McManus, 'a collector of antiques, especially old porcelain', and Jackie 'Mr TV' Pallo, who earned his soubriquet through bit parts in *Emergency Ward 10*, *The Avengers*, and *The Dickie Henderson Show*, were the stars of the show through the 1960s and '70s. The latter days of *World of Sport*, up until the final programme, were blessed with the work of Big Daddy (real name: Shirley Crabtree – hardly surprising, going to school in Huddersfield with that name, that he learned to fight. For further comment on this issue, I recommend the Johnny Cash song, 'A Boy Named Sue'), Giant Haystacks (Martin Ruane), and the mysterious masked man Kendo Nagasaki.

The wrestling continued in its Saturday teatime slot until 1988 when LWT's newly appointed director of programmes Greg Dyke decided its cheerful mayhem was not entirely consistent with the new direction he planned for ITV's weekends, the focus of which he said would be drama, by which he meant middlebrow series like *Poirot* and *London's Burning*. Walton's great gift was to treat the wrestling as if it were real sport, at which he was rather brilliant. In more than a third of a century commentating on men in unappetising underclothes rolling about the canvas in public halls in some of Britain's most desperate purlieus, he never let his own mask slip, even after Jackie Pallo revealed in a 1985 autobiography that all his fights were fixed, provoking a response from the public of whatever the contemporary equivalent of 'No shit, Sherlock' was.

This lack of irony no doubt served Walton well in his parallel career as the anonymous co-producer of soft porn movies, an aspect of his creative output that failed to merit a mention in the obituaries. Walton formed a company called Pyramid Films in the 1970s with Hazel Adair, the creator of the wobbly TV soap opera *Crossroads*, and together they contributed to the pantheon of British cinema such titles as *Can You Keep It Up For*

A Week?, *Clinic Xclusive* (aka *With These Hands*), and *Virgin Witch* (aka *Lesbian Twins*).

Those of you who pretended to be eighteen years old to get into your local Classic (where limp British sex movies were a staple) to sample Walton's oeuvre, no doubt remained blissfully unaware that your genial Saturday afternoon wrestling host was partly responsible for the sinking feeling of anti-climax that inevitably accompanied British (very) soft pornography of the time. Not that *Virgin Witch* was without its fans. On the Internet Movie Database, an admirer writes, 'We get sex, lots of nudity, witchcraft scenes – indoors and out – and a girlie magazine shoot.'

Walton's coyness about his role in chronicling semi-clothed paganism in Britain – al fresco and otherwise – was probably prudent in that wrestling was considered knockabout family entertainment, attracting a similar make-up of audience to that of something like *Harry Hill's TV Burp* nowadays. Its numbers hovered around the six million mark, invariably beating the BBC, who would normally be showing the second-half of a rugby league match opposite it.

Crucially for the BBC, though, sports fans tuning into *Grandstand* for athletics, horse racing, swimming, and so on, stayed tuned for the rugby rather than migrating to the wrestling. An audience research report commissioned by the BBC in 1965 concluded that 'considerably more regular viewers (of *Grandstand*) prefer rugby league to professional wrestling, whereas among occasional viewers the opposite is true. This result accords with earlier analysis of actual viewing behaviour in supporting the view that professional wrestling appeals widely to many persons who are not, in the accepted sense, sports fans.'

Sir Paul Fox, a founding father of *Grandstand*, interviewed for this book, extends this analysis to ITV sport in general throughout the 1960s and '70s, 'Once they put wrestling on a Saturday afternoon, we knew they weren't serious about sport. Their heart was never in it, really. Sport never worked for them because of the commercial breaks, so John Bromley was always swimming against the tide. He never persuaded the bosses, whoever the bosses were at the time, that sport was the answer.'

Like Bromley, Jimmy Hill, Head of Sport at LWT from 1967 to 1972, also found himself kicking against the suits. He clearly meant to compete with the BBC, and smashed in an early goal – to use a wildly inappropriate metaphor – when he beat the BBC to rights to cricket's Gillette Cup final in 1968, which was to be a major part of the early evening schedule, leading into LWT's star performer David Frost's interview programme at 6.45.

This, remember, was Swinging London, and not only was Frost a key figure at the time, he had lined up the editor of *Queen* magazine, the swinging young things' bible, for his weekly flagship interview. According to Clement Freud, who wrote for *Queen*, the targeted reader had long hair, was named Caroline, had left school at age sixteen, was not an intellectual, but she was the sort of person that one ended up in bed with. O tempora! O mores!

Clearly, this was a Frost interview too important to be delayed by a mere cricket match. And so it turned out, as Hill wrote in his autobiography, in some frustration, 'When the last over arrived it was exactly 6.45pm, and the result was still in doubt. The ignoramuses in Presentation, in fear of the powers that be, left Lord's with five balls to go and transmitted the live David Frost interview. What a start for a weekend television company for which, inherently, sport had to be an essential ingredient. What a start too for the new green-as-grass Head of Sport, having to take considerable flak from numerous directions for a decision made above his head by experienced senior executives.'

For anybody still waiting, Warwickshire beat Sussex by four wickets.

If the Gillette Cup turned into whatever the cricketing equivalent of an own goal is – the tournament took its bat and ball back to the BBC – Hill could point to a number of triumphs in television to stand alongside his epoch-making achievements in football.

Hill is probably best known for his role in ending the penury of his fellow professional footballers in 1961, when, as chairman of the players' union, his fierce campaign led to the maximum wage for footballers being abolished. Before Jimmy, a footballer's life really was serfdom. Clubs retained players' contracts and family men were often housed in club houses, which they would lose if they went to play elsewhere. During the close season, players' wages were reduced, often to subsistence level. Even a star like Johnny Haynes, who played alongside Hill at Fulham, would get the maximum £20 in the season, falling to £14 a week in summer.* Thanks to Hill, Haynes became Britain's first £100 a week footballer.

Hill went on to be an innovative manager at Coventry City, where he pioneered match day magazines, pre-match entertainment, and made plans for an all-seater stadium more than three decades before the rest of British football was forced to follow. Hill acknowledged he was not the first choice to deliver sport to London and the ITV network. Bryan Cowgill, Paul Fox, and David Coleman were just three of those approached before Bagenal Harvey got on the phone to Jimmy.

In hindsight, Hill seems a logical choice, given his history of innovation, and deal making. Anyone who could win a battle against the cigar-smoking double-breasted legions of obdurate football club chairmen of the era would surely find the piranha tank of television a walk in the park, if you will forgive the mixed metaphor. But at the time we just scratched our heads, and asked, 'Isn't he the chap with the chin who used to play for Fulham?'

Under Hill and Bromley's stewardship, though, *World of Sport* flourished. If the BBC needed confirmation that Bromley was making waves on the other side – something they might have done well to heed before the Mexico World Cup – it came in a *Times* column in 1969, in which John Hennessy praised ITV's innovative approach to football. His article appeared shortly after the BBC had celebrated its traditional three or four to one victory over the commercial upstart at the 1968 Mexico Olympics.

Hennessy wrote: 'The Mexico Olympics were a disaster for ITV in terms of audience ratings vis-à-vis the BBC performance. But, far from

---

* Another player, asking for parity and being rebuffed for not being as good as Haynes, responded, 'But I'm as good as him in the summer.'

being discouraged, the sports unit have taken new heart. Their advance in the treatment of football has been almost spectacular, with Brian Moore a genial front man and commentator, and Jimmy Hill an eager and intelligent analyst.' He praised the 'inventiveness' and 'shrewd eye for the unexpected' of *On the Ball* (the early Saturday afternoon football preview), noting Barry Davies as 'a relaxed and sympathetic interviewer'.

The BBC promptly snapped up Davies, who was, I recall, quite a factor in giving ITV sport credibility in the late 1960s. I remember him doing the Sunday afternoon commentary on the north-west regional match, and thinking, 'There's a man who sounds like he might have read a book other than the *Charles Buchan Football Annual*.' But apart from that transfer and the tackle from behind on Ken Wolstenholme, a certain arrogance seems to have kept the BBC from any radical changes.

This was despite numerous warnings from football specialist Alec Weeks that ITV was making big strides, and not just in the commentary box and on the pundits' couch. In a memo on 24 February 1969, Weeks wrote: 'As far back as August of last year I wrote to you informing you of my fears regarding ITV's coverage of Association Football, by using specialised units. Since then I have written further memos to Planning and H.E.Tel.O.Bs about the same subject.' While ITV were building up expertise using the same crews for big matches, Weeks, to his frustration, was subject to the vagaries of BBC rotas. However, he applauded Davies's recruitment.

Davies had been brought to ITV by Frank Keating, who was given responsibility for their coverage of the World Cup but didn't have any commentators. So he organised a trial at the Crystal Palace athletics ground, where the National Association of Boys Clubs' cup final was being played, and ITV broadcast it live, giving six novice commentators fifteen minutes each.

For the auditions Keating favoured old Fleet Street buddies whose contributions – thanks to the depth of research for which we sports hacks are famed – were full of comments like, 'There's the young red-headed boy with the ball,' and, 'There's the hefty centre-half.' Davies, on the other hand, had utilised the old Richard Dimbleby trick of actually doing some homework. 'There was a team from Cornwall and one from Derby,' explained Frank. 'He had gone to the trouble of finding out their names, hobbies, and so on.'

More than that. According to Davies's autobiography, *Interesting, Very Interesting*, he had written to both clubs asking not just for biographies of the lads, but six-by-four photographs of them, which spent a week stuck to the walls of the living room in the flat Davies was sharing in Hampstead. 'He was a revelation,' says Keating. 'He got the job, and within two months he was in Middlesbrough commentating on North Korea v. Italy.'

What astonished me, though, about the recruitment process was the thought of ITV broadcasting a boys' football match live. 'We did a number of afternoon things that weren't in the listings,' Frank told me. 'The Labour government back then hated ITV, and made it the law that we had to broadcast a certain ratio of editorial to advertising. If the figures weren't adding up, someone would come to me and say we need four hours of programming in the next fortnight.

'So we'd visit a schools' swimming gala at Crystal Palace or an exhibition at the Design Centre. None of it was advertised in the *TV Times*. They were called traffic spots, ordered by the advertising department to fill our ratio of local programming. We might spot some cricket on, and turn up at The Oval with four cameras for Sussex v. Surrey, and rack up two hours of cricket. We used to pay them fifty or a hundred pounds as a facility fee, and I brought in an old pal, Henry Blofeld, to do the commentary. I remember a mischievous cameraman once catching a woman sunbathing naked on the roof of one of those houses behind the scoreboard, and Henry said, "My God, there's a sight for sore eyes". But it was all live, there was no recording of it, so you never got any flak from the boss.'

Other sports covered included schools' table tennis, and a friendly hockey match at the Lensbury Club in Richmond. I like to think somewhere there is a chap, now in his late fifties or early sixties, desperately trying to convince his mates that some running race he once took part in on school sports' day was shown live on ITV, but, like me, is unable to find any record.

Another memorable broadcasting first for Keating was securing a light-entertainment appearance by the England team manager in Mexico, Alf Ramsey, who famously was rarely either light or entertaining. 'Alf was very difficult to get to, and my job in Mexico up to a point was to keep sweet with him and try and trump the BBC's leg-man, Peter Lorenzo. Fortunately, I got to have a drink with Alf one night and I said to him, "Would you do ITV the honour on the Sunday before the Brazil match of being on *The Golden Shot*?"'

This was a garish game show, hosted by Bob Monkhouse, requiring a telephone contestant to manoeuvre a crossbow into position to shoot at a target. 'Well, his eyes lit up, because Alf was a simple man, and it was the sort of programme he loved so we recorded Alf saying "up a bit", "down a bit", and all that, and sent it off. Alf liked cash in hand, so we paid him a hundred dollars for an interview, and threw in another hundred, and I became his confidant for the rest of the tournament. Dear old Lorenzo and the Beeb were absolutely furious.'

The fusion between sport and light entertainment that characterised *World of Sport* was signalled by its title sequence, which alongside the clips of football and horse racing invariably included footage of people sawing logs competitively, others diving off high platforms into kiddies' paddling pools, and comedians mugging to camera. There was a Christmas Eve show round about the early 1980s when Eric Morecambe was a guest, and Dickie Davies was the perfect foil. He relished the showbiz stuff, having emerged from a background in cruise ship entertaining on the *Queen Elizabeth* and the *Queen Mary*.

From there, he took a job as an announcer on Southern TV, and thence to join Bromley and Hill at LWT. Jimmy actually persuaded him to change his billing from Richard to Dickie. 'Cabbies would shout "Hey, Dickie", when they wouldn't dream of shouting "Hey, Richard",' says Davies. 'Once Jimmy got me to change my name, the whole thing took off, the housewives' favourite and all that stuff.'

He was likeable. Still is. He did not seem quite as intense as Coleman on *Grandstand*, nor as affected as Frank Bough who took over the BBC's flagship in 1968, although Clive James, the TV critic of the *Observer*, and one of the first to review sport programmes, regularly gave him a sound kicking. If anything, more than the other two. James, who liked to draw attention to Bough's tendency to put the emphasis ON his prepositions and break into a shout when you LEAST expected it, was even more scathing about Dickie Davies in his review of the 1978 World Cup.

'What is it about Dickie Davies (*World of Sport*, LWT),' he asked, 'that makes you feel less wretched about Frank Bough (*Grandstand*, BBC1)? By any rational standards, Frank ought to be definitively awful: the whole time that his stupefying ebullience is sending you to sleep, his RANDOM use of emphasis is JERKing you awake. Dickie doesn't do any of that. On the contrary, he speaks with exactly the same degree of measured excitement about every sporting event that turns up on a Saturday afternoon anywhere in the world. Perhaps that's the trouble.

'Understandably keen about the World Cup, Dickie Davies folds his hands, leans forward, and smiles at you from under his moustache. Equally keen about the World Target Clown Diving Championships, he folds his hands, leans forward, and smiles at you from under his moustache.'

Florida's World Target Clown Diving Championships was one of many less than blue riband sporting events featured on *World of Sport* under the banner of International Sports Special. What with this, the cliff diving, and the endless parade of Americans with a death wish mounting motorbikes to jump over other vehicles, the demarcation line between *World of Sport* and *Grandstand* was fairly clearly drawn. 'We used to beat them in the ratings on a normal Saturday, although when it was Wimbledon, for instance, we struggled,' Dickie told me.

Gavin Newsham, writing in the *Observer Sport Monthly* in 2003, recognised the divide: 'If the BBC's *Grandstand* was the first-born son that had flown the nest and found fame and fortune, *World of Sport* was the cheapskate kid brother that was still living at home and sponging off his parents at 35.'

ITV's output was undeniably more racy than the opposition and, like most aspects of British life, there was a class dimension. With betting shops having been introduced in Britain in 1961, the Saturday afternoon flutter had become the working-man's vice of choice, embraced enthusiastically by *World of Sport*. The introduction of the ITV Seven in 1969 was an unashamed invitation to link seven selections from two meetings in multiple bets. The BBC was always a little more coy about betting.

Not that this strict demarcation did anything to prevent the odd turf war. In 1969, when Manchester City played Leicester in the FA Cup final, the BBC paid £1,850 for exclusive post-match interviews with the Manchester team, while ITV claimed to have signed their own agreements with individual players. Jimmy Hill and Bryan Cowgill gave vastly different versions of the impasse, but Alec Weeks, who was actually there, producing for *Grandstand*, describes the disagreement as follows: 'Tempers flared, fists flew. Players stepped over the splayed bodies of television employees. Until we got into the players' tunnel. Then the hard-bunched knuckles really started landing. Players were forgotten as heads were thumped against the tunnel wall. Knees thumped into spines. Elbows jabbed viciously into stomachs. It was a hell of a fight involving about forty men.'

If nothing else, the punch-up began to give sports people an inkling of what they might be worth to the TV companies, and alerted the BBC to the fact that they would face real opposition at the following year's World Cup.

But, rather as the BBC's research concluded in its comparison of the wrestling and rugby league audiences, the true sports fan would continue to gravitate towards the BBC, not least for the authoritative voice of its commentators. People like Harry Carpenter on boxing, Peter O'Sullevan on racing and Max Robertson on swimming, were given top marks by between 65 and 78 per cent of respondents in the document. These voices, along with others like Coleman on athletics and Bill McLaren on rugby union, all hired by Cowgill and Dimmock in TV sport's early days, were in their prime at the end of the 1960s, and would be for at least two decades to come.

As Jonathan Martin, who became Head of BBC Sport, says, this was an era when the commentator was the star. 'Now there is much greater packaging,' he said. 'The presenter not the commentator is the star: Balding not O'Sullevan, Lineker not Motson.' Dickie Davies, despite all the Partridgeness identified by Clive James, may have been partly responsible for the change. By the late 1970s, he was becoming the star of *World of Sport*. I have a *TV Times* from 1970 where, after two years as presenter, Dickie is still billed as Richard Davies. But as the decade wore on only his mother and close friends still called him that. To the nation he was Dickie.

It was Dickie who started us watching sport with an ironically raised eyebrow (see Clive James, above), and, given the paucity of sport that ITV had the rights to, it is a tribute to Dickie that *World of Sport* continued as long as it did. He showed that front of house, as identified by Jonathan Martin, could be as important as behind the mike.

FOURTEEN

SCORING AT HOME AND AWAY

If this book does nothing else, I hope it encourages the BBC to consider a Frank Bough night, or at least a tribute programme like the one they did for Coleman. Bough, who presented around 600 editions of *Grandstand* between 1968 and 1983, defined an era in broadcasting.

As well as *Grandstand*, and the BBC's *Sports Review of the Year* which he hosted for eighteen years, Bough was anchorman from 1972 on *Nationwide*, an early evening magazine format that would skip lightly from an interview with the prime minister to an item about a skateboarding duck, or a mildly satirical song from a chap called Richard Stilgoe, with a neatly trimmed beard, a colourful sweater, and material best described as Tom Lehrer- (extremely) lite.

In some ways, Frank Bough was like one of those easy listening music acts of the 1960s and '70s: the Carpenters, say, or Andy Williams, disparaged in their day and only fully appreciated years later. Like Andy Williams, Frank was often to be found in chunky jumpers and cardigans, especially for that sort of magazine work (for *Grandstand* he favoured a natty shirt and tie), as that was the dress code at the time for middlebrow TV.

Nationwide, in particular, was something of a knitwear fest, as was *Breakfast Time*, Britain's first regular early morning show, which Bough went on to present from 1983 until everything turned very dark for him at the end of the decade. The cosy *Breakfast Time* format, similar to *Nationwide*, suited the time slot, and initially beat hollow ITV's starrier, messier offering.

To cope with the early starts, Bough took a flat in London, which is how the trouble started. With his wife and three sons at home in the Bough suburban pile in Buckinghamshire – his wife Nesta apparently used to buy all his woollies for him from a shop in Maidenhead – our hero was tempted out to parties, where he took cocaine, and was a willing viewer of a spectator sport that had failed to make it onto the *Grandstand* roster, or even *World of Sport*, variously described in the Sunday papers as 'kinky sex frolics' and 'wild vice girl parties'.

A sympathetic piece by showbiz writer Garth Pearce in May 1988, explained for *Daily Express* readers the lure of cocaine: 'To a man so mentally and physically exhausted as Frank Bough was at that point, cocaine can act as a temporary lift,' he wrote. Pearce, who specialised in fire-fighting for stars in trouble, ascribed Bough's unexpected scandalous behaviour not just to pressure of work but also to insecurity. 'Despite his totally professional approach to television presenting which would win him enough work for two lifetimes, he has long feared the sack,' wrote Pearce. 'This completely unfounded and irrational self-doubt kept him hanging on to a *Breakfast Time* show for five years when he should have ditched it long ago.'

Television execs were generally similarly sympathetic. Cocaine, after all, fuelled a fair bit of TV in the 1980s, bringing to mind a joke told by the comedian Bill Hicks, who said people who take the moral high ground on the issue of narcotics should remember that drugs were behind some of the finest rock 'n' roll of all time. The Beatles were so high, said Hicks, they even let Ringo sing a track or two.

Unfortunately for Bough, he got caught out again in 1992, when a receptionist in what our Australian friends colourfully call a wank 'n' spank parlour dribbled her story out to a Sunday paper. And that was more or less the end for Boughie who, at the age of fifty-nine, probably had ten good years left. As Jill Parkin wrote in the *Express* in September 1992, 'He's not a member of the Cabinet, he's not a bishop, pontificating on how we should live. He's a TV presenter. We don't need to know his sexual preferences any more than whether he opens his boiled eggs with a teaspoon or a knife. Why make a whipping boy of Frank? Even if he does enjoy it.'

Gee thanks, Jill. A column purporting to be supportive actually underlined the problem for Frank. He had become a figure of fun. People were making jokes about him, and that was fatal for someone who took the business of television presenting so seriously.

Just how seriously Bough took his work can be gleaned from Bob Wilson's autobiography *Behind the Network*. The former Arsenal goalie, who used to present *Football Focus* at the start of *Grandstand* when Bough was hosting, writes: 'I was fascinated by his pre-programme warm-up when he concentrated simply on perfecting his opening greeting of "Hello" or "Good Afternoon".' ('Look, it says "Good afternoon, welcome to *Grandstand*" here, I'm trying to get a reading. What's my motivation?')

In fairness to Frank, he was at the helm for the glory, glory years of *Grandstand*; and aboard the BBC's flagship, standards were exacting. It does not alter the fact that Frank's description, in his own book, *Cue Frank!*, of the opening to a show he was presenting from Cardiff Arms Park before an international rugby union match is pretty funny. He goes through the build-up and opening to the show – after he's perfected his 'Good afternoon', of course – over several pages, including the genuinely shocking moment when a caption failed to appear at the appointed time. Then he describes his emotions: 'I feel I have survived the opening minutes, but just to get by is never enough. We're not in the business of just getting by on this programme. Was my delivery clear enough, emphatic enough? The viewer only hears the words and sees the pictures once. Was the planning right, was the execution crisp and sure?' After five pages of this stuff, you may be asking yourself if there is much more, to which the answer is an emphatic yes.

He continues: 'The opening of *Grandstand* is the barometer by which we set the standard of performance for the afternoon, and the morale of everybody in the team. If it goes well we're away, up to thirty thousand feet in a twinkling, and flying smoothly. If it's weak, if there's a mistake, then we can waste another hour or so, building ourselves up to the peak we had hoped to climb in those few vital opening seconds, but didn't.'

I don't know about you, but I am anxious to get Frank's verdict on this particular show: 'It was all right today,' *(Phew.)* 'All right. But all right's not enough. Did it show that that damned caption was late on the screen? Did the anxiety show in my eyes or was it hidden? Did I hesitate? Stumble?'

From my limited experience of (pretty awful) television presenting – a few mercifully forgotten shows for Yorkshire Television in the mid-1980s – I should imagine it is enormously difficult to anchor a four-and-a-half-hour live programme every weekend in the circumstances Frank describes, under the scrutiny those chaps endured in a limited-channel world. And no one, with the possible exception of the Dark Lord, Coleman, did it better.

Bough was undoubtedly an extraordinary presenter, the king of all live TV for the BBC, a safe pair of hands on big occasions like general elections and royal weddings alongside all his regular work. Sure, he took some gentle ribbing from Clive James about PUTTing the emPHASis on the wrong sylLABles, but Bough was master of the domain, until that receptionist (the doctor will see you now) sold her story about Frank's relaxation routine, rendering him unsuitable to introduce the Green Goddess with her more conventional keep-fit methods on family-friendly breakfast TV.

Unfortunately, Bough's indecently entertaining autobiography was written in the late 1970s before his life became especially interesting, but the signs were there. As early as page fifteen he is recalling his National Service days in the army, and 'a memorable encounter with a lady in Hamburg whose pièce de résistance was to place six matches in her pubic hair, set them alight, and say "Iss goot, ja? Iss Christmas tree."'

Interestingly, the Everest-conquering mountaineer Chris Bonington joined Bough – the book is full of fascinating incidental detail like that – for this *outré* entertainment, about which Frank comments puckishly, 'Happily she blew the candles out before the whole forest went up in flames'.

Bough's path to the BBC is a typical 1950s success story. A grammar school boy from a working-class background in the Potteries, he worked hard and passed the entrance exam to Merton College, Oxford, where he distinguished himself academically and in sport, winning a football Blue as a centre-half. He joined ICI at Billingham on Teesside as a graduate entrant, and started doing radio reports in his spare time for the local BBC. Like many a bright grammar school boy from the provinces around the late 1950s and the early '60s – Alan Bennett and Michael Parkinson come to mind – the world, or at least the media, must have seemed full of possibilities. By 1962, Bough had abandoned a secure future at ICI to present a new regional news programme in Newcastle, and within two years he was working for BBC Sport. He went to the Tokyo Olympics in 1964 as a commentator and reporter, covering, among other sports, hockey and Greco-Roman wrestling, in which Britain had a medal contender. Coleman, meanwhile, commentated on Britain's big successes: Mary Rand in the long jump, and Ann Packer in the 800 metres. Bough did a filmed piece with Mary for which he took her to a Tokyo marketplace, noting that she wore 'a white sweater and a pair of very brief white shorts'.

I don't know whether you are familiar with the character Bulldog, the sports guy in the sit-com *Frazier*, but, alongside the Andy Williams, there is something of Bulldog in Bough. Back in 1979, when he was writing his book, Bough felt no compunction in expressing his dissatisfaction with the BOAC stewardess on his flight out to Tokyo, who he describes as 'personable enough, but rather a plain thing, to my regret'.

However, said Frank, something happened on the trip to make him reflect on the 'marvellously attractive qualities of English women'. He then launches into a page-long policy statement on relations between the sexes, declaring Bulldog Bough no fan of the subservient role of women in Japan circa 1964. 'For a while, it's grand,' writes Bough, 'but then you simply long for a good, spirited, independent-minded English girl … When I saw that plain English air stewardess stopping over at our hotel on another flight, she suddenly appeared the most marvellously interesting and attractive woman I'd ever seen', to the stewardess's great relief and joy, no doubt.

It was, as James Brown astutely observed, a man's, man's, man's, man's world in those days, and Bough, who worked under the famously hot-tempered Bryan Cowgill, tells many tales of raised voices, industrial language and locker-room badinage. Bough rose above it, though, and with the help of a sterling roster of commentators, to whom he gives full credit – Bill McLaren for Five Nations rugby, Harry Carpenter on boxing, Jim Laker and Richie Benaud on cricket, and so on – enabled the BBC to stay well ahead of the opposition for serious sports fans.

If Bough was Andy Williams, his smooth successor on *Grandstand* was Burt Bacharach, Hal David, and Sérgio Mendes and Brasil '66 – end of the easy listening music references, I promise – rolled into one. Des Lynam told me he was surprised when he was chosen as permanent presenter in 1983, what with Harry Carpenter already acting as holiday relief, and David Coleman and Jimmy Hill, who was now at the BBC, more experienced front men.

Having worked under the demanding Angus Mackay on *Sports Report*, however, Des had proved he could work under pressure, and he had acquired a breadth of experience in a variety of sports. His specialities remained boxing and football but, working under Mackay, who Des recognises as a major influence, he would not have been allowed to escape without building up a decent level of knowledge on sport of all kinds.

Though a radio man, Mackay's is an important figure in the story of TV sport, having brought Gerald Sinstadt to the BBC as his deputy in radio sport. Sinstadt, in turn, mentored both Frank Bough and Barry Davies, like himself grammar school boys, who undoubtedly take some of the credit for helping the BBC tanker steer away from the patrician rocks into the smooth waters of middle England.

Sinstadt was head of sport at British Forces radio before joining the BBC, and was the first person to put both Bough and Davies on the air. After leaving the BBC in the late 1960s, he was an urbane commentator on highlights of Granada's local football on a Sunday and number three at ITV for big foreign matches, behind Brian Moore and the dark brown-voiced Welshman Hugh Johns, who died in 2007, remembered – or, rather sadly, not remembered – for his commentary on the 1966 World Cup final for ITV. While Wolstenholme was doing his 'They think it's all over' shtick on the BBC, Johns was saying, 'Here comes Hurst. That's it. That. Is. It.'*

In the mid-1980s Sinstadt returned to the BBC, and may be able to claim some credit for the groundbreaking coverage of the 1990 World Cup. Like Bough, his career imploded after unnecessary newspaper coverage of an incident in a cinema in Islington, where films slightly – but only slightly – more racy than those you might see in the local multiplex were being shown. A police raid caught Sinstadt relaxing in the gentleman's fashion, offending no one as far as one can tell, and charges were dropped. But the damage was done. In the *Independent* William Hartston wrote a brilliantly sarcastic open letter to Islington police: 'As we lie in our beds and listen to the tinkling of smashed quarter-lights, as we try to ignore the ringing of car and house alarms, we can at least reassure ourselves that the porn cinemas of Islington are being kept safe for our children.'

Does it always end like this? Well no, but often enough to give the living-in-a-Travelodge-by-the-ring-road scenario created by Steve Coogan for the Alan Partridge character the ring of truth.

Des Lynam had his moment under a cloud during the 1998 World Cup, when he entertained a female neighbour to a night in a Paris hotel.

---

* The *Daily Telegraph* obituary described Johns as 'an operator of the old school', whose unvarying routine took in an omelette before kick-off and a post-match drink with his colleagues, one of whom nicknamed him 'Huge Ones' in tribute to the size of his whiskies.

Not just any hotel, but a '£200-a-night' hotel, according to the *Sun*. The hotel's nightly rate might not seem particularly significant in this matter to you or me, but is hugely important to newspapers. One of the first stories I covered, as Chepstow district reporter for the *Western Daily Press*, was one I got through personal contacts, about four boys caught smoking cannabis and suspended from Monmouth School. I thought I had done a bang-up job getting the story, and covering it rather comprehensively and went to the pub to celebrate, only to receive a phone call from the news editor later that night cavilling at my failure to mention how much the school fees were. It was not a mistake I made again. Even if I was reporting on one of *Nationwide*'s skateboarding ducks I made sure I got the age of both the owner and the duck, and if possible the up-to-date market value of the owner's house.

Another important issue in a kiss-and-tell story is frequency of sexual intercourse. In real life, sex can be satisfactory, quite enjoyable, mildly disappointing, routine, infrequent, non-existent, fairly diverting, or any variant, but in tabloid-world there is no room for such shades of grey. The love-rat in question is either 'a flop between the sheets' or a 'six-times-a-night' man. It's the law. Des was fortunate enough to be placed in the latter category. The publicist Max Clifford, who speaks fluent tabloid, said, 'Des has been scoring at home and away', which frankly shocked no one as we always thought of Des as the Leslie Phillips of sport. Ding-dong.

Not that his love romps, as Max would undoubtedly dub Des's indiscretions, seemed to affect his popularity. Des merely shrugged, admitted to a 'serious error of judgement' – or six serious errors of judgement a night over two years if the *Sun* is to be believed – and carried on with his career.

In my view, there has never been a better front man for BBC Sport than Des Lynam, and there is a very good reason why his career failed to flourish when he defected to ITV in 2000. The tone of the BBC suited Des. You are not trying to sell anything on the BBC, other than the excellence and the immutability of the organisation. On ITV you are flogging the stuff in the commercials, on Sky you are shifting subscriptions, working yourself up into a lather over the unmissable quality of the programme so people will sign up, but on the BBC, all you have to do is what Lord Reith prescribed all those years ago: educate, entertain and inform.

If anything, the emphasis at the BBC is on *under*selling. All that stuff Wogan used to do on the radio, about the awful BBC coffee, the mild jibes at management, the jokes about the dodgy weather forecasts, and the jocular deconstruction of the business of broadcasting, does not work on commercial radio – I know, having worked for both – and the same is true of TV.

On ITV, Des would never have got away with his downbeat intros. When England played Tunisia in a midweek afternoon match at the World Cup in France '98, our hero kicked off the BBC coverage with a knowing wink, asking, 'Shouldn't you be at work?' After the hard sell in the commercial break, and the sponsors' bumper (the name check the sponsor gets each side of the ad-break), such underplaying would seem odd. Similarly masterful was Des's intro to the unforgettable Euro '96 semi-final between England and Germany at Wembley. It was a midweek match, a working day when work took second place to waiting for the kick off. I remember suffering PMT (pre-match tension) all day, and Des's welcome cleverly defusing the situation. 'Some of you may have heard there's a football match on tonight,' he said with his trademark nudge, nudge.

By Euro 2000, Des had moved to ITV, citing frustration with the constant moving of *Match of the Day* to a late-night slot, and the BBC's apparent lack of interest, during the era of John Birt (twelfth director general, 1992–2000) in securing important sports rights, especially to big football matches. I was at the BBC on and off during the 1990s, working for Radio Two and local radio. Though I didn't feel obliged to read all the edicts emanating from Birt's office, preferring to catch up with them after they had been leaked to *Private Eye*, I got the impression that the 'entertain' element of Reith's famous dictum was taking a back seat. Flannelled fools and muddied oafs were clearly not right at the top of Birt's agenda.

Until I picked up Birt's autobiography, *The Harder Path*, though, I had no idea exactly how far down. I looked up 'sport' in the index, and found nothing; similarly 'Lynam', 'football', and 'Coleman'. No, I tell a lie. There are two references to 'Coleman', both to *Guardian* journalist Terry Coleman, author of acclaimed biographies of Lords Nelson and Olivier.

Greg Dyke, who became the thirteenth director general in 2000, says in his memoir, *Inside Story*, that sidelining sport was a deliberate policy under Birt. By the time Dyke grabbed the reins, the BBC had lost the FA Cup and Formula One to ITV, cricket, the Derby, and the Cheltenham Festival to Channel 4, and most of the domestic football to BSkyB. 'The BBC had taken the decision not to compete for many of these sports,' writes Dyke. 'John Birt's view was quite logical: that the BBC had limited funds that could be better used in areas like drama and news where the BBC added more value. It was a perfectly rational strategy but, like so many of John's strategies, it ignored one factor: what the audience wanted. Our research showed the British public liked sport on the BBC, without advertisements, and were very resentful it was no longer available. For many of them, that was why they paid their licence fee.'

So Lynam, with ten years of *Grandstand*, and eleven years of *Match of the Day* behind him, as well as having fronted Wimbledon, the Grand National, and Olympic Games from 1980 to 1996, moved on to ITV. A more BBC animal it would be difficult to find, a point echoed in an essay in the *London Review of Books* in July 2000. 'Is it possible to turn from, say, Ian Wright's dreadful Chicken Tonight advertisement to, say, the ruminative countenance of Bobby Robson without feeling the need to interject some Des-like jest?' asked Ian Hamilton. 'Lynam's current technique with each commercial interruption is to pretend that nothing much has happened, that the audience he's now so matily addressing has not, a few seconds earlier, been made to stare at Ian Wright, a former soccer star now flogging tins of yuk.' What I like about the *London Review of Books* – or the *LRB*, as it's known among fans at Upton Park – is that in the following issue, somebody felt the need to write in and point out that Chicken Tonight comes in jars, not tins.

Des was definitely important to BBC Sport, maybe even totemic, although his autobiography does slightly overdramatise his historic transfer. I have read Second World War memoirs by Russian generals expending less time and space on the Battle of Stalingrad. For the record, I love Des dearly, and despite Dimmock's pioneering genius, Coleman's mad intensity, Dickie Davies's wacky cruise-ship shtick, and Brian Moore's loveliness, I would choose Sir Desmond at his peak to present my sport every time, without hesitation.

Now, about television people's autobiographies … the horror, the horror! I must have slogged my way through a dozen or so in preparation for this history – and by the way, you do not know what true embarrassment is until you have been caught by an acquaintance in the café at the British Library reading *Interesting, Very Interesting* by Barry Davies – and I have strong views on them which I mean to share.

Anyway, here is Des on his way to meet Will Wyatt, Managing Director of Television, to break the news to him: 'At my disposal for the dreaded task ahead was the limousine and driver of Richard Eyre, ITV's Chief Executive. Jane [that's Jane Morgan, Des's agent] and I clambered in the back and spoke little as we headed for Broadcasting House. Jane stayed in the car while I went through the back door in Portland Place, showed my ID, had a joke with the doormen, and got in the lift to the third floor. I went through the door … '

Call me old-fashioned, but I had kind of assumed that for his meeting with Managing Director, Television, Des would have entered via the door, rather than parachuting in through an open window. Having successfully negotiated the door, 'his secretary, to whom I'd spoken earlier, greeted me with a smile. I tried to smile back – she probably saw before her the kind of shaky quivering lip that Herbert Lom had perfected in the *Pink Panther* films … '

To précis, she asks Des if he wants tea or coffee (you will have to buy the book, *I Should Have Been At Work!* to find out which), another door opens, and Des is talking to Will Wyatt. He drops his bombshell, 'Will, we've been friends and colleagues for a long time and you've always treated me fairly. But on the list of most difficult conversations I have had in my life, this is definitely in the top five. I'm quitting the BBC as of now. No turning back. I'll be an ITV person by this afternoon,' Des announces.

'Will staggered back and clutched the desk behind him in the manner of a silent movie star conveying shock without words,' reports Des, 'When Will eventually recovered, to find he still had the power of speech, he told me that he could not understand my decision. As I expected, he did not compare ITV Sport favourably with its BBC counterpart. He felt ITV flirted with sports. They had no real commitment.'

In that, Wyatt was at one with every executive interviewed for this book including even David Elstein, fierce critic of the BBC and opponent of the licence fee. Elstein, who has worked for just about every British TV channel yet invented, says ITV's federal structure, with regional companies scrapping for space on the network, left it severely wounded from the start.

'For a long time,' said Elstein, 'there was no ITV sports body. It was years before the network got a sports policy. And when it did put *World of Sport* together it was a ragbag.' For many years different companies shared the London franchise, one taking weekdays, the other weekends, the pickings being too rich not to be shared around: first Associated-Rediffusion and ATV, later Thames and London Weekend Television. LWT was supposed to be in charge of sport, which irritated Thames who then set up their own sports department. Anybody with even a passing knowledge of TV people will recognise that as a recipe for internal politics on a scale worthy of the Borgias.

'The BBC could command its regions,' continues Elstein, 'In ITV you had to negotiate with the independent fiefdoms. So you got incoherence and a lack of commitment and flakiness. Dickie Davies's kipper tie told the story from the start.'

In fairness to Dickie, we were all wearing ridiculous ties in the early 1970s – which in my case I combined with an Afro hairstyle, and a big fake fur jacket, having fancied myself as one of the Stylistics or the Temptations perhaps. But Elstein's analysis bears out what Frank Keating said to me about the screwy and fundamentally unworkable way sport was set up on commercial television.

ITV gradually confined itself to opportunistic raids on sports, according to Elstein. Often it would bid for a sport that had suddenly become high profile, perhaps at an Olympics, and then forget what on earth the attraction might have been. As Elstein put it, 'The coverage of gymnastics and ice skating was so embarrassing that many of the regional companies just didn't want to show them and had to be told it was a contractual commitment.'

Peter Dimmock told me a similar story from the 1960s about an ITV raid on the Horse of the Year Show. 'We were paying very little, and we had been going for quite a long time, so ITV managed to get it away from us one year. But when Harry Llewellyn was doing the big jump – the wall – and he could win if he jumped it, they chopped it short, just as he was beginning to ride towards it, because the agreement with the regional companies was that they would go to the news at exactly that time. Well, the horse people were so angry that they came back to me and said, "Peter, from next year it's back to the BBC."'

Given this history, ITV has from time to time tried to buy some quick credibility by stuffing great sums of money into the orifices of BBC presenters such as Des, his successor on *Grandstand* Steve Rider, Bob Wilson, and more recently Adrian Chiles. We eunuchs at the harem have sat back to wait for it to end in tears, and we have rarely been disappointed.

But back to Des's story (I really feel this would benefit from that backing music the DJ Simon Bates used to play on his Our Tune spot, where people wrote in about their boyfriend dumping them, or being diagnosed with cancer). You may remember we left the BBC's Managing Director of Television, Will Wyatt, clutching the desk. 'I emphasised how sorry I was to have to tell him I was leaving and that my decision was irreversible,' Des sobbed (he doesn't cry in the book, but I think it heightens the drama). 'I said I hoped that when the dust settled our friendship would resume. He showed little enthusiasm for that prospect and found it difficult to shake hands as I left his office. I fully understood.'

Let's not bother with the journey in the back of the ITV limo from Portland Place to ITV's gaff on Gray's Inn Road, and instead join Des already in situ in a side office, calling Niall Sloane, who ran the BBC's football programmes: 'We had worked together on Euro '96 and the World Cup of 1998. Both series were hugely successful for the BBC, and for me,' writes Des, 'we had received much critical acclaim and won several broadcasting awards. Niall had made a touching speech on my behalf at one of the BAFTA ceremonies. We were pals. He listened to what I had to say. His sole response was "OK mate". It would be a long time before Niall and I resumed our friendship. In a way it was hugely complimentary that my soon-to-be-former colleagues were taking my departure so hard. If they had been pleased to see the back of me they would have been rather less aggrieved.'

Right there, in Des's book, is some of what irks me about TV people's autobiographies. For a start, they can't stop going on about their BAFTAs. Almost without exception, every memoir I read, had a story about winning a BAFTA, being nominated for a BAFTA, clambering into the back of a limousine to go and collect a BAFTA, or making a speech at the BAFTAs, which in the pages of most of the autobiographies I read are invested with career-making or breaking importance.

Well, I am sorry to say that these awards, like most awards, mean nothing. I mean, congratulations to Alec Weeks, for instance, for winning a BAFTA for his coverage of the 1976 FA Cup final, but did you win it in 1977 and 1978, Alec? No? Well, maybe it was your turn in 1976. Writing as someone who has never won an award for anything in his life and therefore can look at the subject quite dispassionately, I have to tell you that's how these things work.

Here is some more about how awards work. England, you may recall, lost in its bid to host the 2018 World Cup. The FIFA vice-president Julio Grondona of Argentina explained later on what basis he decided not to support our bid. 'I said, if you give us back the Falkland Islands, which belong to us, you get my vote.' That's how awards work. Merit is only a peripheral consideration. (By the way, my radio programme has been entered for a Sony Radio Academy award. Should it win, please disregard the above.)

The other constant in broadcasters' autobiographies is the conviction that what they are doing is the most important thing in the world. I have lost count of the number of accounts I have read of presenters fluffing their lines, or camera three going down at a vital moment, when only the quick thinking of the protagonist saves the day, for which we, the great unwashed, can only be thankful.

Bob Wilson actually has a very moving story to tell away from the television cameras, having lost two (much older) brothers in the Second World War and his daughter Anna to cancer. He later became a hard-working charity fund-raiser in her memory, and the pages dealing with his personal life are clearly deeply felt. But once in the studios Bob traverses the familiar path from his 'early amateurish experiences', through those days when (ho-ho) everything went wrong, to consummate professionalism and the inevitable BAFTA nomination.

According to his autobiography, he presented *Grandstand* 200 times, which was a surprise to me. I remember him hosting *Football Focus*, but I can barely remember him as a *Grandstand* presenter. Maybe that is a good thing, like being a referee. They say if you don't notice the ref, he has had a good game, and perhaps Bob was playing a blinder all that time I was failing to notice him at the BBC.

He began to make more of a splash, though, when he moved to ITV in 1994, and not always in a good way. For me, Bob seemed a strange choice for ITV, not really showbiz enough. A cheerful host-with-the-most like Dickie Davies, and nakedly commercial animals like Chris Tarrant and David Frost belong on commercial telly. There was an air of courtliness about Bob that did not quite fit, especially when he was presenting the European Champions League on prime time. Bob seemed a little insubstantial, not a big enough personality for ITV, something of a cipher like Chauncey Gardner, the man who rose without trace in *Being There*.

Half Man Half Biscuit, the post-punk football fan band the late John Peel used to champion on Radio One, got it about right, I reckon. They did a song called 'Bob Wilson, Anchorman'. One verse went:

I marvel at the things we find beneath the ground,
And that man can go faster than the speed of sound,
But I still can't get my head around
Bob Wilson, anchorman.

Me neither, particularly because, like some other defectors from the BBC, he seemed uncomfortable with the commercial breaks, which is not ideal, since adverts are what ITV is all about. Sure, there has been a little more sponsorship in recent years and, with rules being relaxed on product placement, ITV may soon be able to pay the rent by the presenter taking a long, cool, refreshing draught from a can of life-affirming Coke, but when the football-loving millions are gathered round the TV for a Champions League match, the main thrust is to advertise stuff to us, quite relentlessly. I am sure when they sold the presenter's job to Bob, they did not put it like this, but to be brutally frank, their only reason for hiring Bob or anyone else is that his face is felt to be the right one to shift more razor blades, new cars, and male fragrances. End of story.

Those of us convinced of the primacy of the adverts on ITV had our suspicions confirmed on 4 February 2009, when during extra time in an FA Cup-tie between Everton and Liverpool, the channel switched from the football to an automated advertising break extolling the virtues of Tic Tac mints, returning to the football just in time to see Everton players celebrating Dan Gosling's goal, the only one of the match. This was obviously a purely technical problem: an 'inexcusable glitch' for which ITV executive chairman Michael Grade apologised profusely, pointing to the hours of football ITV broadcasts without such conflicts. But the balance between the programme and the commercials is always going to be an issue, and needs skilful handling by the presenter to avoid audience migration.

I used to get quite nervous on Bob's behalf when he was presenting a big match. I met him once when ITV Sport invited me up to Newcastle to watch their coverage of a Champions League match against Barcelona in 1997 – Asprilla's hat-trick, the high point of a dismal campaign. It was quite a thrill for me because, what with covering sport on TV, I don't get out much, and they put me up in a nice hotel overlooking the Tyne, and I was able to go and have a drink with my mates from *Viz*. Bob was staying in the same hotel, and we chatted over coffee. He seemed ever such a nice chap, but there was a definite whiff of the BBC about him.

Having met him, I felt I had something of a personal stake in his performance, so when he was presenting, I found myself watching out for that tiny little flashing spinning wheel that appears in the top right-hand corner of the screen when a break is imminent, wondering if he had left himself enough time to make it. His book reveals that he may have been wondering too. 'Soon after my arrival,' wrote Bob, 'I was being counted to the close of the show, overran by a second or two and clipped the incoming commercial. Immediately after the programme, Jeff Farmer, the Head of Football, told me that the advertising company concerned might well object to losing the second or two of air time and claim thousands of pounds in compensation or a free advert. I understood the implications and never made the same mistake again.'

Bob's arrival at ITV coincided with a golden era for football on the channel, with its flagship Champions League coverage bolstered by the acquisition of rights to the FA Cup in partnership with Sky, and to highlights of England internationals. Whether Bob was the right man for the job or not, the audiences for football on ITV climbed – provided the action was exclusive to them. Indeed, the meeting between England and Argentina in the 1998 World Cup, the one marked by Beckham's sending-off and Sol Campbell's disallowed header, peaked at 26.5 million viewers, the highest ever number of people tuning into a television programme on any single channel, averaging out at 23.7 million, the highest for an ITV programme since the channel went on air in 1955.

According to Bob, the 1998–99 season was probably the most success-ful ever for ITV Sport. 'Of the twenty television sports programmes with the highest audiences during that time, sixteen were on ITV screens,' writes Bob. 'For fifteen of those shows, I was the lucky man in the chair.' The broadcasts concerned were all, apart from one, football matches being shown live and exclusively on ITV. The reason Bob is so keen to quote the figures is to set up the uncomfortable conversation he is about to have with his bosses, and underline the injustice of what is about to befall him, another key feature of sports' broadcasters' autobiographies.

In essence, the Holy Grail ITV has been – is still – seeking, in its whirligig of presenters, is a return to the days of 1970 and 1974, when Brian Moore, Jimmy Hill, the famous panel, and producer John Bromley came up with a way of handling sport that offered a genuine alternative to the BBC way of doing things. But it strikes me that is akin to the fruit-less quest to recapture lost youth. And it does seem odd that so often the path they choose is poaching presenting talent from the BBC.

Lynam was their pick, at the start of the 1999 season, after Bob Wilson was perceived to have outlived his usefulness. You may remember we left Des causing much wailing and gnashing of teeth at the BBC through his decision to take commercial TV's shilling. Simultaneously, and as a direct consequence, Bob was having the conversation with his bosses, varia-tions on which you can read in virtually any broadcaster's biography you pick up. As with Des, there are doors opening, hellos and so on, and an uneasy handshake from Head of Sport Brian Barwick, accompanied by an uneasy look. 'There's no easy way to tell you this,' says Barwick, 'Half an hour ago we signed up Des Lynam.'

'It was a hammer blow of great proportion,' wrote Bob, 'the impli-cation was obvious. Des would become ITV's number one football presenter. My first reaction was defensive and emotive. "You've got to be joking. He's tired, lazy and past it!" were the words that came pouring out of my mouth. I followed up this unfair abuse of the great presenter by stating the record figures that ITV had attracted during the past twelve months.

'Brian quickly sought to regain control of the meeting, which was getting out of hand. He said that ITV still wanted me on board and, to prove their commitment, he produced an envelope containing a letter with an increased offer on my contract.' (It's Kenneth Wolstenholme 1970 all over again). 'I threw the envelope back at him without opening it,' continued Bob. 'By now the realisation of what was occurring was sinking in and I was close to tears. I was stupidly beginning to feel sorry for myself but it was no time for that. Brian insisted that I read the new offer and delivered it for a second time in my direction. I took out the letter, glanced at the increased figure and promptly ripped it in two.'

Blimey, hell hath no fury like a TV presenter scorned. Bob was rarely as animated as that, presenting the football. After talking to fellow presenter Jim Rosenthal and Brian Moore, however, Bob decided to take the improved contract, and stayed at ITV until 2003 in a reduced role but with more money – a crime with no victims, I should have said. But that does not stop him ever so gently sticking the boot in to Des.

In 2001, the BBC lost the rights to Premiership highlights, sending its footballing flagship *Match of the Day* into a coma, while ITV put on *The Premiership* at 7pm, a new, promising but untried weapon to be deployed alongside Cilla Black's *Blind Date*, the blockbuster reality show of the era. It was a huge change to the Saturday night routine of millions of football-watchers who had been accustomed to watching the highlights *after* the curry and lagers. As Lynam put it in his opening intro: 'Better for you. Better for all of us. Good evening. New season, new show, new time. You'd obviously heard.' They *had* heard and it didn't suit them. 'Viewing figures were so ordinary,' noted Bob with a deep sense of satisfaction, 'that by Christmas, David Liddiment, ITV's Controller of Programmes, had rescheduled *The Premiership* to 10.30.'

And still, like Arthur Schnitzler's *La Ronde* – although without all the sex obviously – the ITV merry-go-round continues to turn: Bob retired after the 2002 World Cup, Des after the 2004 European Championships. Gabby Logan, daughter of Leeds United's Terry Yorath and wife of Scottish rugby player Kenny Logan, joined from Sky TV in 2004 but after a critical mauling and downgrading of her duties only stayed for two years, making way for Steve Rider, who joined from the BBC to present Formula One and the 2006 World Cup.

By the 2010 World Cup, Rider had gone, supplanted by Adrian Chiles, who presided in South Africa over the two traditional humiliations: ITV's in the ratings and England's in the football. I am sure there will be broadcasting triumphs in Chiles's future, and BAFTAs for us to read about in the inevitable celebrity autobiography – so far he has restricted himself to writing about his support for West Bromwich Albion football club – but in the meantime, Adrian might like to acquaint himself with the story of one of his predecessors.

Elton Welsby was talent-spotted while hosting the local football on Granada, and hired as main presenter when Greg Dyke, then Chairman of ITV Sport, grabbed exclusive live coverage of First Division football – pre-Premier League – at the start of the 1988–89 season. If you look for footage of Arsenal's dramatic 2–0 victory at Liverpool, the match that settled the Championship that season, you will find Welsby fronting it.

He also co-presented the 1990 World Cup for ITV, looking after the Italian end, while London coverage was fronted by Nick Owen, formerly of TV-AM, now reading the local news on BBC in the Midlands (I hope you are taking note of all this, Adrian). Bob Wilson's arrival pushed Welsby further down the presenting pecking order, and he went back to Granada to present regional programmes until 2000, when his contract was not renewed. His most recent work has been presenting crown green bowls for Sky Sports. By 1994 and the World Cup in the USA, yet another presenter had been signed, Matthew Lorenzo from Sky. He was last heard of working outside mainstream television in training and other projects. I am not suggesting the entertainment world's second most famous Elton – or indeed Nick Owen or Matthew Lorenzo – as templates for Chiles's career trajectory, but network TV is an unforgiving business, nowhere more so than at ITV Sport. And one did wonder whether Chiles is an ITV person.

He flourished at the BBC in low-budget shows from which little was expected, like the business programme *Working Lunch, Match of the Day*

2, a football show on which he had to make the most of minimal high-lights, *The Apprentice – You're Fired*, a reality show spin-off, and *The One Show*, a news-lite confection on which Chiles often seemed to be interviewing Alan Titchmarsh plugging a new book. The unaccount-able popularity of this show was probably correctly ascribed to Chiles's sardonic take on some of the features, and slightly spooky sexual chemis-try with his co-presenter. On the basis of this admittedly impressive CV, Chiles was charged at the 2010 World Cup with bringing those 1970s glory, glory days back to ITV. But where Brian Moore had Brian Clough and Malcolm Allison as expert witnesses, Chiles had Gareth Southgate and Andy Townsend.

Chiles's strengths at the BBC – the common touch, an unglamorous image, a certain cynicism, sourness even, about the whole millionaire footballer circus – became weaknesses at ITV, where his weekly brown envelope was reported to bulge with around 30,000 big ones.

That shouldn't matter. Smooth presentation of a live TV show is a difficult knack granted to only a rare few – not as difficult as bomb disposal or keyhole surgery, but let that pass – and the market rate is going to be high. But, in the depths of a recession, Chiles's 'I'm just an ordinary bloke from West Bromwich, me' routine would have to be a lot more entertaining than it was to win over a British public cowed by economic meltdown. The problem was heightened when Chiles was joined by his co-presenter from the BBC, Christine Bleakley, whose inamorato was Chelsea's Frank Lampard, not, beyond Stamford Bridge, Britain's most popular professional footballer.

Thus, at the time of writing, Gary Lineker remains by some distance the most popular presenter of football on television. Nobody who witnessed his rather wooden early media appearances could ever have dreamt he would become part of the TV furniture. And now the audi-ence sticks with him, because it knows what it is going to get. Familiarity breeds contentment. Rather like Terry Wogan, who was on Radio Two for what seemed like a century or two, Lineker has reached the point where the public will stay tuned, almost out of habit. That said, Lineker has Frank Bough's touch for dealing with the unexpected – pundit Emmanuel Adebayor's mobile phone rang during a live segment at the World Cup, and without breaking stride, Gary said, 'Do you want to take that?'

Despite some appalling jokes on *Match of the Day*, which wisely he has been cutting down on of late ('Defoe has become de friend of all Englishmen' was his sign-off after the Tottenham striker Jermain scored for England in a World Cup match), a marriage break-up, and the press sniping at his golf-club cosiness, Lineker survives. 'He is contracted till 2013,' his agent Jon Holmes told me. 'I have no idea what might happen after that, but TV is very searching. It is more demanding than you might think, and Gary will be fifty-three at the end of this contract.

'For the moment, though, he has extraordinary profiling figures. The BBC is surveying these things all the time to gauge the popularity of their presenters, and Gary invariably wins in all categories, age, class, everything, against whoever ITV put up. He has just done his third World Cup as lead presenter. Against Des he won by three-and-a-half to one, last time round it was nearer five-and-a-half to one.'

But, for all Lineker's extraordinary abilities, the words of Simon Garfield ring true: 'Sports broadcasters never get better than the ones we grew up with.' Garfield was writing in 2006 in the now-defunct *Observer Sport Monthly*. To go with the piece, the magazine assembled the heroes of his youth in a studio for a photo-shoot. 'The gang assembled here,' he wrote, 'stand among the microphones in the same way they straddled our weekends years ago: suavely, immaculately, assuredly.' Some were obviously unavailable, and others chose not to attend. There was no Harry Carpenter. 'It would take a substantial sum of money to entice Harry away from the South of France,' his agent said. Or Frank Bough. 'I retired from public life ten years ago, and won't change my mind,' he said. (I believe he softened this stance later. I saw him on a nostalgia show reliving *Nationwide*.)

The last name one expected to find on a list of those too busy to attend was Elton Welsby's, but bizarrely he couldn't make it because he was on a tour of small theatres with Ricky Tomlinson, doing spoof interviews, with the actor playing the Jim Royle character from the TV comedy *The Royle Family*. I am unable to report how that went, but it doesn't sound like a sure-fire winner. Tomlinson is a lovely bloke, but I feel compelled to say he has flogged his 'My arse' catchphrase to death, and I suspect the show didn't keep Elton from the crown green bowling for long.

Jimmy Hill turned up for the photo shoot, though, and Dickie Davies, and Bob Wilson, among others less celebrated. 'Perhaps we have a false memory of propriety and simplicity,' writes Garfield, 'Possibly an imagined sense of gentlemanly conduct. We remember these men fondly, even if some of what they did was absurd, investing the wrestling, the speedway and the ITV Seven with equal and unswerving gravitas.'

But then the whole business of television presenting is pretty absurd. Someone once defined the male TV presenter as any man who looks like he spends more than half an hour a day doing his hair. But who would not become vain with the treatment presenters get?

In the interests of full disclosure, I ought to mention the show I did in the early 1980s, a short-lived series at Yorkshire TV, *Living It Up*, which mercifully appears to have disappeared – even from cyberspace (thank you, God) – when I was given my own dressing room, a dresser who ironed all my shirts and jackets, unfeasibly big taxis to and from the studio, and a good twenty minutes being beautified (within reason, and all that) in the make-up chair.

There is usually a good spread in the green room, too: tea, coffee, upmarket sandwiches, the very best Hobnobs, and booze for afterwards. I was once on a comedy show when all this was laid on, and one of Britain's best-known comedians, who trades on his working-class origins, spurned everything and insisted a production assistant went out in the rain to find him some sushi. Is it any wonder presenters become self-important, occasionally self-deluded, oafs when all the trappings conspire to remind them just how important they are? It is why their ilk are such good subjects for satire – Hank in the *Larry Sanders Show*,

Ted Baxter in the *Mary Tyler Moore Show*, and Alan Partridge in *Knowing Me, Knowing You*.

Television is an unforgiving medium – believe me, I know – and the best presenters are quick-thinking and quick-witted as you must be on live TV. But the harder trick is to convince us, despite the limo to the studio, and the organically grown alfalfa sprout salad delivered to you by a team of Filipino handmaidens, that you care more about the material than about yourself.

Some do this, by achieving a kind of self-effacement like Des Lynam, some like Coleman work hard at it – not to say Des didn't work hard at being casual – bringing us the information we want without frills, and others like Gary Lineker just know that whatever happens on TV will never be as important as being England's second-highest goalscorer.

FIFTEEN

THE BAZZA V. MOTTY WAR!

Extensive research – I asked at least six close friends – reveals that it is common practice when playing street or back garden football as a youngster to commentate on your own actions in the style of the TV voices of the day, subtly inserting one's own name in amongst contemporary stars, as in: 'Law, Charlton, Best … lovely ball through to Kelner … and it's there … what a goal … the goalkeeper didn't stand a chance.'

I used to do this all the time. I remember particularly playing football with my brother in the living room in the 1970s, when I had adopted the practice of screaming, 'Oh yes! Ooooh yes, for the youngster!' every time I knocked one past him against the French windows. I stuck with the mantra until well into my forties, partly for the ironic humour, but also, I like to think, as a tribute to the sports commentator's art. It was not just the words either; I had the intonation and everything. The commentary had been burned into my memory by Barry Davies, on the BBC's *Match of The Day* on the evening of Saturday 9 March 1974, when twenty-one-year-old Joe Waters scored with a spectacular long-range shot in a quarter-final FA Cup tie for Leicester City.

It is possible that Davies used the 'youngster' line merely to buy himself a few seconds to check up on exactly who this nobody was who had just smashed the ball into the roof of the net from outside the penalty area.

Like a goalkeeper, a broadcaster can quite easily be taken by surprise by a sudden strike like Joe's. Whatever the circumstances, they were absolutely *les mots justes*. I think Davies knew what he was doing. His commentaries always were informed by a journalist's instincts; he would have recognised he was on to a big story, and be playing it for all it was worth.

Waters, you see, was a last-minute choice for the tie against Queens Park Rangers, only making the team after the late withdrawal of their star attacking midfielder, Alan Birchenall. Up until then, all his football, since leaving his Limerick home to sign for Leicester as a sixteen-year-old, had been played in the junior and reserve teams. 'Oh, he'll remember that all his life,' continued Davies. 'What a way to start your career in big-time football.' Davies couldn't have predicted that not only would Joe remember it all his life but that I would too. Noël Coward once remarked astutely on the potency of cheap music, on which I would not take issue, but failed to add that for some of us there are moments of sports commentary that are every bit as potent.

Quite a few of those moments can be credited to Davies, the most famous of which he uses for the title of his autobiography, *Interesting, Very Interesting*. On 29 December 1974 (clearly something of an *annus mirabilis* for Davies), Francis Lee, a combative attacking midfielder with a low centre of gravity and a deceptively cherubic face, returned to Manchester City with his new club Derby County. Lee's transfer from City in August of that year had been acrimonious, and as football-speak has it, he had a point to prove.

With the match level at 1–1 in the second half, Lee cut in from the left wing, darting between two defenders. 'Interesting,' said Davies, at which point the shot came in from the edge of the penalty area; 'VERY interesting,' he shouted as the ball hit the back of the net. As the camera followed a joyous Lee in celebration, Davies built on the story. 'Oh, look at his face,' he shouted, 'Just look at his face,' with his voice rising an octave on the 'face'.

Barry Davies is a key figure in the history of sports commentary on TV, bridging the gap between what I like to think of as gentlemen-commentators like Kenneth Wolstenholme and Peter West, and the hard-nosed professionals, who look to stamp their personality on a match with opinions, statistics, and in some cases carefully scripted ad-libs.

I first heard Davies in 1968 commentating on matches in the north-west on ITV's Sunday afternoon highlights show, where he seemed a little racier to me than chaps on the BBC like Wolstenholme and Alan Weeks, but he later acquired a reputation for being pedantic and somewhat schoolmasterly. I once wrote a piece imagining him sitting on a train, doing the *Telegraph* crossword, and tutting at some youth whose personal music player was switched up too high.

Nicolas Sellens reckoned Davies's 'Interesting, very interesting' thing was a conscious technique he had developed during his days at Granada, at the fag-end of the era before action replays, when commentators needed to give themselves a little time to interpret what was on-screen. 'He hangs onto a word or phrase in the hope that something "interesting" happens by the time his lungs finally empty of breath,' said Sellens. 'A standard Gary Lineker effort, whereby the striker would burst through on goal, trip on the edge of the box, stumble towards the penalty spot, knee the ball over the line from two feet, and then throw himself into the back of the net ...' [harsh, I think, Nicolas] ' ... would draw the typical accompaniment, "Linekaaaaaaaa ... SCORES". A variation on this theme is the familiar "tries to curl it ... AND DOES" device.'

Davies's finest moment, in my view, came in the 1986 World Cup quarter-final when England played Argentina and Diego Maradona used his 'Hand of God' to flip the ball over England goalie Peter Shilton. Minutes later, Maradona followed up with something totally different, voted in some polls as the greatest World Cup goal ever. It came after a mazy run, greeted by Davies as follows: 'Maradona, wonderful skill. He has Burrachaga to his left, and Valdano to his left. He doesn't need them. He doesn't need any of them ...' Then the pause, the goal, and, from Davies: 'You have to say that's magnificent. There can be no dispute about that one: that was pure football genius.' As someone on the website dangerhere.com, which studies this kind of stuff, has noted, 'Davies realised it was an expression of low-key wonder rather than boyish excitement that was needed when Diego scored the greatest ever goal.' Just so.

Davies recorded in his autobiography his feeling of relief when he listened back to his original commentary: 'Somebody quoted me as saying "sheer football genius", but I was glad when I checked, that I'd said "pure", for it was the right word to contrast with what had happened a few minutes earlier.'

Good for him. Of all commentators he is the one you would expect to worry about finding *le mot juste* – and, if necessary, checking *Larousse* for the correct pronunciation of *le mot juste* – but as the 1980s became the 1990s this punctiliousness began to grate on some viewers. And by the twenty-first century, the schoolmaster had become a rather ratty one. When Italy bowed out of the 2002 World Cup to South Korea after trying to defend a one-goal lead, Davies said, 'The Italians have only themselves to blame, because they WILL not learn.'

The boys at dangerhere.com thought it all went wrong after 1986. 'Much like Maradona himself, it was largely downhill. His flirtations with lawn tennis, ice dancing, and the Boat Race had always been suspect. And gradually, Bazza's commentaries became two-parts pompous hectoring of cheats and miscreants, one-part look-at-me posturing over every foreign pronunciation [notably Manchester United's Norwegian striker, Ole Gunnar *Sol-shire-a*, as Bazza pronounced it] and three-parts gentleman-at-leisure disinterest in the trivial ball game he has to endure.'

That said – and I feel they overstate it a little – in a list of the top fifty memorable commentary moments in *The Times*, Davies had three entries, while his chief rival at the BBC over the past thirty-odd years, John Motson, had none. The battle between Davies and Motson to be top dog in the BBC football commentary box had echoes of the Wolstenholme–Coleman clash of a previous era, with no significant casualty this time, but with equal bitterness from time to time, what Freud (Sigmund, not Clement) called 'the vanity of small differences'. The rivalry was undoubtedly stoked by a press more alive to public interest in sports broadcasting, thanks to Clive James and those who followed.

Until maybe the late 1990s the FA Cup final was the first prize in an English football commentator's life. It says much about the central role live football plays in sports broadcasting in Britain – and in TV generally – that wherever we have tried to go with this modest history, we have invariably found ourselves dragged back to Wembley on a day in May, and the FAmous Cup, as ITV dubbed it when they won the rights. From 1953 and the Matthews Final, through Bert Trautmann's broken neck playing for Manchester City in 1956, and the heartbreak for Manchester United in the 1950s, to the Crazy Gang beating the Culture Club when Wimbledon beat Liverpool in 1988, the FA Cup has been the ultimate prize for fans – certainly until recently – and even more so for the wielders of the BBC lip mike.

The fact that the battle for this holy grail between Barry Davies and John Motson captured the public imagination says everything you need to know about the national obsession with football and with television, and therefore especially for football *on* television. 'You were either a Davies man, or a Motson man,' says the sports agent Jon Holmes. 'The average football fan in the street was always with Motty rather than Davies, I think. Barry Davies appeals more to the Home Counties audience. He gave you the impression he really didn't like footballers very much, that he would rather be at a cocktail party. Motty had the passion.'

This seems a little unfair on Davies, but Motson does happen to be one of Holmes's clients. And, as Nicolas Sellens points out, 'In between the clever plays on words, Davies punctuated his commentaries with the gasps, whoops, and screeches of the seasoned terrace-dweller. It was a contradictory style that appeared to be caught in a limbo between erudition and populism.' The battle came to a head in the mid-1990s, but according to both men's autobiographies, it went on for decades. Its first major eruption came when David Coleman threw one of his wobblies, threatened to sue the BBC and opted out of the 1977 FA Cup final between Liverpool and Manchester United.

Davies, the more experienced man, and Coleman's number two on *Match of the Day*, was expected to get the nod, not least by Motty.

He describes in his book his first conversation with his rival-to-be after switching from radio to TV in 1971: '"I hear you are coming to join us," said Barry.' I somehow picture Davies saying these words very slowly and pointedly, possibly while stroking a white cat.

'He made some telling points about the differences between television and radio,' said Motty. 'He had done a few months' work experience in Radio Two prior to getting his break in TV. He struck me as confident in his ability and quite ambitious to compete for the top games with David Coleman.' When *Match of the Day* editor Sam Leitch chose Motson for the 1977 final, he went on, 'Barry made no attempt to hide his disappointment. To be honest he was pretty devastated, and I could understand why. He, like many others, had seen himself as the natural replacement – successor even – to David Coleman. It didn't take long for the newspapers to spot a story. One of them solemnly reported that Barry would be going on holiday, "unheard of for a commentator during the season."'

Davies's autobiography does not dispute Motson's account: 'The minor soap opera, which frequently took the attention of the television critics, lasted for a quarter of a century, ending with the European Championships in Portugal in 2004, when the fact that I was not invited to commentate on a single one of England's matches, not even recorded, made my position absolutely clear.

'It began in April 1977 with newspaper headlines proclaiming: "Davies Does Not Get the Cup Final". The negative is significant. With David Coleman declining the new contract he'd been offered, it had been expected that I'd deputise. What the newspapers didn't know was that a month before the announcement Sam Leitch had told me that the final was mine and that a statement would be made in due course. Nothing more was said between us. The announcement came as a bolt from the blue. I sent a letter of resignation, not because Motty had been given the final but because of the way I had been treated. I was sent for by Cliff Morgan, Head of Outside Broadcasts and Events, who did his best to placate me while making it clear that the BBC would hold me to my contract. The following Sunday, David Hunn wrote an article in the *Observer* quoting Morgan berating commentators who came to him to whine, and how they should appreciate their privileged position, which was the envy of many.' Which, I must say, seems entirely reasonable from where I am sitting.

Davies went on: 'I protested that it was Morgan who'd asked to see me, but I achieved nothing; and Alan Hart, Head of Sport, put out the BBC spin that in giving John the Wembley final and me the European Cup final we'd been treated fairly and equally. Much as I enjoyed the evening in Rome on the Wednesday following, the FA Cup final then stood above everything else in the British game. The die had been cast.'

Motty's turn to be angry and bitter came in 1994, when after a run of sixteen FA Cup finals and three World Cups, he got a telephone call during the World Cup in the United States telling him that Barry Davies was the choice for the final. 'The word soon went round that I had lost the final,' writes Motty. 'It had taken the BBC such a long time to make the decision that many people believed it would be a defining one. "Motson – That's Your Lot Son", trumpeted one tabloid headline.' Messages of sympathy poured in for Motty from friends back home, and there was support, he reported, from other members of the BBC team at the tournament, such as Des Lynam and Tony Gubba.

Des, Tony, and Motty had bonded at the start of the tournament in Dallas, when all three, he said in the book, 'turned tourists and visited the Texas School Book Depository on Dealey Plaza from where Lee Harvey Oswald shot John F. Kennedy in 1963.' (If you are still undecided about the Kennedy assassination, ignoring the powerful body of evidence that Lee Harvey Oswald acted alone in favour of one of the many conspiracy theories, maybe the fact that Motty seems to be supporting the lone-assassin reading of the outrage will help make up your mind.)

'I'll always remember Tony, who is quite useful with a rifle, expressing amazement when he looked down from the window of the room where Oswald had stood,' writes Motty. '"Bloody hell, I could have shot him from here," exclaimed Tony. He, like the rest of us, had always believed that Oswald had had to set his sights over a much greater distance.' There is something deliciously Alan Partridge about John Motson giving us his take on the Kennedy assassination. It is the kind of thing we love him for.*

The sports writer Will Buckley claims to be responsible for reinventing Motty as a vaguely comic figure. 'In the early 1990s I was ideas man at the lads' mag *Maxim*, which was an absurd magazine open to all sorts of nonsense, so I suggested Motty as our agony uncle, helping people with their personal problems,' Will told me. 'Over a three or four bottles of Chardonnay lunch on the magazine, he took the job. From that moment on, he stopped taking himself too seriously, at a time when sports coverage was becoming less reverential. The post-modern Motty was an idea that had found its time.'

But which post-modern ironist knew that Tony Gubba was a marksman? Gubba was one of those anonymous sports broadcasters, never more than fourth, fifth, or sixth banana in the roster, who would step in and do a job when needed without making a hash of it, but without any producer grabbing him by both arms, and saying, 'You went out there a kid, but you're coming back a star.' 'Tony Gubba's place in the pantheon is clear,' concluded the magazine *When Saturday Comes*. 'He is the BBC's supply teacher figure – versatile, available, and not particularly heeded.' Not a big beast of the jungle like Motty and Davies, who both insisted in their autobiographies that there was nothing personal in their rivalry.

Buckley, however, tells a slightly different story, 'When Motty lost one of those cup finals to Barry Davies in the 1990s, he took the sport-on-TV writers out to lunch at a restaurant in the City of London. A lot of wine was drunk – and Motty was clearly on some kind of charm offensive. He was very upset about losing the cup final, and while it might be overstating it to say he was briefing against Davies, he certainly was not

---

* Partridge was the fictional sports reporter created by comedian Steve Coogan, originally for the radio show *On the Hour*, who would pepper his reports with irrelevant detail, delivered without a trace of irony.

discouraging the anti-Davies lobby. It may be one of the first examples of a sports broadcaster using the media for his own ends.

'As I recall,' Buckley went on, 'it went on till about five in the afternoon. Motty had invited journalists thought to be sympathetic to the Motty cause. Because I had written a few things about him he had liked, I was thought to be in the Motty camp. It was a strange lunch all round, reminding me of a 1950s movie, where a bunch of chaps gather together to plan a bank heist.'

The more you read about broadcasters feuding, the scores settled between paperback covers, inter-network tugs-of-love, and the massive importance attached to the glittering prizes handed out on awards nights, the more you realise why other bits of TV stations and newspapers often refer to Sport as 'the toy department'. There is definitely a touch of the playground about some of the characters in our story – a playground with massive egos.

Which explains why my own stuff in the *Guardian* about sport on TV has occasionally provoked what feels to me like disproportionate anger from some of the *dramatis personae*. The main aim of my weekly column is to provoke a little mild amusement. My credo I take from my brother, a fine newspaper editor, who once advised, 'Get a joke in the intro, and then run like fuck for the end', advice he had acquired from the former sports editor of the *Observer*, Peter Corrigan. Which is what I do, and why I am surprised when broadcasters take offence.

TV clearly invests people with a monstrous sense of self-importance – all those attractive youngsters hoping for a permanent place in the gilded palace, running round with clipboards and getting you coffee (or sushi), and then the sitting down in a chair with a bib on, being made up. So the battle to be king of the castle, between Wolstenholme and Coleman, and later Motty and Davies, is entirely understandable. 'It is ridiculous that anyone could become exercised by a split between two commentators, but you could almost define yourself at one time by whether you were in the Motty camp or the Davies camp,' said Buckley, in an echo of Jon Holmes's recollection.

It has never gone away. As recently as 2008 Rob Smyth posted a piece on the *Guardian* website, comparing the Davies v. Motson question with other great conundrums of our time: Blur or Oasis? PCs or Macs? Pepsi or Coke? and so on. It provoked more than 200 comments. Smyth places one foot at least in the Davies camp, though he accepted that his sermonising and obvious middle-classness could be irksome. 'Yet Davies's background has nothing to do with anything,' Smyth went on. 'He "felt" football as acutely as anyone, and many found his sporadic crankiness an integral part of his overall charm, like an endearing, eccentric uncle predisposed to unprompted expressions of contempt for modern society from behind an impenetrable fug of pipe smoke.

'This is not to criticise Motson,' Smyth insisted, 'who for most of his career was a superb broadcaster. But Davies simply had more going for him. Davies wore baldness with a roguish majesty; Motson wore a sheepskin. Davies had a wonderfully expressive, almost operatic voice; Motson spoke like someone whose mouth had been invaded by Chewits. Davies focused on detail, narrative and character; Motson often commentated by numbers in more than one sense. Davies was chic, Motson a geek. Davies, like Richie Benaud, spoke little and often; Motson spoke lots and often. Davies, you imagined, had a dictionary by his side; Motson probably had a Rothmans.' (Not a cigarette, you understand, but the sponsored yearbook of football statistics.) The comments on Rob's piece were more or less evenly split. The results are in; the nation remains divided.

Interesting to note, though, that it is Davies's middle-classness on which he is constantly marked down, a fate also suffered by another of the BBC's veterans, Peter Alliss. The classless society former prime minister John Major spoke about clearly never reached the Voice of Golf. The journalist Matthew Norman dubbed Alliss 'suburban' (about as damning a criticism as you can get from the metropolitan chattering classes), and placed him at the top of a list of sporting irritants. And there is a substantial body of opinion that goes along with Norman.

During his commentary on the 2011 Open, Alliss mentioned he would be eating a Dickinson and Morris Melton Mowbray pork pie at lunch, and I wrote what I fancied was a light-hearted piece about the old-fashioned English salad that might accompany it – floppy lettuce leaves, a sliced hard-boiled egg, Colman's mustard made from powder, that kind of thing.

Predictably, salad-related issues were ignored by those commenting on my piece on the *Guardian* message board. Instead, argument raged over whether the BBC's chief golf commentator is a middle-class golf-club bore, 'the editorial column of the *Daily Mail* given legs and voice', as Norman puts it, or a national treasure, and on this issue, once again the Kingdom was shown to be less than united. I was even accused of being some kind of quisling for writing affectionately about Alliss. To me, though, he is both insufferably Home Counties, and the indisputable Voice of Golf. I feel about the sport the way Thomas Beecham reckoned the British felt about music: 'I don't understand it, but I love the noise it makes' – and for me Alliss is that noise. As for the great Motson–Davies battle, I am calling it a score draw.

SIXTEEN

IT'S ALL GONE WEST

The schism – for it is nothing less – between Motty and Bazza devotees seems a peculiarly British obsession, like *The Archers* or the correct pronunciation of the word 'scone'. Is it any wonder we sometimes cast longing glances westwards from our tight little island to the wide open spaces across the Atlantic, and sideline sport in favour of sports.

I have never had hoop dreams – to quote the title of a fine basketball documentary – myself, nor baseball diamond or gridiron dreams come to that, but share the British reverence for aspects of American culture: Clint Eastwood, Sinatra, inch-high sandwiches, and their comedy, especially Woody Allen, through whom I developed a latter-day interest in American sports.

My love of Allen goes right back to his stand-up days, when I tried every shop in Manchester before finding his LP, which included a routine about how he prolongs his love-making by thinking of baseball players, whom he named, and I later discovered to be from the New York Yankees, his team. A scene in *Annie Hall* also reflects Allen's love of sport. Woody sneaks away from a dinner party to watch the New York Knicks on TV. 'What's so fascinating about sitting around watching a bunch of pituitary cases stuff a ball through a hoop?' asks his wife. 'What's fascinating is that it's physical,' is the response, which I felt acted as a kind of get-out clause for all those of us who sometimes spurn worthy discussion – the guests downstairs are chewing over modes of alienation – in favour of sport on TV.

In his 1971 film *Bananas*, meanwhile, there were references to ABC's *Wide World of Sports*, and a guest spot from the show's biggest name. The Woody character gets caught up in a revolution in Latin America, and from time to time, a slow-talking sports reporter pops up to comment on the action and seek interviews. Who, I wondered, was this exotic blazered creature, with a line in insensitive questions, and a toupee resembling a small mammal on his head, always there with his microphone, even for Woody's wedding night? ('I have never seen action like this. That's it! It's over! It's ... all ... over! The marriage has been consummated!')

I later discovered it was Howard Cosell, of *Wide World of Sports*, and *Monday Night Football*, as uniquely American as Sinatra, but minus the universal love. In fact, he was widely reviled, as opinionated commentators on sport often are. The nearest we have had in this country was Jimmy Hill, whose stint on *Match of the Day*, and later on Sky's *Sunday Supplement*, allowed him space for the occasional rant; but would he ever ask a sportsman a question like the one Cosell put to British heavyweight Brian London before a title fight against Muhammad Ali in 1966? 'Brian, they say you're a pug, a patsy, a dirty fighter, that you have no class, that you're in there for the ride and a fast payday, and that you have no chance against Ali. Now, what do you say to that?'

ABC's Head of Sport, Roone Arledge, who brought Cosell to the network, described in his memoir the day he signed him in 1965, in defiance of his superiors who thought Cosell too loud, too pushy, too New York. 'All the things that make him Howard,' wrote Arledge. He added that when he told Cosell he was giving him a chance, the pushy New Yorker replied, 'Roone, we are today witnessing an occurrence on the scale of Milo T. Farnsworth's invention of the cathode ray tube: you are to be congratulated, young man, on your sagacity.'

Actually, that 'young man' brings to mind another home-grown figure similarly unburdened by self-doubt, Brian Clough, but unlike his US counterpart, he was part of the game he was pontificating on. When Arledge introduced Cosell to *Monday Night Football*, he used him as a gadfly alongside a pair of experts who looked after the moves, increasing commentary box occupancy from two to three. He also doubled the number of cameras, and introduced action replays.

Arledge's description of the coverage goes some way to explaining why the sport became so popular in Britain in the 1980s when Channel 4 showed it: 'those dazzling unforgettable images I'd always imagined, the helmets gleaming, the colours of the uniforms magically bright against the bright green carpet of the turf, and the cheerleaders, the fans roaring …'

Until Channel 4 came on the air in 1982, the only American football on British TV had been two or three minutes of highlights of the Superbowl in amongst the cliff diving and snooker trick shots on *World of Sport*'s international sports special. The first ever American football game to be shown live and in full on British TV was Superbowl XVII, Washington Redskins v. Miami Dolphins, in January 1983. It was brought to Channel 4 by its first commissioning editor for sport, former Olympic silver medallist Adrian Metcalfe, whose other great coup was to bring the Tour de France to the network. Both helped not only establish in Britain sports that were previously considered alien, but also ensured the values of Channel 4 were not abandoned in the toy department.

Yes, a television station with values. Ironic, is it not, that the organisation that did more than any other to popularise a great American pastime should be set up in such a typically Limey way? Though it was a commercial channel, a large measure of its funding came from its competitors – American readers gasp in disbelief – via a levy on ITV's advertising income. In return, it had to encourage 'pluralism', and provide 'a favoured place for the untried', and the 'new and experimental in television'. Unlike other broadcasters, it did not make its own programmes, but commissioned them from independent producers, many of whom promptly switched their focus from game shows and lame-brained comedy to anything that reeked of public service.

The presenter Tina Baker told me the story of how she went for a screen test to host a 'feisty, feminist' magazine show, *Watch the Woman* for Channel 4, and was told her test was excellent, but that the company was really looking for someone disadvantaged, possibly disabled, to present the show. 'I'm from Coalville,' replied Tina, 'how disadvantaged do you want?' Paul Gascoigne, I suppose, would count as disadvantaged when he went to play for Lazio in Italy in 1992, with his well-advertised mental health issues, and the effects of his self-destructive tackle on Nottingham Forest's Gary Charles in the 1991 FA Cup final. And he was indirectly responsible for one of Channel 4's most successful forays into sport, *Football Italia*.

'I would say that Channel 4 changed the face of football in the UK,' says Metcalfe's successor, Mike Miller, commissioning editor for sport from 1989 to 1998. 'We put foreign football on terrestrial TV in Britain for the first time. This was when satellite television was just beginning, not mainstream like it is now. It was Gazza going over there to play for Lazio that inspired it. A chap called Neil Duncanson from Chrysalis came to me and proposed a programme following Gazza around and maybe showing his first game. I said I'd rather show the first year, the whole experience, so he went and bought the rights for it. We showed all the top games, and I think it changed people's view of what foreign football was. I think it opened the way for the influx of foreign players here.'

Football Italia was an instant success. With Sky TV having snatched top-flight English football, the only live action terrestrial viewers had left was ITV's piecemeal coverage of the old Second Division, so the programme was pushing at an open door. Grimsby or the San Siro? No contest. Three million of us watched the first match, a 3–3 draw between Sampdoria and Lazio. Before that, there had never been a huge appetite for Italian football in Britain. The popular perception was that it was all about solid defence, and in attack, a bunch of jessies falling over. Like espresso coffee, fine for foreigners but not for us. *Football Italia* changed these attitudes, and incidentally made a minor star of James Richardson.

Richardson was to be found on Channel 4 on a Saturday morning in Rome's Piazza Della Rotunda, sipping the previously unfancied espresso, translating chunks of *La Gazzetta dello Sport* for us, while looking back at the previous week's action in *Serie A*, and ahead to the live Sunday afternoon fixture. He was relaxed, knowledgeable, and prepared to see the funny side of the whole business. As the *Guardian* journalist Sean Ingle wrote when Channel 4 gave up Italian football in 2002, Richardson 'should by rights be a well-cultivated moustache away from being the next Des Lynam'.

That did not exactly happen, but the 1990s were great days for Richardson and *Football Italia*. We may have started watching to follow the progress of homegrown favourites like Paul Gascoigne, Des Walker, and Paul Ince, but we stayed for a fascinating *scudetto*, and learnt to respect its characters, some of who went on to play leading roles in our own football.

In his quest for the 'untried', Miller commissioned minority sports like kabaddi – a kind of South Asian version of the playground game British bulldog. There was also Sumo wrestling, and Eskimo Olympics, a variety of disciplines that seem designed with sado-masochists in mind – stressing endurance to pain alongside athleticism – but a key element of Eskimo culture. 'When you're out ice-floe hunting and you cut your finger you have got to patch it up somehow and carry on, never mind the pain, and that is where these sports derive from,' says Miller. He also televised without irony – well, not much anyway – table football ... the Subbuteo World Cup, normally no more than a 'finally' item on the news.

Metcalfe and Miller's commissioning of sports previously ignored even in *World of Sport*'s most desperate moments helped convince sceptics at the channel that sport was one way in which the culture of a country is manifested, and that the channel could fulfil its obligations by covering it in a slightly different way than other broadcasters.

Derek Brandon, an executive at Cheerleader, the company that produced the American football programme through the 1980s and '90s, told the *Observer* they took their lead from US TV, 'they make it fun, they make it stylish and they make it a family occasion. These are the things that we've lost from British sport. If LWT (London Weekend Television) had done American football, they'd have been back to the presenter in the blazer with the glass of water.' Gary Imlach, presenter for nine years, told me the entire production team went to live in America for the season – unthinkable in today's economic climate – getting under the skin of the sport and its culture to an extent unprecedented in British TV.

At the time, it felt like a revolution. The British audience was wearying of football, a game whose reputation was being shredded by violence and tragedy off the field and tedium on it. They were searching desperately for an alternative. But the counter-revolution was just round the corner. And it would not be led by a channel with a public service mandate and a social conscience.

SEVENTEEN

SKY-IFICATION, THAT'S THE NAME OF THE GAME

One day in the late 1980s I picked up a message, asking me to telephone someone at British Aerospace urgently, which came as something of a surprise as I had previously, as a pinko liberal *Guardian* reader, no contact with their industry, which I believe is defence systems (defence being a euphemism for attack). Turned out this call was the beginning of my short-lived career in satellite television.

The company had bought one of Britain's six Specialised Satellite Service Operator (SSSO) licences, granted in 1988, and planned to use its satellite expertise to broadcast sport rather than bomb the bejesus out of people (disclaimer: I have no idea that this is what they do exactly, just guessing). For a fee of £3,000 a year, pubs and clubs could sign up for British Aerospace's service, Sportscast, for which they would get a feed of sporting action not available anywhere else.

There was, however, a good reason this sport was not available elsewhere. It was not exactly what you would call premium content, consisting mostly of second division rugby league and young pugilists no one had heard of, scrapping away at places like York Hall, Bethnal Green.

In many ways, this was reminiscent of the pioneering days of ITV when crews used to go out and cover schools' sports days and nondescript county cricket just to fulfil their licence obligations. Surprisingly, though, there was a flicker of interest in the service, and a few hundred venues signed up, mostly around the North of England for the rugby league, and in East London for the boxing.

So, for the year or so that the venture lasted I would turn up at places like Whitehaven, Dewsbury, and Barrow – memory plays tricks, but it always seemed to be a wet Monday night – and co-commentate rather badly alongside Keith Macklin, who was very good. At the time there was not even that much interest in *first* division rugby league, so the second tier – where there still endured the proud tradition of front-row forwards built on the lines of Fatty Arbuckle, but without the grace – was not a natural audience winner.

My brother tells me he once went to a pub called The Ring in Black-friars where they had the service, obviously for the boxing, begged them to switch it on for a rugby league match, and sat on his own watching it, while avoiding eye contact with any of the regulars. 'Was I commentating?' I asked him. 'Don't be stupid,' he said, 'If I'd asked them to switch the sound on, there would have been a riot.'

Conscious that maybe its subscriber pubs needed something more for its three grand, Sportscast started doing pub quizzes, some of which I also presented. We went to Sportscast venues all over the country to present these events, which were shown live in all the other Sportscast pubs. I cannot for the life of me believe anyone watched them, but I racked up lots of money in expenses. I remember once going up to Whitehaven for a rugby match, then driving to Plymouth for a quiz, and then back up to Edinburgh for another quiz.

It was nonsense, and not at all cheap once they had booked all of us into hotels, fed us, paid us, and kept our cars running. Maybe it was a tax loss but, as suddenly as it started, British Aerospace pulled the plug on the venture. I learned a few lessons from this forgotten footnote in broadcasting history, namely that commentating on live sport is quite difficult, that I am not awfully good at it, and that Britain at that time was not the most fertile ground for the growth of satellite TV.

Tellingly, a piece in the *New York Times* in 1989, welcoming BAe's venture, made just that point: 'If it proves a success, the company will start looking for other opportunities of the same sort,' according to the paper, 'there should be lots. In America, broadcasting deregulation has allowed special interest group television – narrowcasting – to flourish. Forthcoming launches for lucky Americans include a cowboy channel (all Westerns) and a chiller channel (all sci-fi). Stuffy regulation stops the same thing from happening in Britain.'

Quite. It was several years before that sort of narrowcasting took hold here. As we have learned in the course of this history, every new broadcasting development in the UK is treated with fear and suspicion. Before long, the great and the good get hold of it and start regulating, fitting it into the straitjacket of redeeming social importance. If we are lucky, an Australian or two, or an American, will come along, let it loose, and get the thing going properly. And so it was with satellite television.

We were undeniably sniffy about it. You may remember the joke going round in the early 1990s: What's grey and hangs off the end of a Sky dish? Answer: A council house. That was a joke that said more about us, and our class-consciousness than it did about the Sky dish which, through a combination of good fortune and business acumen, has gone from being a membership card of the lumpenproletariat, to an essential piece of kit for sports fans, whatever social group we think we belong to.

This could not have been achieved without management that could hold its nerve during some shaky times. It helped that the two chaps driving the business forward, Rupert Murdoch and Sam Chisholm, were spiky, hard-nosed Antipodeans who cared less than two hoots about the British class system.

Sky launched in Britain in February 1989, and merged with its struggling satellite rival BSB in April 1990 to become BSkyB, and it is easy to see where the jokes stemmed from. Occasionally, I stayed at friends' houses, or hotels with a dish – I was not an early adopter – and found little to watch apart from some skiing on Eurosport, and German soft porn on RTL late at night, mostly films of large-breasted blonde girls

211

being chased around Alpine ski-lodges by chubby moustachioed Teutons. There were rumours that slightly more outré pornography was available by re-positioning your dish, but I always find it difficult to explain myself when friends find me climbing all over their roof.

Like much of the rest of Britain, the Kelner family had what I believe the newspapers like to call a wait-and-see policy on subscribing. My wife feared fixing a dish to the side of the house would lower the value of the property, cause us to be shunned by friends, and maybe microwave our brains, to say nothing of reinforcing my fetish for Alpine porn.

And most people in Leeds where I lived seemed to take a similar view to mine – about Sky dishes, not the girls in the ski lodges. Another popular joke at the time asked: what's the difference between the Loch Ness monster and Sky TV? Answer: some people have *seen* the Loch Ness monster.

Actually, Leeds was unusual in that alongside the very few Sky dishes, you also saw a couple of squarials, the less obtrusive, more tasteful, but largely useless square-shaped dishes favoured by Sky's rival, BSB. This was because BSB had bought the rights to rugby league, a contract taken over by Sky on the merger, and currently the longest-running sports rights deal held by the network.

Nick Hunter left the BBC to be Head of Sport at BSB, the worst year of his life, he tells me. The sport was provided by Champion Sport, part of Mark McCormack's IMG group, and there was never any clear deline-ation, says Hunter, of who was responsible for what. He soon found himself with a big car and an expense account, but not much of a job, about which he is philosophical. As a man in his fifties, and a BBC lifer – he started as a studio manager, spinning the discs for the likes of Pete Murray – the chaos of BSB, he says, was not for him, 'We got on air, and that at least is an achievement I am proud of, although we were more than six months late.'

When I was a young reporter, I would occasionally interview people complaining about the local council, which they would dub 'a right Fred Karno's' – a reference to Fred Karno's Army, a music hall troupe whose joyously anarchic routines delighted Edwardian audiences. Nobody talks about anything being 'a right Fred Karno's' these days, which is a shame because the jibe fits BSB perfectly. I know nothing about satellites – I have only just come to terms with decimal currency and round tea bags – but I gather BSB went for the wrong one: where Sky hitched a lift on the Astra satellite, a cheapo European job using comparatively primitive technology, run by a company based in Luxembourg; BSB put its faith in its own British-built Marcopolo satellite, which for all I know is still orbiting the earth as a memorial to the ill-fated venture. 'A proud British satellite,' according to the journalist Matthew Engel. 'It was bespoke, state-of-the-art, technologically whizz-bang, and, of course, didn't work properly.'

I have never met anyone who watched BSB, but my friend Tony Quinn was on it. Quinn is an incorrigible practical joker widely known in north Leeds, who I first met after he had made several telephone appearances on my radio show, under a variety of false names and accents. In an idle moment one week, he changed his name to Zachary Z. Zzzzzzzpster to ensure last place in the phone book. The story made some of the more desperate tabloids, and BSB booked him to fly down to London and appear on a live Friday night chat show on which Radio One DJ Mike Smith interviewed 'interesting' people in the audience who had been in the tabloid press for some reason.

When our genial host finished his chat with the chap who said he planned to have his head cryogenically frozen in the style of Walt Disney, and moved on to Tony, there were two issues of which he was unaware. First, that the north Leeds funster had consumed all the imported Dutch lager left in the green room fridge; and secondly that the warm-up man had come out wearing an identical suit to Tony's, about which there had been much joshing. So when he quizzed our hero about his claim to fame, Tony ditched the story Smith had on his clipboard, and proudly asserted that he had invented 'a self-replicating suit' to general hilarity and the bewilderment of the host, not helped by Tony patiently explaining the suit was radiation-proof, and came with two pairs of trousers.

What it must have cost to fill an audience full of nutcases and publicity seekers on a Friday night is unknown, but stories of excess in those early days are legion. Peter Chippindale and Suzanne Franks, in their book *Dished*, reported on BSB's lavish launch party, for which £80,000 was spent on designer peppermints and which was attended by more people than actually had squarials. While Sky was based in unfashionable, economical Isleworth, BSB had the ritzy Marco Polo building in Battersea. The serial TV executive Michael Grade observed the scene in the BSB car park: 'Everyone had a BMW and a chauffeur. They were all on a gravy train, and they weren't focused at all.'

One thing BSB did do was bequeath to Sky some of its sports broadcasters, who were later to become big names on serious channels, like Andy Gray and Richard Keys on football, and the former tennis champion Sue Barker. These were among the people who saved Sky, after its own disastrous launch on the back of expensively acquired Hollywood movies, for which it had entered a damaging bidding war with BSB.

The 1990 World Cup in Italy proved to Sky what a massive audience football could reach, and with the Premier League starting in 1992, the timing was just right for them. Later acquisitions of cricket and golf were arguably even more important to Sky, because they delivered a middle-class audience (and an end to the council house jokes).

David Elstein, however, Head of Programmes at BSkyB from 1992 to 1996, says it was neither football nor movies that saved the business. 'It's a myth that football made Sky,' Elstein said. 'The major increases in subscriptions came when Sky multi-channels launched, showing things like CNN, UK Gold, and TNT, lifting the number of channels from four to seventeen.' But he agrees that the cricket rights were also vital: 'That's when Surrey found Sky.'

Mathew Horsman's book on the early satellite era, *Sky High*, tells the story of how one weekend in 1990 Sam Chisholm, the fearsome workaholic who ran Channel Nine for Kerry Packer, flew from Australia to meet Murdoch in Los Angeles, where I like to imagine the head of News International sitting in a big black chair, surrounded by a bank of screens, in his secret headquarters built into the side of a volcano. He offered Chisholm the job of Chief Executive at BSkyB.

After the meeting, Chisholm flew straight back, and was at his desk in Sydney first thing on Monday morning, fielding inquiries from his colleagues about why he 'looked a little tired'. He accepted Murdoch's job offer, and never rested from then on until stepping down in 1997, a decision that lowered Sky's share price significantly. Horsman described Chisholm as 'a Kiwi James Cagney', and told how the firebrand used to fly to New York for English bank holidays because he could not stand to see our shops shut, and people not working. Chisholm himself described his management style as 'delegating, then interfering', which his near-superhuman stamina enabled him to do. To use the modern parlance, he was constantly 'on it'.

The strength of feeling aroused by Chisholm's 'interfering' is best indicated by an interview the former *Sun* editor and Sky managing director Kelvin MacKenzie gave to the *Independent* in 2005. Chisholm, at the time, was back at work running Channel Nine in Australia, after a successful lung transplant. 'I notice that Chisholm is back and regrettably still alive,' said MacKenzie. 'He should have had a bloody head transplant – then he would have been more handsome. Put that in – it will aggravate the shit out of him.'

MacKenzie was Murdoch's appointee, having edited the *Sun* for him with no little élan. He spent just seven months as managing director of Sky in 1994, before resigning after a number of colourful spats with Chisholm. Eleven years later, and the wounds, it appeared, were still reluctant to heal. Chisholm's nickname for MacKenzie, meanwhile, was reported to be 'unfit to print in a family newspaper'. In truth, the internal politics at Sky were far more dramatic than most of the programmes.

Like most people in those early days, I tended to watch it in the pub, in my case the Rose and Crown at the top of my street. Those were the days when pubs could get Sky by paying a normal domestic subscription, and this was a typical old-fashioned local where everybody knew everybody. It was packed for matches, with banter flying back and forth, especially if Leeds United or one of the local rugby league teams was in action.

David Elstein says, 'What football did was it embedded Sky.' I guess he is referring to those days when people like me went to the pub to watch football, and became used to the style, and the ubiquity of it. One of Chisholm's many shrewd moves was to wait before piling the fees on to the pubs. Nowadays, I doubt that the Rose and Crown could afford to offer Sky, but that doesn't matter, because like most pubs of its type it has closed down.

I do hope I was not partly responsible for this because when Sky – recognising me as the kind of media-savvy opinion-former it needed on its side – installed all the tackle for me free of charge, I often avoided the pub in favour of the hearth.

Like most journalists I know, I am more or less incorruptible, so I was never 100 per cent in Sky's corner, often observing in my column that they were prone to overselling their football, pitching the tone of their coverage of a Monday night match between, say, Charlton Athletic and Leicester somewhere between the chariot race from *Ben-Hur* and the Second Coming.

A key figure in establishing the Sky Sports style was Vic Wakeling, a soft-spoken Geordie with a reputation for steeliness, who joined Sky in 1991 as Head of Football, having been sports editor of evening papers in London and Birmingham. His background meant he was a shade removed from the culture of his new colleagues, mostly TV or technology types, and also had a contacts book stuffed with names steeped in the culture of English football.

Legend has it that it was thanks to those contacts that Sky was able to snatch the rights to televise the embryonic Premier League from under the noses of ITV. One of them, Alan Sugar, chairman of Spurs at the time, wrote in his autobiography about the deal, worth £304 million over three years, a record for British sport.

As a manufacturer of satellite dishes, Sugar had a stake in Sky's success, but inside the Lancaster Hotel in May 1992, the momentum was with ITV, until Sugar allegedly disappeared to a public telephone cubicle opposite the meeting room and called Chisholm. Sugar recalls the conversation: 'ITV had somehow found out the details of BSkyB's bid and wanted to top it (they raised their bid from £205 million to £262 million). I told Sam, "There's only one way to clinch the deal – you'll have to blow them out of the water!" Little did I know this call would go down in the annals of football history as "the phone call that irrevocably altered the history of sport and media in Britain."'

'It is one thing winning the rights to the football,' Wakeling told me, 'but then you have to do it properly. We had a deliberate policy in our first season of doing it in great depth. We had a two-hour build-up to a Premier League game, behaving exactly like a bunch of chaps going to the match might. What we had that free-to-air TV did not was time, and we made the most of it.

'It did not happen by accident. We looked at sports coverage around the world: the NFL, football in Germany, rugby league in Australia. This helped us get our coverage just right. We learnt the most from Germany, where a lot of the matches were from grounds with athletics tracks around them. They made more use of low-level cameras than we did over here, because our grounds were more traditional football grounds and you couldn't get them in, so we started negotiating with football teams about finding space. They also had super slo-mo on German TV. We saw it, and said, "Christ, what is that?" so we copied them, and bought in the system.'

In that respect, Wakeling was not a million miles from Peter Dimmock, the father of TV sport, who had scoured the world almost fifty years previously to bring in developments like zoom lenses and autocue. On a more basic level, simple developments like a clock and scoreline in the corner of the screen were introduced by Sky. You could argue that they brought a pioneering spirit back to a sport-on-TV land-scape that was ossifying.

That is certainly how David Elstein sees it. 'Pre-Sky, the coverage of sport was grudging,' he said, 'If you're not paying anything for the rights why would you pay anything for the production costs? Sky, having spent all that money on the rights, decided to spend as much again on promotion and marketing.' From the start, Sky's promotions hit you between the eyes, and have influenced BBC and ITV to throw off some of their British reserve, and be a little more flamboyant in hawking their wares. They also inspired a brilliant sketch on the comedy show, *That Mitchell and Webb Look*, in which David Mitchell walks round a football ground, shouting into the camera, with fevered excitement, 'Watch the football. Every football team will be playing football several times in various combinations, and you can catch all of that football here, where we'll be showing all the football all the time. Catch all of the constantly happening football here. It's all here, and it's all football, always. Constant, dizzying, twenty-four-hour, year-long football.'

And Sky Sports made the most of their supremacy. Those low-level cameras bring us close-ups of every sliding tackle, and the low-level shot we enjoy so much, up the nose of the losing manager. We could also hear every kick, which was impossible pre-Sky. 'We decided to work on making the sound better,' Wakeling told me. 'We had directional mikes that could pick everything up. Also, around the time we started, all-seater stadiums were coming in and we were worried about losing atmosphere. We didn't, because even though we were playing in some stadiums with dead ends and dead sides as they rebuilt, we worked harder on the mikes to keep that sound level up.' (Some of you may remember the giant mural of fans on the north side of Arsenal's Highbury ground, which was later amended after complaints that the artist had neglected to include any women or black faces in his work. Some Tottenham supporters said the painting was actually livelier than the original North Bank.) Sky also put in extra camera positions, giving them the capacity to have more than twenty cameras at a big match.

With the benefit of hindsight, the football deal, which Chisholm negotiated with Mudroch's backing, seems like what Vic Wakeling calls a 'slam dunk'. But that is not how it felt at the time, even to Sky. 'It was a huge gamble,' says Wakeling, 'We had just merged with BSB, and losses were running at £11 million pounds a week. More than one news-paper said it was ruinous, and Greg Dyke over at ITV, who had lost the rights, called all his troops together and said, "Don't worry, they've paid far too much, we'll get the football back. We'll just sit here and watch them go bust."'

Whether by luck or judgement, though, everything about the foot-ball deal was right. Because Sky dishes were still far from universal, the worries sports bodies had in the 1950s that TV might keep crowds from live games were less prevalent, so far from keeping TV at a distance as in the Wolstenholme years, football behaved more like partners with Sky, pushing forward a great project.

'Sky and football found themselves in a not entirely predictable virtu-ous circle,' said Elstein. 'The money enabled the clubs to buy top players from round the world. Football became more popular again, and TV couldn't damage the crowds because the grounds were full, and anyway too few people could see the games on Sky, so the dividends put both sides on a rising curve of success.'

It was the start of a golden age for English football, if you did not object too much to England failing to make any impact in international competitions, to lavishly rewarded footballers behaving like alley cats in high-end hotels, and to paying the thick end of a hundred quid to take your son to a match. 'I think all this would have happened in any case,' said Wakeling. 'Football was ready for change. We merely accelerated the rate of change. We pushed the Premier League ahead of the opposition in Italy and Spain. Back in the early 1990s Italy was seen as the big TV market, now it's a distant third.' On the other hand, Italy and Spain have won the last two World Cups, due, at least in part, to Premier League riches crowding out young British players in favour of foreign talent.

The 1992 deal was only the start of it. To give you an idea of the kind of money sloshing round the Premier League, the *Sunday Times* quoted research in October 2010 showing income from overseas rights at £479 million a year – on top of the £2 billon a year from domestic rights – with potential further income thanks to pay-TV rivalries and the fascination for English football in the emerging economies of Asia; its nearest rival, *La Liga* in Spain, earned £132 million. Wakeling finds it difficult to see the downside of any of this, 'Look at some of the players we have been lucky enough to see. Sure, dreadful amounts of money have been wasted, but overall the game is better than ever to watch, and we are sitting now in better stadiums than we could ever have dreamed of.'

On the other hand, although it was not Sky's intention that its bounty would create a new breed of footballer earning more money, to quote 1970s pop legends Dr Hook, than a horse has hairs, living in gated communities, building up property portfolios in Abu Dhabi, taking out super-injunctions, emerging every so often at the behest of the club's PR to bestow his celebrity graciousness on some 'project to help inner-city kids'. ('This game's given me so much, I wanted to put something back.') But that is what has happened. Indirectly, he is Sky's creation, that footballer who allegedly set fire to £50 notes to show off in a night-club. It is probably urban myth, but supporters tell the story about their *own* players. That is what Sky's money has done.

With a very few exceptions, we don't love our footballers the way we used to. Sky's involvement – not just the money but also the way they cover the sport – has changed the relationship between fans and football.

David Mitchell's 'constant, dizzying, twenty-four-hour action', together with its aggressive promotion, and the need to fuel the Sky Sports News channel all day and all night long with constant sports 'news' – not news at all, but gossip and speculation – has created an atmosphere in which football takes on an importance the game, beautiful or not, may be just too fragile to handle.

The extended punditry before and after games, the constantly evolving visual aids, and the bizarre 'You're on Sky Sports' phone-in forum for the misguided, the medicated, and the just plain mad, have all contributed to an overheated climate in which a player can be on the skids after two poor matches, a manager after one and a half.

Roy Keane observed as much in an interview with the *Independent* in 2008. 'Punters are getting brainwashed by what's real and what's not real. That gets to the players sometimes,' he said. 'We're on about teams losing two games, it's "a crisis". There was a debate yesterday about Arsène Wenger on Sky. How crazy is that if you step back from it? I think I've done it once for Sky. Never again. I'd rather go to the dentist. You're sitting there with people like Richard Keys and they're trying to sell something that's not there.' Keane's point is a good one, if undermined slightly by his frequent appearances as a pundit on ITV.

Ironically, it was the overheated atmosphere around football, fostered by Sky itself, that led to the hullabaloo when the channel's two main football broadcasters, Keys and Andy Gray, were caught making sexist remarks about a female official, which ultimately led to the departure of the two chaps most identified with satellite football. And the Sky-ification of football, if I may call it that, has spilled over into radio too. At times, during the post-football phone-in frenzy on a Saturday evening, if you flip between BBC Radio Five Live and Talksport, you feel like a prisoner in the back of a taxi, even when you are driving your own car.

I would argue that back in 1957 when we saw Peter McParland put Ray Wood out of the FA Cup final, depriving the Busby Babes of the then historic league-and-cup Double, but still switched off the TV at five-to-five and got on with our lives, it was healthier for us, and healthier for football – although not financially, of course.

Alongside the 'whoosh' sound effects, the multiple camera angles, and the constant, dizzying, twenty-four-hour-ness of it all, the contribution of Sky's presentation and commentary team to the success of the enterprise should not be underestimated. Wakeling's choice of the experienced and commendably unfussy Martin Tyler, a signing from ITV, as lead commentator, was inspired. As Sky's whistles and bells sound around him, Tyler remains a calm presence. He had seen it all over more than forty years in the business, and had the benefit of learning from the master, Jimmy Hill.

Tyler's life in football began in the 1960s, as a staff writer on Marshall Cavendish's *Book of Football*, later ghost writing Jimmy Hill's column in the *News of the World*, and also covering some matches himself for

The Times. A chance meeting took him to London Weekend Television, where he took a job as editorial assistant, working on *The Big Match* and *On the Ball*. 'I was offered the job, and initially turned it down, because I wanted to continue playing football on Saturdays,' Tyler told me. 'But I discussed it with Jimmy, who had just left LWT to go to the BBC. He said it was a real opportunity, so I got on the phone and asked if the job was still going.

'I then broke what I thought was the bad news to my teammates at the Casuals, who were disappointingly relaxed about losing me.' Tyler got a chance at commentary on 28 December 1974, when Southern Television's Gerry Harrison was unavailable for a match between Southampton and Sheffield Wednesday.

'I spent the whole of Christmas being nervous,' said Tyler. 'It was my big chance and I was determined to make the most of it. Every year, even now, at Christmas time I get a little wobbly, remembering what it felt like. Fortunately for me, there was only one scorer, a red-haired Sheffield Wednesday winger called Eric Potts, who was the only ginger-haired player on the pitch, so identification wasn't a problem. The director, a chap called Steven Wade, who was not a football man at all – in fact, he normally directed things like *Sunday Night at the London Palladium* – asked if I could come back and do another match a month later, and it has been like that really ever since.'

A measure of Tyler's self-effacement is that Nicolas Sellens' comprehensive *Commentating Greats*, which covers virtually everyone who ever wielded a microphone on a sporting occasion, somehow manages to omit him. After the first ten years of the Premiership, however, Tyler was voted Commentator of the Decade both by fans and a panel of football experts.

Beside Tyler in the commentary box, since the early 1990s, was former Aston Villa, Everton, and Scotland striker, Andy Gray, whose value to Sky is best indicated by the lengths Sam Chisholm went to keep him when Gray was offered the manager's job at Everton in 1997. He spirited Gray away from his agent and the two met in Chisholm's flat in Hyde Park where, according to Mathew Horsman, 'he talked about Gray's importance as the ultimate interpreter of what was going on out on the field. Gray was very taken with this, accepted the compliments and a pay rise (though it still did not match Everton's offer) and stayed.

I blame Gray for much of the ill-informed drivelling about football that has followed in Sky's wake. Gray, of course, had the pedigree to validate his views, but it was his forcefully expressed opinions, especially on referees, that seemed to make it all right for managers to spend their post-match press conferences cavilling at decisions, with fans echoing the complaints. Gray's departure has had little effect on the practice.

His replacements, the intelligent and personable former Arsenal striker Alan Smith and the urbane Ray Wilkins don't seem to work as well with Tyler, but maybe it needs time. Gray and Tyler used to dovetail nicely, Tyler's even Home Counties tones acting as counterpoint to Gray's excitable Glaswegian.

'Whatever anybody says about Sky Sports,' says Wakeling, 'they cannot criticise us for the way we do things, the standards we set, the cameras we put in, the sound, and the commentary teams we put together: Tyler and Gray, Miles Harrison and Stuart Barnes on rugby union, Eddie Hemmings and Mike (Stevo) Stephenson on league.' Harrison and Barnes work much like Tyler and Gray, one (Harrison – an excellent commentator) keeping his head, and the other losing his. Eddie and Stevo, on the other hand, are capable of losing it both singly and severally. 'We needed fireworks,' shouted Stevo, of England's performance in the rugby league World Cup, 'but so far it has been a bit of a damp squid.'

The rugby league contract, says Wakeling, helped establish Sky in the sport's strongholds of Lancashire and Yorkshire, despite the fact that 'the rugby league community', as I suppose we have to call it, viewed Sky with the deep suspicion normally reserved for southerners or rugby union fans.

I was among them. As someone who grew up with names like Bradford Northern and Warrington, seeing them renamed the Bulls and the Wolves, complete with cheerleaders and fireworks, offended something deep inside. This was not helped by the fact that my team, Swinton, has spent most of the Sky era on life support, when sometimes it seems it would be a mercy to switch the machine off altogether. But the decline would have happened anyway, for reasons unconnected with TV. In my team's heyday, Swinton was an old-fashioned northern industrial town, built on cotton and coal, with jobs for all in factories of all sorts, in mining, and on the railways, in engineering. We reputedly had the largest concentration of chip shops per capita anywhere in Britain. Now it is one of Manchester's less salubrious suburbs with above average levels of unemployment, and drink and drug problems, and you are never more than a minute away from a doner kebab. Not the most fertile ground for a traditional northern sport.

So I bear Sky no ill will. In fairness, in recent years I have fulminated just as much about multi-screen cinemas, TV talent contests and the rise of Nando's. An age thing, I expect. And there is little doubt that the Sky deal for rugby league – £50 million over three seasons – has helped sustain a sport particularly vulnerable to economic misfortune, because of its geographical base. Because of the co-dependency of Sky and rugby league, innovations such as the video referee, miked-up officials, and top-eight play-offs have been incorporated fairly smoothly into the sport, making the BBC's coverage – the BBC still cover the Challenge Cup – seem positively stone age.

And while all this was going on – the twenty-four-hour dizziness of the football, the cricket from overseas, the sexy rugby – the BBC could do little but sit and watch (if they paid the subscription). While the Corporation's income rose by around 3 per cent per annum, the price of top sporting events was rising by 30 per cent, which was an impossible sum for an organisation depending on a licence fee, which is taxpayer's money by another name. Will Wyatt, Managing Director, Television, who we last met gripping the table at Des Lynam's departure to ITV, talked of 'retreating in good order to prepared strongholds'. As it turned out, reports of the death of BBC Sport were greatly exaggerated. What I have heard described as 'the nuclear winter of John Birt,' has passed. As this book went to press, 2012 shaped up as being a year when BBC Sport returned to its glory days – or took great barrowloads of licence payers' money and made a big bonfire out of it, depending on your point of view.

Clearly, little expense has been spared in coverage of the Olympics, with live coverage of every event on BBC1, BBC3, and on digital platforms, meaning that at times, twenty-four different programmes were being made available. In London, Glasgow, and Bradford, big screens were due to show some events in super hi-vision, reckoned to be sixteen times sharper than HD.

Roger Mosey, the former Director of Sport, left his post in 2008 to prepare for the games. He was not prepared to give me a figure on the overall cost – difficult to do at the BBC anyway, with so many different departments picking up separate tabs – but 'people expect the BBC to deliver the Olympics properly and not randomly cut costs'.

Mosey quoted the BBC Executive's consultation process DQF – or Delivering Quality First for those of you not quite as enamoured of initials – to decide how the Corporation could live within its means: £3.5 billion a year. Fewer, bigger, better, said Mosey, was the formula decided upon, which meant cuts in some fringe activities, but not when it came to big events, including sport, and especially the Olympics.

A great summer of sport, as we heard repeatedly on a series of lavishly produced trailers, but coverage eats into that £3.5 billion, so it will not be a surprise if other broadcasters nibble away at some of the BBC's rights, as Sky has already done with Formula One and golf. There may be trouble ahead, as the song goes, and one thing is for certain, it is doubtful that cricket, the sport conspicuously absent from the BBC this great summer, will be returning any time soon.

EIGHTEEN

TEN POUNDS DOWN

My dad never played French cricket on the beach with me when I was a kid. But neither did he lock me in a cupboard or subject me to Satanic abuse, so I guess I don't have much in the way of a misery memoir. But still I feel deprived.

I have been reading the book *Fatty Batter* in which the actor Michael Simkins recalls boyhood games of cricket in the park with his father, who kept a sweetshop in Brighton. At weekends, the future RADA graduate would sit with a Thermos flask, and the sandwiches his mother had made and wrapped up for him in greaseproof paper, watching county cricket and keeping score. It was the start of a lifelong passion, and the kind of idealised English childhood some of us can only dream of.

My dad was from an immigrant family – neither of his parents spoke English – and he was in a hurry to better himself and so had little patience with cricket. He tried, bless him, taking me to a Test match at Old Trafford some time in the early 1960s, but K.F. Barrington batted all day for something like eight runs. We were both bored, and decided to stick to our favoured ways of passing the time: football, rugby league and sarcasm.

Mind you, he was as keen as any immigrant parent to haul us all out of the shtetls, and he regularly passed on to me very English books to enjoy, like Frank Richards' boarding school stories – Billy Bunter and Tom Merry – and any P.G. Wodehouse he had managed to enjoy on rare breaks in his labours. But cricket remained a closed book to me until comparatively recently when I have been drawn in by the coverage first on Channel 4 and then Sky, which seems to make more concessions to cricket agnostics.

Up until 1990, the BBC had been the place for cricket, happily tootling along since 1938 when they covered the two London Tests against Australia and caught Len Hutton grinding out his world-record 364. BBC coverage was undeniably aimed more at the Michael Simkinses of this world than the Martin Kelners, remaining single-ended until Kerry Packer's World Series in 1977 pointed the way to the future.

In 1990, though, as we know, there was a change. The fledgling satellite broadcaster Sky covered England's tour of the West Indies, something hitherto untouched by the BBC. It was the first live television broadcast from abroad of an entire Test series, and to the great glee of Messrs Murdoch and Chisholm, England scored a surprise victory under Graham Gooch in the First Test in Jamaica in February, leading sports lovers to scratch their heads and seriously consider whether it was worth fixing one of those ugly Sky dishes to the side of the house.

Even before the football deal in 1992, Sky saw off the BBC to show the Cricket World Cup in Australia, and 100,000 dishes were sold in a few weeks. England reached the final and, as with those early FA Cup finals, people at least began to wonder which of their friends might have been daft enough to shell out money for this gimmick. Sky's tanks were now circling Television Centre looking for parking spaces, and in 1994 they bought the rights for home one-day internationals and county cricket, with the BBC retaining home Test matches – still, at that stage, protected by the listings regime.

Cricket, says Matthew Engel, editor of *Wisden* at the time, was beginning to fall a little bit in love with the satellite broadcaster. 'Sky took cricket seriously. It did not keep disappearing for weather forecasts and the 2.30 at Goodwood. Its production values were higher and its ideas fresher.'

But the sport did not fall immediately into the arms of Sky. In what can be seen in retrospect as a kind of halfway house deal, Channel 4 first got a slice of cricket. By 1998, the grandees of English cricket had successfully got home Test matches removed from the roster of 'listed events', which could not be taken away from free-to-air TV. There was, however, 'a gentlemen's agreement' between the England and Wales Cricket Board and the government that 'a substantial amount' of cricket would stay on free-to-air. There was nothing to stop it going to a commercial station, though, and Channel 4, sensing an opportunity where ITV feared to tread, nipped in with Sky, and cut the BBC out of cricket after sixty years.

'Some would say the BBC had got a little slack, and complacent in its coverage,' said John Perera, of the Board. 'Channel 4 came in with new ideas, new production teams, and a number of innovations: the snickometer in 1999, then Hawkeye in 2001, and all sorts of new camera angles, including a stump camera and one for run-out decisions.'

Replays of those pictures were not just for the TV, but also for the audience in the stadium watching on big screens, a prime example of how TV alters the nature of a sport even for people actually going to the game. 'All those "is-he-in? is-he-out?" debates started during Channel 4's coverage,' Perera told me. 'Those are the sort of things that have taken the game to another level. Things like the analysis of a bowler's length and line have been made available by TV, which appeals to the statistically minded follower, of which cricket has lots.'

But, notwithstanding the hugely entertaining Ashes series of 2005, which delivered excellent ratings, by 2006 Channel 4 was finding it increasingly difficult to schedule live cricket. You only have to go back to those arguments from the early days of BBC TV about clashes with Children's Hour to recognise just how problematic that can be. Like Ken Barrington at Old Trafford in 1964, or whenever it was, it just goes on too long and to its own timetable. And for Channel 4, there is the added complication of needing to make money out of advertising breaks as well. Its half-hearted bid for three more years fooled no one.

Since 2005 the only live cricket on British TV is on Sky, which Engel says is 'catastrophic' for the sport. 'I remember how my son would watch Wimbledon, and then rush off to try out his shots against the wall,' he says. 'That's the magic of sport on TV. For cricket that is no longer possible, because almost no one will seek it out on satellite unless they are already committed cricket lovers. For football, it's a different story. There is still a huge chunk of football on BBC and ITV. It is also much more deeply rooted in the community. It's still played informally in every playground and park. There are still fathers who take a bat to the beach, but there are not many kids who play with one when dad's not around.'

Mike Miller was the BBC's Head of Sport from 1998 to 2000, replacing Jonathan Martin, and admits ruefully that his position in the TV executives' pantheon will always be 'the man who lost the cricket for the BBC'. 'By the time I joined the BBC, the whole business of television sports rights had changed radically,' he told me. 'Jonathan Martin and his predecessors basically ran everything, because the BBC ran sport. He would decide how much each sport would get, and what would be shown. Yes, there was *World of Sport*, but the serious stuff was *Grandstand*, *Sportsnight with Coleman* and all that. But that was no longer the position when I took over.

'Losing the cricket was not actually my doing, but I was in the unenviable position of being at the BBC when the BBC lost it to Channel 4, and I was the one who was put up publicly to explain the reasons why.'

The reasons, says Mike, were quite simple: Channel 4 had a new boss – Michael Jackson had replaced Michael Grade and wished to make a splash – but more importantly, the channel simply outbid the BBC, and the cricket hierarchy was in the market for a change anyway. 'A lot of sports at that time thought the BBC took them for granted a bit, and wanted to give it a bit of a kick. Cricket thought the approach offered by Channel 4 might help revitalise the sport, and they did it very well.'

I suspect Miller's position at the BBC was not helped by the fact that he had arrived there from Channel 4, having been commissioning editor for sport from 1989 to 1998. There was a sense that he really ought to have known what they were up to.

As we know, Channel 4 got lucky, holding the cricket rights until the end of 2005, covering England's thrilling triumph in the Ashes series, which made heroes out of Freddie Flintoff and Michael Vaughan, and culminated in a street parade, a reception at Number Ten, and a fair degree of laddish drunkenness. By the time it hit the nation that cricket could once more be such a part of the national conversation, that controversial deal taking the exclusive rights to England's further progress, from 2006 to 2009, had gone to Sky. Cricket's successful campaign to get itself delisted had trumped the gentlemen's agreement.

The listing system, under which events deemed to be of special national interest like the Grand National, the FA Cup final and the Olympic Games, must be available on free-to-air television, is defended by the former BBC Head of Sport Jonathan Martin: 'It may have seemed anticompetitive, but it worked'. But it is fiercely attacked by David Elstein: 'Listing was invented by the BBC for the BBC. It is illogical to instruct sport to accept a bad deal. Why would the government know what is good for the sport? What duty does the sport have to the TV viewer who stays at home and contributes nothing?'

The self-induced downgrading of cricket actually passed without much comment at the time. Following the 2005 Ashes, however: the open-topped bus, the drinking, joy being unconfined and all that, cricket's Sky deal came under attack, especially from cricket-loving MPs. Though my natural position is not to defend Mammon against universal joy, I do become profoundly suspicious when politicians hitch their wagon to a sporting cause. I am old enough to remember the godfather of British spinmeisters, Harold Wilson, making maximum capital out of England's 1966 World Cup win, while more recently French prime minister Jacques Chirac implied that France's 1998 World Cup triumph said something about the state of the nation under his stewardship. 'This is a France that wins,' he commented.

Downing Street actually contacted the BBC's *Match of the Day 2* programme in March 2010, offering Gordon Brown as a guest for the show, ostensibly to talk about England's bid to host the 2018 World Cup. However, the BBC, in an uncharacteristically old-fashioned Reithian way, resisted, saying it was too close to a general election. Some of us, however, had stopped taking notice of politicians' pronouncements on sport after Tony Blair brought us to a kind of nadir in this area when he guested on the *Richard & Judy* morning TV show in 1999, appearing to support calls for the sacking of England football manager Glenn Hoddle.

In the May 2010 issue of *Spin* magazine, ECB chairman Giles Clarke said: 'It would be a disaster for English cricket if home Test matches had to be broadcast free-to-view. I've seen a few dumb cricketers saying how wonderful that would be, but they won't think like that if their salaries halve. The amount of money Sky put into the game is huge. It really is a good deal for cricket. Without the Sky money, cricket at all levels would be hit: women's cricket, disability cricket, kids' cricket and first-class cricket.'

But in the same issue, the then *Wisden* editor Scyld Berry said: 'I seriously object to the ECB propaganda, the weeping and lamentation over the prospect of the Sky contract being cancelled, the suggestion that no one will ever play cricket again, women will never play again, no one blind will ever touch a ball again.' Berry agreed that the money has benefited the amateur game, but believes role models are more important to the future of the game than new facilities and qualified coaches. 'You can always find somewhere to play cricket with a tennis ball and a piece of wood. That's the worldwide experience of the game.'

Since the pluses of the Sky deal are countable, and the objections theoretical, there has never been any question of ECB wanting to switch back. In 2010 an advisory committee, under the former BBC sports presenter and FA official David Davies, had recommended that Ashes Tests should go back on the A list. The Labour government, then in its dying days, did nothing, fearful of the election-time wrath of Rupert Murdoch, Sky's effective boss and owner of four national newspapers.

A year or so later, after the phone-hacking scandal, Murdoch's wrath would have seemed less of a threat but by then Labour was out of power and the coalition government had no interest in the subject. Early in 2011, after England had retained the Ashes, a leader in the *Guardian* echoed the Berry thesis and fulminated: 'The paywall means that cricket becomes even more the preserve of the corpulent and the corporate than it is already … England's Ashes win produces no seedcorn for the future. Meanwhile, Mr Murdoch laughs all the way to his tax-avoiding offshore bank.'

Vic Wakeling, you will not be surprised to hear, does not see it quite like that. 'It is a difficult equation for the rights holders. On top of everything else, they have to take into account their sponsors' views. Channel 4 seemed a good home for cricket, but they clearly couldn't make it work on the money they were paying.

'I know that because someone from Channel 4 phoned me and asked if we could get together and talk about Test matches being reduced to four days. I said sorry, five days is not a problem for us. But I can see it would be for a commercial channel. You sell your airtime, and suddenly it is raining, what do you do?

'Apart from us, the only place for Test cricket would be the BBC,' said Wakeling. 'But they didn't bid for it.' David Elstein is another who thinks cricket should be on the BBC, but on a different kind of BBC, 'I would like to see a premium sports channel, and digital TV makes it possible,' he told us. 'The BBC has been thinking about it for twenty years. Around 40 per cent of our leisure time is spent watching TV but only 4 per cent of the household budget is spent on it. Either the BBC changes its funding mechanism over the next five to ten years, or Sky will just become more and more powerful.'

One thing is certain. The appetite for live sport on television is showing no immediate signs of diminishing, and David Elstein is not alone in predicting a change in the way we might pay for it to appear on our screens. I discussed this with Will Buckley, who has slightly more experience in TV than I do. Only slightly, since he presented a short-lived yet fondly remembered American football-themed sports quiz show called *Quiz Bowl* on Channel 4 in 1991, contested by teams of sports journalists – the channel favouring the disadvantaged and oddball once more – who gained yardage for correctly answered questions. The point is neither Will nor I know one-tenth as much about television as Elstein, yet feel confident in predicting a slightly different future for sport on TV than he does.

From the 1970s to roughly the end of the '90s, sport was in thrall to booze and fags – cricket had the John Player League and Benson and Hedges Cup; rugby league had the Silk Cut Challenge Cup, the Regal

Trophy and the John Player Cup; snooker had more cigarette-sponsored events than there is space to mention; and the darts world championship, like snooker's, was bankrolled by Embassy. Formula One, meanwhile, was basically contested by mobile fag packets, and there will be football fans of a certain vintage who remember the Watney Cup – and indeed the big Watney Party Seven can of beer, without which no 1970s student party was complete. Jump racing had the Whitbread, Mackeson and Hennessy Gold Cups and even the Stone's Ginger Wine Handicap Chase.

Tobacco companies loved sports sponsorship, because they were already banned from conventional sites. When even that avenue started to be closed off, sport fell into the arms of financial companies, especially the big banks: Barclays took the Premier League, RBS the Six Nations rugby, NatWest became big in cricket and by 2012 Investec had both the Derby and Test cricket.

But by the second decade of the twenty-first century even the banks were insecure. And the most reliable source of money lies elsewhere. We are now in an era when gambling has taken over from booze and fags, and where the bookmakers hold sport's purse strings, with deep implications for the future of televised sport.

For the moment we are talking mainly about sponsorship and advertising. Where Embassy sponsored the world professional darts championship, it is now under the auspices of Ladbrokes; Betfred sponsors snooker's world championship. My team, West Ham, is sponsored by a betting company I have never heard of – SBO Bet (they also sponsor Cardiff), global leader in Asian handicap sports betting, apparently. Meanwhile, watch any football match on the TV and you will be urged ad nauseam by übergeezer Ray Winstone to put a bet on the next scorer, how many corners, final result, and so on, which, with smartphones and tablets, is now the work of a moment.

Booze and fags were quite clearly separate from the sport: the rugby league sponsors were interested only in getting some nice shots of their Silk Cut branding at Wembley – and making sure my ten-year-old son had enough gaspers for the journey back to Leeds. Now the lines between the sports broadcast and the bookmaking sponsors are becoming very blurred. Take the recent Ladbrokes ad based on the slogan, 'Everyone's got an opinion, what's yours worth?' It is set in a transport café with four hard-hatted geezers, looking like real workmen – or a Village People tribute band at a pinch – sitting round discussing who might win the Premier League.

The geezers were Chris Kamara (Sky's *Soccer Saturday*), Ian Wright (BBC, ITV, Absolute Radio), Ally McCoist (BBC pundit at the time of the ad), and Lee Dixon (*Match of the Day*). Other sports broadcasters had also been signed up by the betting companies, even if only as voiceovers: Colin Murray (*Match of the Day 2* and BBC Five Live) did one for William Hill as did Tim Lovejoy (ex Sky's *Soccer AM*). Though Betfair just use ordinary fans arguing about the odds, the message is clear: viewing no longer need be a passive experience.

As an enthusiastic user of Twitter, I can confirm this. I now watch *Question Time*, the BBC's political debate programme, purely to tweet. When I am not tooled up, and unable to comment, I find it a very flat experience. I know I am not alone. There is a genre of TV show – the dating game, *Take Me Out*, for instance – that seems to exist primarily for social networking. I am sure the TV companies now look at Twitter potential when programmes are first pitched.

I watched the 2012 Australian Open tennis final with my laptop not only on Twitter, but also on William Hill's in-play betting page. When the match seemed to be slipping away from Nadal, I spotted something in his body language that convinced me he was not out of it. I was about to tweet this, but noticed he had drifted to 9–1 in the betting, so put ten pounds on instead. Turned out, I was right, it was far from over for Rafa, and as the match continued, he got progressively shorter. It was fascinating watching the odds change shot by shot, until I was able to tweet smugly that I had got the 8–15 favourite at 9–1.

As we know, Rafa lost, and I ended up ten pounds lighter, but had I known how to work the exchanges, and had my investment been bigger, I could have won. The point is, I was able to watch, tweet and bet – and it seemed a perfectly natural way to view sport.

So is there not a chance that the future of sport on television is that events will be created by or bought up by bookmakers? They already show 'virtual racing' in the betting shops, made-up computer-programme races from fictitious courses, to fill in the gaps between genuine races. They could go one step further and stage their own real events on their own web-based TV, or actually pay broadcasters to televise their events. That is what Will and I decided.

'You only had to watch the 2010 World Cup on ITV to see the way the wind was blowing. I have never seen so many adverts for gambling on terrestrial TV. You couldn't move for Ray Winstone telling us about the next bet,' said Will. 'There is in fact a nice circularity about gambling fuelling all sport in the future, because 200 or 300 years ago sport as organised competition only started as a means of gambling. One gentlemen would bet another he could walk a hundred miles.'

Kevin Mitchell, the *Guardian* sports writer, agreed, 'Cricket started as a gambling venture,' he told me. 'The very term "match" meant a match between one set of money and another set of money. There always has been betting in cricket – and corruption – going back to Georgian times. It's a paradox that we think of cricket as the cleanest game, play up and play the game and all that. And the danger is that there is so much cricket on TV now, from all over the world, there are so many more opportunities for corruption.'

A succession of scandals over the past two decades has made cricket painfully aware of the problems, although almost powerless to resolve them because the Asian betting market is large, cricket-obsessed and theoretically illegal, and thus unregulated.

As far as the home market goes, the only thing we can say for certain is that betting opportunities on sport – and beyond – will proliferate, and it will become easier than ever to lose while you view. If even someone like me old enough to have stuck his head out of the train window and get a piece of coal in the eye can manage effortlessly to lose a tenner on the Aussie Open without missing a point, the die is definitely cast. This could be bad news for me. My name is Martin and I am a mug punter, a habit I learnt at my father's knee, and other low joints, as the joke goes.

NINETEEN

WHAT'S YOUR
OPINION WORTH?

The irony is that in this new television landscape of unfettered gambling, the sport that started it all is in a struggle for survival. Horse racing is no longer part of the television furniture, as it once was. Channel 4 sticks with it on Saturdays, but has cut down midweek coverage. The BBC, meanwhile, is only really interested in the big events: the Grand National, the Derby, and Royal Ascot.

And from 2013, even this residual involvement in horse racing will end. Money is, of course, the key, with Channel 4 more willing and able to stump up the £15–20 million for a four-year deal than the BBC Sport department, buckling under the cost of the Olympics and its move to Manchester.

In these circumstances it did not entirely surprise me that the BBC lost the horse racing, but I confess to a little surprise they let the Grand National slip away with barely a whimper. When you consider the travails of Peter Dimmock in bringing the race to television, and its importance in the BBC's historic role of uniting the nation in front of the TV, you are led to the conclusion that this is not so much selling the family silver as hawking a much-loved granny.

About the Derby and Royal Ascot I am less exercised. As John McCririck, betting pundit, remarked in a radio interview in March 2012, the Derby was on Channel 4 right through the 1990s with few complaints from racing fans, who would also be quite happy, he ventured, to accept Ascot from a commercial broadcaster.

More than happy, I should think, as the BBC tended to treat Ascot as combination hat-fest and forelock-tugging sycophancy. I often found myself reverting to the revolutionary socialism of my student days, as Her Majesty the Queen and her chums – the Earl of Romney, Mr and Mrs Anthony Duckworth-Chad, that lot – arrived each day in their horse-drawn carriages, and the BBC dutifully gave chapter and verse on every last one of them. Its commentators cooed about how wonderful the Queen and Prince Philip look for their age, how heart-warming it was that they insist on sitting in an open coach to allow the hoi-polloi to get a decent butcher's, and how marvellous that they all love racehorses. Maybe this is the Royals' payback for letting those primitive cameras into Westminster Abbey in 1953, and giving television its big kick-off.

If Channel 4's coverage of the Cheltenham Festival is anything to go by, racing's big occasions are safe in their hands. If, however, you want to watch the workaday 2.45 at Catterick or Pontefract, you have to seek it out, like porn, and pay for it. There are two satellite racing channels, one of which is part of the Sky Sports package, the other charging an extra fee. According to an enthusiast I know, you can sit around in your underpants all day and night, if you want, watching racing from every UK course, and round the world (which I think he does).

But for how much longer? Horse racing is dangerously dependent on the betting industry, which pays a levy to help finance it. That has been falling in recent years as some bookies move their operations offshore. Others have voiced their resentment at the charge. Ralph Topping, chief executive of William Hill, Britain's biggest high-street bookmaker, calls the levy 'a nonsense'. He argues that racing is in decline as a gambling product, replaced mainly by betting on football. And my son, who is one of his employees, tells me the same story. Those chaps whose Saturday afternoon flutter used to be on the TV races are now just as likely to have an accumulator on the football.

I am one of them. I like to tweet my selections to my followers as well, although sadly Twitter does not allow enough characters for me to add the warning that the value of investments can go down as well as up. But I can't remember the last time I backed a horse.

I remember the first bet I ever made: a horse called Oxo in the Grand National in 1959. My dad put the money on for me, and the horse won, which is probably the worst thing that could have happened, presaging a lifetime of backing my worthless opinion with hard cash. In the days when racing was the mainstay of *Grandstand* and *World of Sport*, that would have been exclusively on horses.

If you were a gambler, the horse racing on TV on a Saturday was an indispensable part of your weekend routine. After some years of pain, I formed the opinion, which I am happy to share with you now, that it is extremely difficult to predict the winner of a horse race. I am not sure the horses even know they are in a race.

This runs counter to the views of the BBC's chief racing presenter Clare Balding, who was brought up with horses (possibly even *by* horses), and whose comments lean heavily towards anthropomorphism. One Grand National she even introduced thus: 'We'll be talking to the trainers, the jockeys, the horses ...'

My father died too soon to enjoy the work of Balding, but he would have been with her all the way. He laboured under the delusion that he was a good judge of horseflesh, and liked to back his judgement. I can picture him now at breakfast on a Saturday morning squinting over the racing pages of the *Daily Express*, the intense concentration causing him to drip a little fried egg onto his cardigan; lost in thought, but still alert enough to pretend to be doing the crossword should my mum suddenly materialise over his shoulder.

He was not a habitual *Express* reader – he would be outraged at the suggestion, God rest him – but an extra morning paper, something a touch racier than the *Guardian*, was part of our Saturday treat, along with the football, and Mum maybe bringing something nice to eat back from town. That was the rationale anyway, although the extra reading matter may have had more to do with the *Guardian*'s reluctance back in the 1960s to publish race cards.

And the BBC was just as sniffy about gambling as the *Guardian*. The corporation's Peter O'Sullevan (later Sir Peter, the only knighted racing commentator) recalled in his autobiography, that throughout the 1950s and into the early '60s, the BBC barred him from mentioning the odds of a horse, and certainly did nothing as vulgar as quoting starting prices.

'Without the introduction of ITV, the announcement of starting prices might have remained unacceptable to the BBC Board of Governors indefinitely,' wrote O'Sullevan. 'As it was, resistance to any indication of pre-race betting moves was sustained for a further two and a half years – placing BBC TV racing coverage under a handicap, vis-à-vis the opposition, which was virtually doubled on Saturday 29 October 1960 when, as one paper put it: "The farce came to a head with the commercial boys gleefully dealing a knockout blow for the BBC by giving the betting at both the Corporation's televised meeting and their own."'

My dad certainly knew the odds, whichever side the race was on. As noon approached, with the antecedents of the participating animals thoroughly mulled, the advice of the *Express*'s 'useless' tipster The Scout pointedly ignored – The Scout was actually the pen name of O'Sullevan's colleague Clive Graham, who was not a bad tipster at all, if you remembered to back only his winning selections – and preferably with Mum now safely out of the way, my dad felt ready to make his selections for the afternoon's sport. He would settle down with a cup of very strong tea and possibly a crumpet or a matzo cracker and commit his wisdom to a scrap of paper, usually the back of an old birthday card.

His bet of choice was something called a yankee, the details of which need not concern you too much. The key point is that four horses were involved in a combination of bets, and at least two of the selections had to win for there to be any return at all on the investment. Ideally, to make it worthwhile, you had to choose three or four winners. For a man who, on all the available evidence, found it well nigh impossible to predict the winner of even one race, gambling on his ability to select three or maybe four live prospects was either an act of folly or of almost heroic optimism. I like to think the latter.

The son of Polish immigrants who came to England in the early years of the twentieth century, my dad left school at thirteen to be apprenticed to a cabinetmaker. He was never short of a heart-rending Dickensian story; usually involving his pushing a heavy piece of oak furniture up Waterloo Road in Salford while his master – a fugitive from the shtetls of Eastern Europe like his parents – beat him, and cursed him in Yiddish.

After the war, he sold stuff, any stuff: encyclopaedias, subscriptions to newspapers, government surplus greatcoats, until in the late 1950s he and his brother eked out a living making raincoats, until Broderick Crawford rode to the rescue. His factory was, not to put too fine a point on it, a sunless, airless shit-hole. The atmosphere, a heady cocktail of asbestos dust and clothes fibres, must have completed the job done on his lungs by the forty Senior Service a day. The point I am making is that Dad's experience must have told him he was not a person on whom life's gifts were routinely bestowed; yet he expected that same good Lord, who had lobbed nothing but slings and arrows of outrageous fortune his way these many years, to now oblige with three or four winners at Kempton Park.

The names and numbers of the largely hopeless beasts on which he had decided to pin his hopes were read out over the telephone to a bookmaker who I pictured guffawing behind his hand at the other end, calling his mates round to listen in. At Dad's end, the conversations were conducted in serious, hushed tones, as if they were matters of national importance, or as if Mum was liable to reappear at any time. Sometimes Dad would take me to a rugby or football match on a Saturday afternoon, without losing sight entirely of the day's investments, seizing voraciously on the late edition of the *Manchester Evening News*, and scouring the Stop Press for the late winners, or in his case losers.

With Mum safely out of the way, we would watch an early race before leaving for the match, which taught me the joy of a shared secret with a parent – terrible parenting I know, but it is too late now – and also the important life-lesson that just because the first leg of a yankee comes up, there is no guarantee that the day will not end in defeat and disappointment, as I have found in a number of areas where horses were not involved at all. I loved those Saturday afternoons with my dad. There is definitely a social aspect to gambling, and I think that is what I am, a social gambler, in the way that some people describe themselves as social drinkers.

Let me give you an example of social gambling. One day I was in an Italian restaurant with a friend, who remarked on the fact that a decade earlier when we had lunch in the same restaurant all the waiters and waitresses were genuine Italians, but now, while the restaurant still took care to employ people who looked vaguely Mediterranean, half the waitresses were newly arrived from Poland.

'No, ours is too good-looking to be Polish,' I said (so hang me for racism, those bastards set fire to my grandparents' village), 'I bet she's Ukrainian,' at which he uttered the two words he knew would reel me in: 'How much?'

'A tenner. Why, where do you think she's from?'

'Spain,' he replied.

Apparently, while I was in the toilet, he had heard her pronounce 'bill' as 'vill'. Also, there was a mention of 'Waterloo Estation.' So we ask her where she is from. 'Espain,' comes the answer, and there is another £10 down the gambling drain.

There is a lesson here for gamblers everywhere. Information is important. Make it your business to acquire it, and act on it swiftly. Another lesson worth absorbing at this point is one normally applied to poker games, but pretty apposite in this Italian restaurant. 'If you look around the table and you can't see who the sucker is, it's probably you.'

From May 1961, the key venue for social gamblers was the newly legalised betting shop, 10,000 of which opened in the first six months. In fact, the first piece I ever wrote for the *Guardian* was about the experience of watching sport in a betting shop, where you could enjoy a whole six-months' worth of passive smoking in one afternoon. When I was a student I actually had a holiday job in a betting shop, as a chalker-up, listening to the commentary from the track for changes in odds – those were the days before shops were allowed screens, drinks machines, toilets, and other such luxuries – and chalking them up on a board. There was a definite sense of community in there: thrillingly multi-ethnic too.

I don't know whether it is just Jews and Chinese, or whether it applies to other immigrant communities, but gambling does rank high on the roster of vices to which we people are prey. Thanks to those days in Mick Dines' bookies' shop, I became one of the few in my circle who had regular contact with Manchester's recent arrivals from Hong Kong outside the context of takeaway shops. Stan Hey, who suspected his father, ostensibly a respectable employee of English Electric, of being a bookie's runner, wrote an elegiac history of the betting shops in the *Independent* in 2008, in which he rehearsed the contrasting feelings they arouse:

> Depending on your point of view, they are either the equivalent of the wardrobe through which you enter a Narnia of wealth and enchantment, or of Dr Caligari's Cabinet, full of horrors and disturbing visions. Supporters will point to the harmless entertainment the shops provide to people who, otherwise trapped in drudgery, can pop in to watch a bit of sport and try to win some money. The naysayers will point to the real possibilities of addiction and to dark pits of debt for people trying to escape whatever their plight may be by gambling.

I used to be in the harmless entertainment camp – my father-in-law, who is seventy-eight, spends whole afternoons in his local bookies, chatting with his mates, and cheering on his ridiculous multiple bet covering all the races and costing about a fiver. But then came what the betting industry calls 'fixed-odds betting terminals' – fruit machines to you and me – which have nothing to do with sport, are highly addictive, and generate a high proportion of the shops' profits.

It all conspires to help push horse racing further out towards the fringes of the sporting menu, the tragedy being that horse racing still believes it is important to TV. Negotiations between TV and the sport were going on all the time I was researching this book. Channel 4 pundit John McCririck best summed up horse racing's problem saying: 'There is no centralised control and too many people looking after their own interests'. The racing authorities comically believed they were negotiating from strength, but every comment from TV executives seemed to indicate this was a dangerous delusion.

Even Sky remains barren ground. 'We would certainly never bid for anything like the Derby or the Grand National,' Vic Wakeling told me. 'We did a bit of racing in the early days, but it was far more valuable for us to have night racing from Exeter or Towcester, rather than big one-off events like the National, which people would go down to the pub to watch. We need to give people a reason to take out an annual subscription. We had to look at every sport and consider what it would do in terms of driving subscriptions and dish sales, and horse racing was never that prominent. It is something that might be looked at again, but I doubt it's at the forefront of anybody's plans.'

It is even rare to see horse racing take pride of place in the window displays of the High Street bookies, unless it's for the Cheltenham Gold Cup or one of the other red-letter days. But on any day of the week you will see odds advertised for the day's football, especially for matches live on TV. In some respects, it is another of Wakeling's innovations at Sky, *Soccer Saturday* with Jeff Stelling, that has contributed to this. The programme began in 1992 as *Sports Saturday*, but only really took off two years later when the excitable Stelling took over.

'I got the idea from Bloomberg TV,' said Wakeling. 'They would do what they were doing, talking away, with stats scrolling through at the bottom of the screen, and tables and whatnot on the right. We had all these feeds of football matches coming in, and I thought we could do something with them.'

The idea that people would watch people watching football seemed patently absurd, but with Stelling's Colemanesque joy in statistics, and well-chosen panellists, including Rodney Marsh (later sacked for a bad taste joke), the late George Best (before he left to deal with his alcohol problems), and others with varyingly colourful backgrounds including Matt LeTissier, Paul Merson, Charlie Nicholas and Phil Thompson, the show became a hit. (It's difficult to decide which is the more transfixing on Sky: Thompson's hyperactive style, or the screaming skull of Chris Kamara, reporting from the grounds.)

More importantly for horse racing, *Soccer Saturday* meant the viewer with a penchant for a punt had a ready-made replacement for the ITV Seven. It is all a far cry from the world vividly brought to life by O'Sullevan, one of the great figures of television sport: 'Among early *Grandstand* producers,' he said in his book, *Calling the Horses*, 'racing was to such an extent a linchpin that one of the dynamic (or do I mean manic?) orchestrators, Bryan Cowgill, would change location overnight when winter racing was threatened by bad weather. On one occasion when there were to be early Saturday morning inspections at Windsor and Sedgefield, he had me drive to Nottingham (which I was happy to do) so as to be within striking distance of whichever meeting got the go-ahead.'

Sir Peter was the doyen of horse-racing commentators. His voice was vividly described by the critic Russell Davies as 'perhaps the only hectic drawl in captivity'. Like Coleman on his long walks around the countryside, Bough rehearsing his 'good afternoons', or Dimbleby taking a boat on the Thames to prepare for the Coronation, O'Sullevan's craft owed much to thorough research. As Nicolas Sellens wrote: 'His paranoia over mis-identifying a horse led him to prepare himself extraordinarily assiduously for each race. He chose the osmosis approach, surrounding himself with race cards and colouring in silks by hand in the hope he could absorb the critical clues in the horse-rider-owner equation. While the requirement to be able to distinguish crimson cross-belts from bright pink polka-dots may not appear too daunting, external variables such as rain, mist and fog can queer the pitch at almost a moment's notice. Depending on the prevailing meteorological extremity, his monitor – providing it was functioning – offered him, as he puts it, "white mice in a snowstorm or black mice in a coal mine".'

Bryan Cowgill, the aforementioned manic producer, said of O'Sullevan, 'I've worked with him for over twenty-five years, and I've never known the bugger to be wrong.' On top of which was that magnificent 'hectic drawl'. Sellens says 'only rugby union's Bill McLaren rivalled O'Sullevan in terms of vocal allure. Those uniquely velvet tones, lauded variously as "Savile Row" and "honeyed gravel", always built a smoothness of crescendo attributed normally only to Rossini. It was a voice that oozed class and breeding but that crucially retained the common touch.'

That is so true. When O'Sullevan was the sound of Saturday afternoons round our house, we never thought of him as upper-class, not like Peter West who we spurned as the voice of posh sports like tennis, and the then-hated rugby union. Maybe it was because of the unique democracy of horse racing, the only place in the class-conscious Britain of those days where peers and peasants – and Jewish bookmakers – would happily mix.

O'Sullevan personified that inclusivity, and ITV tried to poach him. This passage from his book gives you some idea of how different the world was in 1968 – both for horse racing, and in television. Jimmy Hill was keen to sign O'Sullevan for ITV, and starting writing letters: 'We got on particularly well and enjoyed a series of excellent lunches, making serious impact on Henri Sartori's stock of most notable Bordeaux at Le Coq d'Or. Foolhardily I was reluctant to quit the BBC for cash and must have been very tiresome to negotiate with. Jimmy changed tactics towards the end of the year. "I have already made arrangements for a yacht for you in the Mediterranean," he wrote.'

There is more of this stuff about yachts and the Seychelles, and offers coming over the phone, as Glen Campbell so memorably put it in his hit song 'Rhinestone Cowboy' (not talking about Peter O'Sullevan), all a million miles from my dad in his egg-flecked cardigan scrawling the names of his desperate selections on the back of a birthday card. Very occasionally my dad went through a phase of attending synagogue on a Saturday morning, primarily when a bar mitzvah or similar occasion was imminent and he needed to keep the elders of the tribe onside, but soon stopped going again when new-found piety failed to have a beneficial effect on either his business or his attempts to crack the ITV Seven.

But here too, I was made aware of the joys of social gambling through the chaps Dad hung around with outside the synagogue, mostly first-generation immigrants like himself, discussing the prospects for the day's sport, who seemed much more fun to be with than the guys in the tan brogues and nicely pressed suits paying attention to the service. A couple of the gambling types used to go to the rugby with Dad and me, and would place side bets among themselves on whether goals would be successfully kicked or not. Which, to all intents and purposes, is what, in a more technologically sophisticated way, Ray Winstone is currently doing on TV, and I am doing by sharing my opinions on Twitter.

My son, who is a producer on Hill's web-based radio broadcasts, often works on something called *In-Play*, a free-form zoo-format radio show (rather like those programmes on pop radio where a gang of syco-phants whoop at the presenter's *bon mots*, and are referred to as 'the crew' or 'the posse') where a team of three or four people, on duty live for four or five hours, will discuss sporting action from around the globe, talking about what might happen next, and the odds being offered against that possibility.

Here is just a selection of some of the events *In-Play* was following on a fairly standard Monday afternoon: a Russian league match between Spartak Nalchik and Zimbru Chisinau, a Turkish cup tie – Ankaragucu v. Bucaspor, Polish women's volleyball – the big one between Impel Gwar-dia Wroclaw and KPSK Stal Mielec, youth football from Brazil – Santos FC Under-19s v. Rio Preto EC Under-19s and international handball between Croatia and Australia.

That is just a small sample, and there can be up to sixty betting markets on any one of them. Live pictures from all these events come into the studios of William Hill – and similarly to other bookmakers running an equivalent service – which the team watch and comment upon, obviously in terms of odds. More and more, pictures from these events, streamed live on the bookies' websites, are offered to customers, on payment of, say, a £10 subscription fee for the live sport, refunded – sort of – by way of a £10 free bet.

How long before convergence between our computers and TVs means people can watch this stuff all day long if they so choose? But who, you might feel tempted to ask, is going to be interested in watching Danish second division football (one of the events my son covered on *In-Play*)? You may well ask, but that presupposes we are only going to be interested in the sports and the competitions in which we have always been interested. If you think that, I would refer you to the hundreds of thousands of spectators who flocked to speedway and county cricket in the years between the end of the Second World War and the 1960s. What happened to them? Sports can wither on the vine. No sport is guaranteed a spot on TV.

When the magnificently acerbic TV critic A.A. Gill gave a talk at the Edinburgh Television Festival in 2007, he was asked what a new TV channel might do to attract viewers. He suggested inventing a new sport, an idea greeted with ridicule by his audience of television grandees.

'Actually, I still think it's a first-class idea, and I offer it to any passing channel gratis,' Gill wrote in the *Sunday Times*. 'Though in general I loathe sport, I can see that, combined with the box, it's a marriage made on the Elysian Fields. It grows outside its ordained slot with leagues and competitions, it produces heroes and stars and it sells merchandise. Sport is the one programme you can try at home (not so easy with *Pride and Prejudice* or *Panorama*). And if you did invent a new game, it would be under copyright, there'd be none of that hysterical bidding, you could lease the concept to foreign channels and have internationals.' Television, complained Gill, has always been content to be a passive fan and pay the ticket price. Maybe it needs someone like him, not steeped in sport, to see the future clearly. Football and cricket, of course, are still highly attractive to TV because they are at the centre of the national conversation but equally, so are *The X-Factor*, *The Apprentice*, and *Big Brother*.

Strictly speaking, all your new sport would need would be a master manipulator, like Christof, the character played by Ed Harris in *The*

Truman Show, or indeed Simon Cowell, capable of seducing a supine press, and also using the blogosphere, the twittersphere, and all that, and your network might be on the road to being freed from the need to hand over billions to the people who run organised sport.

I was watching the quiz show *The Weakest Link* the other day, and thought how much more interesting the show would be if we could bet on it. Using our skill and judgement of the human race – or even their hairstyles – we might speculate which contestant the team would choose to eliminate next, whether the next contestant would get his or her question right, how much money the team might make in a particular round, to say nothing of betting on the overall winner. There could be a whole plethora of markets adding an extra layer of interest onto what is already an entertaining show.

I am not a gambling addict – five or ten pounds on the football at the weekend and the occasional bet on tennis or reality television is my limit – and I am fully aware it is an addiction as corrosive as any other. I further hold the betting companies responsible for exacerbating the problem through their highly addictive fixed-odds terminals and online bingo games. There might need to be some government control on that sort of activity. But not prohibition. That, as the movies teach us, is destined to end in tears, and possibly a hail of machine-gun bullets.

All the indications are that gambling will grow in popularity as a leisure time pursuit, and play a growing part in television sport. That Ladbrokes question, 'What's your opinion worth?' (which I seem to be following a family tradition in overvaluing) is becoming the salient one for TV viewers these days.

TWENTY

THE IMPORTANCE OF SALT 'N' VINEGAR

Jerry Seinfeld, the American comedian who more or less invented observational comedy in the 1980s, had an interesting observation about snacks: 'I like the idea,' he said, 'of just eating with one hand, without looking.' This is why TV sports fans love snack food so much, especially those suddenly ubiquitous big bags of potato crisps that can last you a whole innings, in bizarrely specific flavours like Sea Salt and Cracked Black Pepper, or Slow Roasted Lamb with Moroccan Spices ('Shopkeeper, can you assure me the black pepper is cracked, or is it maybe just mildly eccentric?')

No statistical evidence is available on the number of those consumed during a Sky Super Sunday or a cricket all-nighter from Australia, but the shocking fact is that we British consume more potato crisps – and near-neighbours like Quavers and Monster Munch – per person than any other nation on earth, including even the artery-hardened USA.

Statistically, in fact, there is a better than even chance that by the time I have finished writing this chapter – and you have finished reading it – we may both be eating a packet of crisps. Figures provided in 2010 by Walkers, Britain's most popular brand, show that we get through around 150 bags per person per year in Britain. That is three bags a week: every person, every week, and given that there are those – Olympic athletes for instance – who forswear them, some of us are eating even more.

Walkers are rather pleased with these figures, as the company commands roughly half of this one-and-a-half billion pound market. Yet, just twenty years ago Walkers of Leicester was primarily a regional brand in the English Midlands, rubbing along on around 19 per cent of national sales. It is now owned by PepsiCo, which might have surprised the original Henry Walker, who had started out as a butcher in Mansfield.

What helped pitchfork the company to potato crisp prominence was the inspired choice in 1994 of a local lad, the former England international footballer Gary Lineker, to advertise Walkers' crisps on British television.

Seventeen years later, Lineker is still the face of the brand, and this is the longest-running personality endorsement in British advertising history, worth more than half a million pounds a year, probably quite a lot more. The deal gives Walkers exclusivity: Lineker is barred from endorsing, advertising, or in any way associating himself with another company's products. To borrow an expression from our American cousins, Walkers own the former international's ass.

It appears to be money well spent. According to the Food Commission, an organisation campaigning for 'healthier, safer, sustainable' food in the UK, a spokesman for Walkers told them that two years of the Lineker commercials had helped shift 'enough crisps to cover the whole of Holland'.

Lineker's long-time manager Jon Holmes, who negotiated the arrangement, was less eager to pursue the 'Today Holland, Tomorrow the World' line when I spoke to him (in view of the so-called obesity crisis, this is probably not the ideal time to be propounding a policy of snack food *Lebensraum*), restricting himself to saying Walkers were 'very pleased' with the work of his charge, which they expected to continue for the foreseeable future.

Lineker's first nationally networked commercial in 1994 – he had done a few regional spots in the 1980s – was nothing more than a simple gag really, the visual equivalent of a one-liner, which nobody foresaw as the start of one of British television's longest-running series. His retirement from football, after two injury-plagued seasons with Nagoya Grampus Eight in Japan's J League, coincided with Walkers' product manager Martin Glenn's idea for a campaign taking advantage of the crisps' provincial origins. With Lineker having been born in Leicester – he used to help his dad sell fruit and vegetables from a stall on Leicester market – and having started his career at Leicester City, his return from Japan provided a topical peg for the commercial.

In the ad, a jaunty, smiling Lineker arrives back at Leicester station to a hero's welcome, and a soundtrack of 'Welcome Home' by Peters and Lee, a toe-tapping number one hit from a folksy duo who had won the TV talent show *Opportunity Knocks*. The clever twist was to subvert Lineker's cheery wholesome image at the end of the commercial, by showing him stealing a packet of crisps from a young boy. 'With crisps this good, there is no more Mr Nice Guy,' runs the copy line. And there, ladies and gentlemen, is your classic moment of intersection between televised sport and bare-naked commerce – because it was television that created Mr Nice Guy.

Though Gary Lineker was never once booked during fifteen years as a professional, with Leicester City, Everton, Barcelona, Tottenham Hotspur, Grampus Eight and the English national team, that will not have planted the Nice Guy image so firmly in our crisp-eating consciousness. Few of us will have seen many of those matches in more than highlight form, and so will not have registered Lineker as anything more than an honest professional with a knack for goalscoring. However, when a British television audience of 26.2 million witnesses a moment, cash registers begin to register. In the case of Gary Lineker that moment, the incident that emphasised his niceness and took him from clean-cut marketability to national treasure/lottery winner, occurred on 4 July 1990, nine minutes into extra time in England's World Cup semi-final against West Germany.

Lineker himself had scored an eightieth-minute equaliser in the tie, showing the opportunism and deft control that had characterised his World Cup. But he only rose to mythic status when England's charismatic, hyperactive midfielder Paul Gascoigne was booked for a lunge on Germany's Thomas Berthold in extra time. When Gascoigne realised the booking, his second of the tournament, would rule him out of the World Cup final should England reach it, he first bit his lip and choked back tears like a little boy getting a Chinese burn from a bigger one, and then, red in the face, found himself incapable of preventing the gusher.

As the camera focused on the tear-stricken Gascoigne, Lineker drifted unknowingly into shot, wearing an expression that was part-resignation, part-sympathy for his teammate, at the same time signalling to the England manager Bobby Robson, tapping the side of his head and pointing to his eyes, a gesture Lineker says he gets asked about more than any other moment in his career.

Footballers do not often impress anyone with their intelligence, awareness and, well, niceness, in the way that golfers and cricketers occasionally do, but Lineker did at that moment, before the biggest TV audience of the year, which was undoubtedly among the factors helping make the 1990 World Cup a landmark event. The image of Gazza blubbing like a child, and Lineker, the concerned parent, moving to take charge, is seared into the mind of Britain's snack-loving public in a way such incidents can never be when you merely experience them live. I use the word 'merely' advisedly. As *The Times*'s Simon Barnes suggested, there are times when the live experience is not the half of it.

Lineker's moment – usually referred to in discussions of the World Cup under the umbrella term 'Gazza's tears' – is often mentioned when the 1990 World Cup is talked of as having rescued English football from the predominantly male, rather threatening atmosphere which prevailed in the 1970s and '80s.

Italia '90 – Gazza's tears, and so on – gentrified football, runs conventional wisdom, making it a game fit for families, and paving the way ultimately for the Premier League, millionaire stars from all over the world arriving in Britain, the cult of Beckham, the success of Nick Hornby's book *Fever Pitch* (1992), and toilets in football grounds that occasionally boasted washbasins. But it is the televised version of 1990, not the tournament itself that deserves the credit.

For those who were out there, there was little indication that Italia '90 was going to be what is now popularly referred to as a game-changer. Defences dominated – the goals tally was the lowest in World Cup history – with teams seemingly bent on hanging on for 120 minutes and then taking their chances in a penalty shoot-out. Argentina progressed twice in this way.

The Republic of Ireland managed just two goals in five games, destroying in three weeks a nation's reputation for blithe spirit and careless abandon. A record sixteen red cards were handed out during the competition, including one for Argentina in the final, while off the pitch it was business as usual for football's roughneck followers, despite – or perhaps because of – the widely advertised enthusiasm of the Italian riot police for their work. In Sardinia, where England were based for their group matches, Dutch hooligans, keen to take the title of Europe's most feared, engaged the English in a modest rumble, as did the Irish, also in the same group. There was violence in Rimini, too, before England's second-round game in Bologna against Belgium.

Few signs, then, that the national game had moved on significantly in the five years since the *Sunday Times* characterised it in a famous front-page leader, as 'a slum sport played in slum stadiums by slum people', words echoed by Lord Hill-Norton, Admiral of the Fleet, arguing in the House of Lords in March 1989, that football was not fit to be called the national game, since it was 'a slum game played by louts in front of hooligans'.

The admiral's fulmination boasts some of the patrician flavour of prosecuting counsel Mervyn Griffith-Jones's words in the *Lady Chatterley's Lover* obscenity trial in 1960, when he asked if it was the 'kind of book you would wish your wife or servants to read'. By common consent the 1990 World Cup, a tetchy, defensive, badly behaved contest, was the mysterious agent that helped make football a game fit for your wife, your children, your servants and even your Admiral of the Fleet. And ultimately helped shift industrial quantities of snacks.

It also gave the term The Beautiful Game, first used in the title of Pele's 1977 autobiography *My Life and the Beautiful Game*, wide currency in this country. This had little to do with the football and every-thing to do with the BBC's coverage, not least the choice of a recording of *Nessun Dorma* by Italian tenor Luciano Pavarotti as the theme tune for its broadcasts.

Over a sequence of dancing nymphs on stage in an old-fashioned opera house, mixing to footage of some of football's greatest names like Cruyff, Pele, and Maradona, the hummable bit of *Nessun Dorma* is belted out. Then a simple title card reading *World Cup Grandstand* heralded the BBC's front man, then at the height of his powers, the moustachioed matinee idol Des Lynam. Puccini, Cruyff, and Des; forget the football, this was beautiful.

Des claimed in his autobiography that his long-term partner Rose was responsible for the Pavarotti brainwave, but the credit for choosing the actual piece is shared by the BBC's house opera buff Gerald Sinstadt, and Brian Barwick, the Corporation's football editor at the time, and later chief executive of the Football Association.

Before Pavarotti, no one was calling football The Beautiful Game: not after the Bradford City fire in 1985 where fifty-six people died in a decrepit stand, nor after the riot later that same month at Heysel Stadium in Belgium where thirty-nine people, mostly Juventus fans, died before the European Cup final against Liverpool and nor after the Hillsborough disaster in 1989 where ninety-six fans were crushed to death before an FA Cup semi-final.

The music was key. Ask any TV viewer what is noteworthy about the BBC football highlights programme *Match of the Day*, as it approaches its fiftieth anniversary, and the chances are he or she will hum you a few bars of the theme tune. I could not care less about skiing on TV, but just as radio's *Sports Report* theme evoked memories of tea and toast on childhood Saturday evenings, so the *Ski Sunday* theme, a tune called 'Pop Looks Bach' by Sam Fonteyn, immediately transports me to those few blessed sleepy hours between Sunday lunch and the working week, and the sight of idiots in spandex throwing themselves off mountains. Similarly, if I hear the first few insistent bars of the BBC's *Sportsnight with Coleman*, it is once again a misty February night some time in the 1970s and I am waiting by the TV for brief highlights of a West Ham cup replay. What a little piece of almond-flavoured sponge cake did for Marcel Proust, David Coleman does for me.

The former Head of BBC Sport, Jonathan Martin, agrees on the importance of the right theme, having chosen 'The Chain', a Fleetwood Mac instrumental, to introduce the BBC's Formula One coverage, after it was suggested by his assistant producer Bob Abrahams. 'Bob had a good ear for music,' said Martin. 'And I wanted something that reflected motor racing. The first time I heard it, I just jumped at it – it was absolutely right. The first few seconds are threatening, in anticipation of the start and then it bursts into life as the cars go off – it just explodes.'

Italia '90 was the first time a classical piece had been used as the theme for a televised sporting event. Now no big football or rugby occasion in Britain is complete without a classically trained singer and an anthem. The 1990 World Cup made it possible for artistes like Russell Watson and Katherine Jenkins to break into the mainstream. Though they would no doubt have become celebrated in their specialist field had sport not taken opera to its bosom, they have Pavarotti and Italia '90 to thank for sell-out stadium gigs and pictures on the cover of the *Daily Mail*'s *Weekend* magazine.

And there is no doubting the potency of sport on TV. Ralph Bernard, the founder of the radio station Classic FM, tells me he and others first started thinking about a commercial classical station in the wake of the 1990 World Cup. 'Suddenly, there was an operatic tenor at number two in the charts,' Ralph told me. 'Clearly, a popular classical music radio station was an idea whose time had come.' Bernard's GWR radio group – later called Global – started researching their market straight after the World Cup, and launched in 1992.

Non-musical beneficiaries of Italia '90 included not just Lineker, but the other two protagonists in the Gazza's Tears moment, Robson and Gascoigne himself, who had cameos in a Walkers commercial: Lineker stole the crisps off Gascoigne prompting floods of tears from one of those suction pump devices. But it is Lineker's subsequent career that is of particular interest to followers of televised sport, not only the millions from the crisps, but the steady progress that now sees him as the BBC's – and by extension, Britain's – pre-eminent TV sports presenter.

You might think that the rise of a lower-middle-class lad from Leicester who left school with just four O levels, a blameless and industrious England international footballer with a decent goalscoring record, to a position of prominence in the media would be cause for celebration. But, as tends to be the way in Britain, that has not always been the case.

Quite apart from the flak he attracts for pushing salty snacks at our kids – he has been dubbed a 'jug-eared crisp whore,' a soubriquet he wore lightly in a *Daily Mirror* interview in 2009 – his hosting of *Match of the Day* has been criticised for being too chummy by half. In September 2010, the *Daily Mail* devoted two pages to comments by former Liverpool and England striker Stan Collymore who branded *MOTD* under Lineker as 'stale, clichéd, smug pap'. He said the team of presenters looked like 'a golfing clique who have a passing interest in football', words echoed by the *Mail*'s chief sports writer Martin Samuel who described the programme as 'a cosy golf and social club with a football show attached'. Lineker and his associated pundits, Alan Hansen and Alan Shearer, do play golf together. And there may be a little envy at work too, because Lineker seems to be rather good at the game. I am no golfer, but I am sure I have heard him say he 'plays off four', which I gather is rather impressive.

Jon Holmes explained that this is not just a matter of natural ability. 'Most people go to a golf pro, he says "let me see your swing," they swing and he says "I want you to do it more like this," and they do it a couple of times, and then go back to doing it how they were doing it before. It's different with Gary. He does it exactly the way the guy tells him how to do it. If you tell Gary something and he thinks you know what you are talking about, it's immediately put into practice, and it sticks. Gary is the best learner of anyone I have ever worked with.'

Holmes is as close as we have to a modern day Bagenal Harvey. In fact, he got into the business in much the same way as Harvey. After a short spell as a trainee reporter with the *Leicester Mercury* in 1971, he joined a friend at a company of financial advisers – mostly flogging insurance – and took on as a client the then Leicester City goalkeeper Peter Shilton in 1972, at around the time Shilton became England goalie.

His role model in those early days was Mark McCormack, the boss of IMG. McCormack, an American lawyer who died in 2003 with his title of 'the most powerful man in sport' still intact, founded his empire on a handshake in 1960 when, having spotted the potential for athletes to make large incomes from endorsement in the television age, he signed the golfer Arnold Palmer as his first client. Gary Player and Jack Nicklaus followed, forming the bedrock for a multi-million-dollar worldwide corporation whose activities in the business and marketing spheres are beyond the ken of a humble lounger on sofas like me.

McCormack was proof that timing is all, because – unlike Bagenal Harvey who only had one TV channel to play with – he was also able to create the offshoot TWI, Transworld International, a worldwide television empire producing and distributing 6,500 hours of original programming to more than 200 countries.

The old Jimmy Hill tactic of signing up the stars and then creating the event yourself is a favourite of TWI, whose programmes include *Trans World Sport*, *World's Strongest Man*, *FIFA Futbol Mundial*, *American Gladiators*, and many others you will have found in the more distant regions of the Sky menu. The fifty-odd sponsors who signed up for the 2012 Olympics are, to some extent, products of the empire McCormack created. Every time it sticks in your craw when you hear something described as 'the official beer of the England World Cup squad' or the 'official snack food' (usually McDonald's) of some festival of athletics, that is a little nod in the direction of McCormack.

When Holmes started opening Peter Shilton's mail for him, and looking for opportunities, McCormack was his guide. Soon the two other local heroes joined him: cricketer David Gower and, in 1980, Lineker. 'He was twenty then, and very shy, so shy in fact that he brought a friend with him to act as spokesman,' said Holmes. 'But we hit it off straight away. He was quite obviously someone who would go a long way in whatever he chose to do.'

It is remarkable how many sports broadcasters' careers are defined by one moment that almost becomes part of folk history, and no matter what else they achieve in life, continues to define them. For Kenneth Wolstenholme, it was 'They think it's all over'; for rugby league commentator Eddie Waring it was his comment 'Poo-er lad, 'e's a poo-er lad' when Wakefield's Don Fox missed the last kick of the 1968 Challenge Cup final, handing the cup to Leeds; for John Motson, it was not even anything he said, but his report from Wycombe Wanderers in 1990 when he stood in the centre circle in his sheepskin coat while a blizzard raged around him. The ITV summariser Gareth Southgate, meanwhile, will forever be remembered for his penalty miss against Germany in 1996, which – irritatingly for some of us – he turned into hard cash, shooting a fashionably ironic pizza ad on the back of it. But that was as nothing compared to Lineker's moment, which is still paying dividends more than twenty years later.

'Gary was always adamant, even while he was still playing, that he did not want to manage a football club,' said Holmes. 'He was actually quite interested in writing about sport, so I told him to read anything he could, and Gary being Gary, he set about it quite methodically. He started hanging around the journos a lot, seeing how they worked. After the 1986 World Cup, BBC producers Niall Sloane and Brian Barwick, who had been impressed with Gary's interviews and had seen him around the press area, came to me and said that any time he wanted to go into broadcasting, they would be happy to help train him.'

When Lineker went to play for Barcelona in 1986, Holmes was able to give him more experience of live radio: 'I used to appear on a Sunday sports show on Gem AM, a local radio station, and I suggested we get Gary on each Sunday round about five o'clock to report on what was happening in *La Liga*, and he proved he had a real talent for it.'

By the time Lineker returned to England to play for Tottenham, Holmes was able to get him on a variety of TV shows. 'We went on Des O'Connor,

Wogan, Parky – and he was getting better all the time. I was building up relationships with producers and assistants, and Gary was learning how to make sure he got asked back.' This was all part of Holmes's big plan, he says, to 'broaden the constituency' of his clients, much as Eddie Waring had done for himself in an accidental, more haphazard way a couple of decades earlier.

Lineker's early broadcasts were a little wooden to say the least, but he began to blossom on the sports comedy panel game *They Think It's All Over*. This had started life in the early 1990s as a fairly gentle radio show hosted by the courtly and amiable Des Lynam, and mostly celebrated for Rory Bremner's wickedly accurate impersonations of Richie Benaud and Geoffrey Boycott. Two of Holmes's star clients, Will Carling and David Gower, appeared in the show, so he obviously had an interest in its transfer to television, a suggestion he put to his friend Brian Barwick in BBC Sport.

A TV pilot was made, but both Rory Bremner and Des Lynam declined the chance to be in the show, and it was not until two years later, 1995, that it made it to BBC1. 'I thought all the subtlety we had in the radio version was lost on the TV pilot,' Lynam told me. 'The radio show was a celebration of sports people, on TV it was too contrived and seemed to be all about insults. Also, I felt that if I was doing proper sports programmes, it would not sit well taking the mickey out of people, and then maybe having to do a serious interview with them.'

When the show did appear, Des's place was taken by comedian Nick Hancock, and David Gower and Gary Lineker were team captains. It was a huge success, though Lynam never dropped his reservations. 'I thought David and Gary, whom I like and respect as broadcasters, always looked ill-at-ease on the show.' But Gower and Lineker did fifteen series in all, before retiring from the show in 2003.

Running gags were that Lineker was nothing but a goal-hanger, and that Gower was lazy. 'This central joke only worked because the two of them were among the best at what they did,' said Holmes, 'From their point of view, it was fantastic experience because they were sitting next to comedians each week learning how to deliver funny lines.' The comics on the show – Rory McGrath and Lee Hurst mostly – also got much comic mileage out of the toe injury that prevented Lineker playing much football when he moved to Japan for £3 million.

Holmes was credited as a consultant on *They Think It's All Over*. He also devised with Gary Lineker a six-part BBC series called *Gary's Golden Boots* in 1998, about fellow winners of the World Cup Golden Boot award, and was consultant on an unjustly neglected BBC show about a Holmes-like sports agent/manager, *Trevor's World of Sport*. Trevor/Holmes was played by Neil Pearson, and the series was written by the cherishable Andy Hamilton, a Chelsea fan who once told me, when I asked him how he felt about Roman Abramovich's questionably acquired billions: 'When I am enjoying Chelsea's pursuit of football's glittering prizes, I try not to see the turf stained red with the blood of Russian peasants.'

From 1998 to 2006 Holmes was chief executive of the European division of the hugely powerful American SFX entertainment agency, who bought his company. At SFX, he oversaw David Beckham's major sponsorship contracts, as well as acting as Beckham's representative on earth during the great man's protracted transfer negotiations. When the frenzy over Beckham's move to Spain was at its height, Jon was usually on hand with a quote. Having helped sell the Beckham brand across the world, Holmes may be the perfect man to clear up for me the mystery of celebrity endorsements.

Take razors. About six or seven years ago, I attended the *What the Papers Say* awards, a lunch at which members of my profession – not me, obviously – were honoured by the now defunct television programme for significantly good work, or for knowing one of the judges.

As is the way of these things, all attendees were given a 'goodie bag' on leaving; nothing grand like at the Oscars, where you might receive fine jewels and *objets d'art*, but a collection of tat, including a Gillette Mach3 razor. At the time, this was the latest in shaving technology, which I had been steadfastly resisting as I felt content with my two-blade model.

But, as it was free, I decided to switch – and, by the way, I do know the deal with razors is that you get the shaver for next to nothing, and then they screw you on the blades – and was thrilled with the results. Of all the choices I have made in my life, this is the one with which I am most unequivocally pleased. And yet, through the seven years my Mach3 and I have been together, a constant parade of newer, brighter, more advanced shavers endorsed by some of the handsomest, most celebrated people on the planet has processed before my eyes: three blades, four blades, five blades – I am waiting for some shaver company to unleash the nuclear option – and even one with a little electric motor.

Most recently, Roger Federer, Tiger Woods, and Thierry Henry have been the very expensive turns trying to persuade me to abandon my Mach3 in favour of something a little younger and more racy. Talk about mixed messages. Tiger is suggesting to me (subliminally, obviously*) that if my chin is as smooth as the one he is stroking, any number of compliant cocktail waitresses may come my way, while Roger Federer's message is that a stubble-free skin may be the key to a successful rock-solid marriage. So I am sticking with my Mach3. They will have to get Woody Allen, Groucho Marx and God in their advert before I consider changing.

But why the millions spent on celebrities? Surely even young males watching sport are not stupid enough to believe using the same shaving tackle as Tiger Woods will improve their swing, or their strike rate with comely young blondes? Or that Tiger even uses those blades?

Well, according to a piece by Matt Cowen in the *Independent*, it is not as simple as that. 'The presence of a familiar face in a TV campaign can quickly raise a client company's profile as the audience learns to associate a well-known figure with a product,' wrote Cowen. 'The advertising also has the potential to work hard for a company long after a commercial break ends. Once a celebrity has been associated with a consumer item, then their every subsequent appearance on television produces a

---

* Possibly the subtlest oxymoron you will ever come across.

reminder of the campaign.' So your high-cost celebrity is the gift that keeps on giving.

Lineker and the crisps, meanwhile, was a marriage made in heaven. 'Though Lineker may subvert his nice guy persona in the Walkers ads,' writes Cowen, 'We still know that this is the fresh-faced boy next door whom we can comfortably associate with a game of football in the park and a packet of crisps on the way home.'

It is indisputably the growth of sport on TV that has drawn Gary into the crisp trade, Tiger into razor blades, and David Beckham into more or less anything you care to mention. The Food Commission, the charity that pictured the whole of Holland being covered with potato crisps, gave Gary Lineker its Greedy Star award in 2003, for his assiduous and highly lucrative work on behalf of Walkers, pointing out that one-third of each packet of crisps is fat, and that there is half of a six-year-old's recommended daily intake of salt in just one small packet.

Lineker responded by pointing to parents' role in tackling the so-called obesity crisis, blaming them for allowing their children to lead a sedentary lifestyle, but he failed to impress the Commission much. 'What do you think Gary Lineker's favourite food is?' they ask. 'Not Walkers' crisps, of course, but healthy and delicious paella.'

When I visited Holmes, the 2010 World Cup was on and he was watching closely, as at least half a dozen clients – commentators, pundits – of his new company, Jon Holmes Media, were in action in South Africa. More than that, though, for someone in his business it was a thrilling demonstration of how commerce and sport on TV are not only in bed together, but turning a howitzer on anyone who tries to enter *their* bedroom. Sport's new reality makes the crisp deal he set up for Gary look not so much like the work of the devil, but the work of the devil's younger, nicer brother.

While I was with Holmes, he learned of a scandal that had broken over one of ITV's pundits, Robbie Earle, some of whose complimentary tickets for the Holland v. Denmark match found their way into the hands of a mob of young women in matching orange mini-dresses working for Dutch beer brand Bavaria, trying to break Budweiscr's monopoly of in-stadia beer advertising. Budweiser paid around fifty million euros to FIFA for their rights, and it is the work of FIFA's paid goons (all right, that's a little harsh) to make sure nobody muscles in on their action, so for Robbie the World Cup was over.

And Budweiser was not even a leading FIFA sponsor. There are two levels at which big corporations can hitch their star to the World Cup: firstly, as a long-term FIFA 'partner,' like Coca-Cola, Visa, Emirates Airlines, Hyundai Motors, Sony and Adidas, who are each committed to paying between a hundred and two hundred million euros for a four-year partnership, guaranteeing that anybody caught drinking a bottle of Pepsi at a FIFA match, or parking a Toyota, will be taken out and shot. Not really, but Coke insists on exclusivity in all markets. The other level at which you can fill FIFA's coffers is as a 'corporate sponsor', like Budweiser, Continental Tyres, and McDonald's, who each pay around fifty million euros.

And that is before you even get started on the money poured into FIFA member nations by the kit manufacturers. In his report, *The Football World Cup of 2010: Destination South Africa*, the Argentinian sports marketing expert Gerardo Molina said that it was profitable for them to pay exorbitant sums because of the size of the audience: 'Without doubt, it's a gold mine.'

But those of us who have seen John Huston's 1948 film, *The Treasure of the Sierra Madre*, know what squabbles can brew up around a gold mine. In England, Mars, the official England sponsor, threatened legal action against rivals Nestlé, who linked their Kit-Kat bar to the England football team with a campaign in which the chocolate fingers were crossed for England. Mars claimed 'passing off' of an association with the England football team without having paid for the right to do so. Without comment, here is what the English football establishment said when Mars signed their five-year deal in 2009. Sir Trevor Brooking, FA director of football development: 'These are exciting times for the England team and to have Mars, an iconic brand that's loved by football fans, on board as a sponsor is a positive thing. We are looking forward to a successful long-term partnership.'

The Olympics operates in similar fashion. Pringles were made the official crisps of the London Olympics, not, in my expert view, the ideal choice for those of us watching on TV, requiring some hand-eye co-ordination to manoeuvre the crisp from the tube, necessitating the snacker to remove eyes from the screen. Snack choice is a matter of some importance on my sofa, my recommendation being for a kettle chip type of product, or maybe a ridged crisp, a premium item anyway, built on more substantial lines than those in the little packets that Gary flogs, and less prone to crumbing.

When England played Argentina in the 1998 World Cup we put on a little World Cup party at home for the in-laws, and bought some bags of posh crisps – roast Wiltshire ham and whole grain mustard, I believe (but with no guarantee of provenance, a little Dorset ham might have crept in there) – which we placed in bowls around the lounge. When Sol Campbell appeared to have won the tie for England in extra time, I was so overjoyed I began to jump around the room forgetting I had a bowl of the crisps in my hand. The crisps ended up in my mother-in-law's hair, a circumstance relatively easy to rectify with a comb and an apology. Imagine if we had decided on those crumbly crisps, or even worse, pizza.

We can look back at the incident and laugh now. In fact, we laughed at the time. And maybe that points to one of the reasons we are in thrall to sport on TV. It gives us a chance to share the agony and ecstasy with family, friends, and like-minded others. Baddiel and Skinner's song 'Three Lions', written for the 1996 European Championships about the thirty years of hurt and so on, was probably the hit it was because it said just this. The snippets of commentary in the song undoubtedly helped. The work of Coleman, Bough, Lynam, Motson et al resonates as loudly over the years as Gazza's tears, Ali's shuffle, or Jules Rimet still gleaming.

Clearly, in a multi-platform, time-shift, niche-market world, there will be fewer of those landmark occasions when the nation unites in a common cause, and increasingly the experience will be shared through social networking. But sport will still create unforgettable moments, like Gazza's tears, that live more vividly on TV than at the live event. The tears were not even visible to those in the stadium.

There will undoubtedly be new ways of watching those moments, and of sharing the experience, on Twitter perhaps; but McDonald's, Coca-Cola, and Budweiser will never be far away, thinking of ways to make a buck.

It is no longer 1957 – a fact with which some of us are striving hard to come to terms. Whether the 3-D television set I have just acquired will make the experience more vivid than those black and white pictures of Peter McParland barging Ray Wood into the back of the net we watched with our bogus aunts and uncles is open to question. But, whatever the technology, one thing is certain: sport will continue to be as important to the future of television as it has been since its very earliest days.

TWENTY-ONE

THE FUTURE'S BRIGHT ...
THE FUTURE'S SPORTSEX

There was a television play in 1968 called *The Year of the Sex Olympics* written by Nigel Kneale, which was remarkably prescient about television's future. The mass of the population were known as 'low-drives', anaesthetised by a constant diet of TV, kept in thrall by programmes like *Artsex* and *Sportsex* where attractive young people competed for a place in the Sex Olympics.

The TV controllers, or 'high-drives', planned to follow the qualifiers, who were left to fend for themselves on a remote island, foreshadowing reality TV by some thirty years. If you were pitching it now, you would describe it as *The Truman Show* meets *Big Brother* meets *Lord of the Flies*. The BBC in 1968 was not quite ready to have a Sex Olympics at the end of it, the title being merely a metaphor for a TV entertainment based on the vicarious thrill we might derive from essentially pointless competition between fit young people – not unlike, for the sake of argument, the actual Olympics.

'Try standing back a moment and looking at the Olympics as if you'd never seen or heard of them before,' wrote A.A. Gill. 'Why do we watch it, what is the fascination?' he asks, 'I can understand the World Cup: lots of people follow football, know the players, understand the rules. But whoever follows 2,000-metre medley swimming, who has posters of airgun target-shooters in their bedrooms? It isn't the sport we watch, it's the repeated small nursery-rhyme dramas of winning and losing that we plug into; the small adrenal doses of disappointment and excitement, the soft-centre satisfaction of tears and flags and national anthems.' Gill and I are as one on this.

As for the spectacle of the Games on TV, Leni Riefenstahl set the standard for filming the event in 1936, says Gill. 'Say what you like about the Nazis,' he adds, 'they knew how to throw a decent sports day. An awful lot of how sport is filmed and presented is a homage to Riefenstahl.' Which is more or less where we came in.

Hitler, by the way, would have loved the idea of holograms; great blonde Amazonian women ruling the world through their athleticism, and sticking it to us, right in our faces, in the sanctity of our very own living rooms. But I feel fairly safe in saying they – holograms, that is, not big Aryan women – are not the future, despite a number of newspaper pieces claiming them as televised sport's final frontier.

According to a cover story in the journal *Nature* in November 2010, a team at the University of Arizona's College of Optical Sciences has developed a new type of holographic telepresence that allows the projection of a three-dimensional, moving image without the need for 3D glasses or anything like that. The technology, claimed the college, could have uses ranging from telemedicine to entertainment.

'Holographic telepresence means we can record a three-dimensional image in one location and show it in another location, in real-time, anywhere in the world,' said the leader of the team, Professor Nasser Peyghambarian. Well, bully for them, but without wishing to sound like the chap from the *Daily Express* who dismissed John Logie Baird as a nutter, I don't think this is technology that will have much of an application in sport on TV.

I am not a natural technophobe, having embraced enthusiastically such innovations as the Internet, mobile telephones and cordless pyjamas, but I am fairly sure 3-D – and by extension holographic TV – will turn out to be gimmickry. Golf and tennis enthusiasts speak highly of 3-D, as it gives an idea of depth of field. But this technology likes the predictable, so the camera can be judiciously placed for maximum effect: tennis works because you know that at the start of each point, someone will be serving, and someone receiving serve. For a flowing game like football or rugby, though, you only really get the benefit on set pieces. 3-D may turn out to add a little value to Sky's product, and sell a few more subscriptions, but I would be surprised.

History tells us Rupert is more likely than Martin to be right about the future of TV, but, for what it is worth, I believe the future will be led not by technology, but by the convergence of sport, television, the Internet, and, as I have already argued, gambling.

The influence of pioneers like Peter Dimmock, who spent ten years persuading the owner of the Grand National, Mrs Topham, that television was the future, and Jimmy Hill, whose urgings turned football into a more entertaining, more TV-friendly game, will continue to be felt. But in a multi-channel, multi-platform world, there are bound to be changes in the way we watch sport, and certainly in the way we pay for it.

The changes will be on all sides. In the future, no sport will be able to expect TV to pay handsomely merely for a seat in the stand. Whatever the sport – even the almighty football – it will have to welcome television metaphorically, and in some cases even literally, into the dressing room. Goal-line technology and miked-up referees are the very least of the changes I expect to come football's way in the near future, and they will undoubtedly enrich our experience.

But this is not to deny our history. It was the appeal of sport that helped Britain through all the ages of television: from the FA Cup finals of the 1950s that fuelled the first wave of TV ownership, through the green of the Wimbledon grass that persuaded us to switch to colour, the ITV panels of the 1970s, whose to-and-fro banter is being replicated today among reality show judges, and the cricket piped in by satellite from the Caribbean in the depths of an English winter that opened wallets to pay-per-view television.

And what a rich cast of characters sport on television has brought us. Of course, those of us who have lived through it all remember most fondly the characters with whom we grew up: Murray Walker, Bill McLaren, Coleman, the Davies boys, Dickie and Barry, Motty, Frank Bough, O'Sullevan, Rickman, Wolstenholme, the wonderful Brian Moore, and the tragic-comic Eddie Waring, whose 'poo-er lad' commentary may be the finest moment of empathy between commentator and sport television has ever provided.

Modern sports broadcasters will never build up a store of goodwill like their predecessors. We are more critical now. A whole industry has grown up ridiculing the figures who bring us sport these days. I know; I am part of it. And television itself is no longer a wonder to us, so there is no automatic respect or affection for the people on it.

For one thing, there are too many of them. There will never be another Dickie Davies or David Coleman, not because TV lacks skilled sports broadcasters, but because the BBC, for instance, with its twenty-four different screens of sport running simultaneously at times during the Olympics, ensures a fragmented audience. And there will be viewers ignoring all twenty-four to watch old football on Sky or ESPN instead, not forgetting my friend in his underpants tuning into one of the subscription racing channels.

And what of the 2012 Olympics themselves, the biggest TV sporting event of all time, the first social network games, with the BBC putting huge effort and resources into its websites, message boards, and Twitter feeds. But at what cost?

We are told we will get a dividend in terms of the reputation of Britain abroad, and that the games will do wonders for the morale of the nation. Putting on an event like this makes us feel good about ourselves. But as the comedian Frankie Boyle said, 'For that money, we could have written, "Fuck Off, Germany" on the moon.'

There were concerns that London's famously creaky transport system, which has difficulty coping at the best of times, would be stretched to breaking point. I did my bit to help, and you could have too, by staying at home where the action is. Where the action always is. On the TV.

ACKNOWLEDGEMENTS

This book is memoir as much as history, which is just as well, because although I have enjoyed almost half a century of sport on TV, the history of it has usually played second fiddle to snack selection and getting the beers in.

So a million thanks to everyone who helped provide historical perspective. In an entirely fortuitous touch of circularity, I spoke to Peter Dimmock, responsible for much of the BBC's coverage of the 1948 Olympics, and to Roger Mosey, who looked after the 2012 games for the Corporation. Thanks to both, and especially to Peter for his impressive recall and scrapbooks full of newspaper cuttings. I am also grateful to other executives who helped: Niall Sloane, Head of Sport at ITV, and Jonathan Martin, Paul Fox, Michael Grade and David Elstein, who between them have held some of the top jobs in TV.

Mike Miller, former head of sport at Channel 4, helped me fit kabaddi, Eskimo Olympics and Italian football into the story, while Vic Wakeling, midwife at the birth of the behemoth that is football on Sky, told me how it all came to pass. Thanks also for factual information, dates and the like, to Chris Haines, press chief at BSkyB.

I also spoke to some of the commentators and presenters who have been there and done it – and in some cases still are. Des Lynam, Dickie Davies, Peter Drury, Gary Imlach, Clive Everton, and Martin Tyler all added to the story, and I thank them.

Frank Keating, one of the pioneers at ITV Sport, gave me a fund of funny stories and useful suggestions, and thanks also to his former colleague at ITV, Steve Minchin, who surprisingly was able to act as secondary source to some of Frank's more outlandish tales. I also got some good stories and pointers from friends Will Buckley, Kevin Mitchell, Andy Jacobs and Tony Hannan for which I am grateful.

Nick Hunter, ex-BBC and BSB, helped with his memories of the glory days of *Grandstand*, and filled in great gaping holes in my knowledge of cricket, as did John Perera at the ECB.

Thank you also to Lucy Smickersgill for her invaluable research in the BBC's written archives at Caversham, to Philip Turner for his *World of Sport* wrestling memorabilia, and to Jon Holmes, for enlightening me on the world of the manager/agent.

Much of this book was written in a holiday flat in St Annes, Lancashire, the quietest place on earth out of season, so thank you to the landlady Gillian Kilburn, who keeps a tip-top establishment. Thanks also to Jamie Blackshaw at the Mocca Moocho coffee house, Wakefield, whose free wi-fi helped out when BT internet failed me.

Most of all, though, I am grateful to my editor Matthew Engel for some fine jokes, and for insisting I bring some solid research and intellectual rigour to the exercise.

Finally, thanks to my wife Janet, my children, my friends Tony and Corinne, and all my workmates at the BBC in Leeds, for putting up with my constant whinging about Matthew's insistence I bring some solid research and intellectual rigour to the exercise.

INDEX

279